Faith in Theory and Practice

Essays on Justifying Religious Belief

Edited by

Elizabeth S. Radcliffe
and
Carol J. White

Open Court
Chicago and La Salle, Illinois

OPEN COURT and the above logo are registered in the U.S. Patent and
Trademark Office.

Printed and bound in the United States of America.

Library of Congress Cataloging-in-Publication Data

Faith in theory and practice : essays of justifying religious belief / edited by
    Elizabeth S. Radcliffe and Carol J. White.
       p. cm.
    "This collection of essays derives from a 1991 conference held at
Santa Clara University"—Preface.
    Includes bibliographical references and index.
    ISBN 0–8126–9246–2. — ISBN 0–8126–9247–0 (pbk.)
    1. Faith and reason—Congresses. 2. Religion—Philosophy—
Congresses. I. Radcliffe, Elizabeth S. II. White, Carol J.
BL51.F318 1993
231'.042—dc20
                                               93–33067
                                                CIP

Contents

Preface

This collection of essays derives from a 1991 conference held at Santa Clara University on the topic of the epistemology of religious belief and the subsequent volume of our journal *Logos*. All of the essays, in one form or another, were either presented at the conference or included in the journal. We were prompted by two features of these papers to make them more widely accessible than they otherwise would have been. One is that these essays together constitute a more unified discussion of a single topic than conference papers typically yield, with several of the authors exploring common themes in the justification of religious faith. The other is that the papers individually raise questions central to both epistemology and philosophy of religion and address them in a way of significance to philosophers in both areas. Our Introduction aims to display these two virtues of the volume, to give an overview of the theses and arguments the papers offer, to show what common themes grow out of them, and to steer those uninitiated to the field through them.

We would like to thank several individuals who helped in the production of this book. We are grateful to those who served as readers for the many papers submitted for the 1991 conference. This group of referees includes William P. Alston, who occupied the Austin J. Fagothey Chair in the Philosophy Department that year, as well as several colleagues in our department: James Felt, S.J., Philip Kain, Christopher Kulp, William Parent, and William Prior. The judicious advice of these people is evidenced by the caliber of the contributions assembled here. We thank Phyllis Cairns, who meticulously edited the manuscript for *Logos*. We are also grateful to Shiela Speciale, philosophy department secretary, who cheerfully assisted in many facets of the production of this book.

Elizabeth S. Radcliffe
Carol J. White

Santa Clara, California
May 1993

Introduction

This collection offers at least two views of religious faith and its justification. Some of our authors see religious faith as a set of beliefs about God and seek justification for these beliefs that will meet the demands of traditional theories of knowledge. This notion of faith in the hands William P. Alston, Alvin Plantinga, Richard E. Creel, William Lad Sessions, Stephen Grover, and James F. Sennett raises the classic issues concerning the foundation of knowledge. Having sound philosophical grounds for religious belief consists in finding the foundational propositions or experience upon which such beliefs rest, or in determining the beliefs themselves are foundational, or in showing they are formed through a method whose reliability is not questionable. Francis J. Beckwith and Jesse Hobbs add a discussion of the role of anecdotal evidence in both religious and scientific knowledge to round out this analysis of justification.

However, another view of religious faith at least tacitly emerges from these essays, including those of Alston, Sessions, and Creel. This view is most directly discussed in the essays by Joshua L. Golding, Linda Zagzebski, and Michael A. Brown. Faith can be seen as not just a set of beliefs but a special way of living. Under this characterization, justification may be quite different from finding support for propositions. Instead, it is situated in the quality of life of the believer and manifested in her understanding of herself and her relationships to others. For example, Creel briefly contrasts faith as a passion, the subject of his essay, with faith as an action, and Sessions notes beliefs are only one component of faith along with feelings and dispositions to behave. Golding specifically addresses the rationality of living religiously, not simply the rationality of religious beliefs, and Zagzebski discusses intellectual virtue as both an admirable way of attending to evidence and a disposition to have certain feelings, attitudes, and motives characteristic of a person who excels at knowing. The connection between these two views of faith is an intriguing theme winding throughout the collection and one addressed explicitly by Michael A. Brown in the last essay of the volume.

Our volume opens with **William P. Alston**'s paper, "The Fulfillment of Promises as Evidence for Religious Belief," which focuses on a neglected justification of religious belief that played an important role in the Biblical accounts of important religious figures from Abraham to Jesus. Directing us to the presence of this type of justification in an individual's life, Alston examines the fulfillment of God's promises of moral and spiritual development as evidence supporting religious beliefs.

Love, joy, peace, patience, kindness, goodness, fidelity, gentleness, and self-control are, according to Paul, the promised results of the Christian's belief, not seen as an extrinsic reward but as the "fruits of the spirit" developed in the relationship to God. Addressing the connection between the two views of faith distinguished above, Alston looks at characteristics of a way of life as evidence for the belief that God exists. He assesses the adequacy of a justification of religious belief drawn from the empirically observable manifestation of these qualities in a person's life and the testimony of the believer confirming their presence. Although Alston concludes that the evidence of fulfillment of divine promises does offer some justification for religious beliefs, he shows we must carefully consider its limits.

Next **Alvin Plantinga** begins "An Evolutionary Argument Against Naturalism" by noting that, despite the "occasional dissenter" in the grip of "a cognitive malfunction," we all assume that our minds are capable of grasping the truth and indeed do so over "a vast portion of our cognitive terrain." But popular as Darwinism in science and naturalism in metaphysics are, Plantinga points out that the theory of naturalistic evolution, i.e., an evolution ruled by blind forces and random chance rather than divine plan, raises doubts about our easy assumption that we know what is and is not real.

Darwin himself was bothered, he said, by the recurring "horrid doubt" that the conclusions of our minds are no more likely to be true than those of the monkeys with whom we share genes. Billions of years of evolution ruled by the blind processes of natural selection and genetic drift may have produced a creature fit to survive in its surroundings, but the ability to survive does not entail the ability to perceive reality as it is, only success at meeting its challenges—a conclusion also more recently reached by Patricia Churchland and entertained by

Stephen Stich. Plantinga notes Quine and Popper think otherwise, but he argues that the theory of naturalistic evolution gives us reason to estimate the probability of our cognitive faculties' being accurate as fairly low or simply unknown.

Plantinga shows that "Darwin's Doubt" in various reformulations is not easily laid to rest. Once we have raised such radical doubts about the functioning of our minds, the ghost haunts any belief we might use to regain our security, constantly retracing the path of the Cartesian circle. Indeed, the theory of naturalistic evolution gives us reason to doubt the accuracy of our belief in it, making it a self-undermining hypothesis. Plantinga points out that no such doubts beset the theist's starting point or propel him into the "appalling loop." The theory that God creates us in his image, and thus gives us the capacity to know a broad range of things, raises no internal doubts about its own credibility. Neither does the theist need to set foot on the first step of Descartes's circle. Our conviction that our faculties do grasp the truth counts in the theist's favor and against naturalism.

In "Faith as Imperfect Knowledge" **Richard E. Creel** argues that Thomas Aquinas's claim that faith is a form of knowledge is true if faith is a gift from God. Agreeing with some other contemporary epistemologists, Creel identifies the crucial condition justifying a claim to knowledge as the appropriateness of the cause of our belief. Of course, on this model of knowledge, the problem for the claim that I know God, or know that He exists, comes from my inability to prove God has caused me to have this idea of Him.

Thus, even if I have been given the gift of the idea of God, I cannot claim to know this; without knowledge of the cause of my belief, the conclusion that I know God exists is left without crucial support. Creel concludes that at most we may claim to have "imperfect knowledge" of God under our current epistemic limitations. We may indeed know God, but we cannot be certain that we know Him. However, adding to Creel's quotes from I Corinthians 13, we could say that although we may only "see through a glass darkly" now, this does not mean that we may not have certain, perfect knowledge in some future state when we are "face to face," our limitations graciously removed.

William Lad Sessions observes in "The Certainty of Faith" that faith may also denote a personal relationship to God rather than simply a type of belief we might assess solely to see whether it meets a philosophical criterion for knowledge. Sessions conceives faith as our relationship to God on the model of a relationship "between two distinct existing persons qua persons." Such faith encompasses trust, acceptance, commitment, love, a longing for ever greater intimacy, and a desire to act in ways that express all the crucial aspects of this sort of relationship with another person. Sessions's analysis suggests we might consider this form of faith, too, as a gift, as did Creel in following St. Thomas. The "object" of this type of faithful relationship may be conceived as an active agent "proposing articles of faith for belief, producing belief in such articles, awakening natural capacities to believe, bestowing new or even 'supernatural' capacities, and so forth."

Sessions adds a new but familiar distinction to our authors' discussion: He contrasts "epistemic certainty" with "psychological certainty." The former refers to our recognition of being in the best possible position to justify a belief while the latter indicates our feeling of confidence in beliefs and personal relationships. Just as the trust, commitment, acceptance, and so forth, that such relationships manifest vary over time, so, too, does psychological certainty; unlike epistemic certainty, psychological certainty comes in degrees. Sessions notes we would be considered obsessed or fanatical if we did not have doubts at times since we have all experienced the influence of "hidden thoughts and unconscious motives, self-deception and wishful thinking, the opacity and inchoateness of intention, the elusiveness of feeling, and the conspiracy of others' silence." However, he argues we can be psychologically certain of our beliefs even though we are not epistemically certain of them. Sessions then considers various possible relationships between the two kinds of certainty and their relationship to faith.

In reflecting "On the Rationality of Being Religious," **Joshua L. Golding** also focuses on the religious life, not on religious belief justified either cognitively in traditional attempts to prove God's existence or pragmatically in Pascalian wagers. He articulates five conditions that must hold if we claim a person is a "God-oriented religious person" and assesses the rationality of each. The first condition is that the person "has some conception of God and . . . of what would constitute for him the best relationship with God." Golding points out ways in which a concept of God could be incoherent either by not representing a possible being or by not being consistent with other conceptions the believer holds, such as notions of good and evil. He then shows, however, that if certain constraints are met, it can be rational for a person to hold a conception of God and of the best relationship to God.

Golding examines the other four conditions with a similar aim. The religiously oriented person must also believe (2) that God could exist and that he can attain the envisioned relationship, (3) that being in this relationship would be more valuable than being in any other state, and (4) that certain actions increase his probability of attaining the relationship. The fifth condition is that the God-oriented person does certain actions which he believes will increase the probability that he will attain a relationship with God, and Golding assesses its rationality according to his modified version of the Principle of Expected Value used in decision theory. He concludes with some Pascalian twists of his own, this time on wagering one's life, not merely one's beliefs, on the existence of God.

In "Religious Experiences: Skepticism, Gullibility, or Credulity?" **Stephen Grover** focuses on the rationality of basing conceptions of God or religious claims on certain kinds of evidence, and he warns us that the justification of religious belief confronts epistemological danger in the thicket of gullibility and the bog of skepticism. Assessing whether Richard Swinburne's Principle of Credulity "represents a suitable guide along the narrow path" between the two, Grover examines the adequacy of this claim that, in the absence of special circumstances or considerations indicating the contrary, "what we seem to perceive is probably true." Grover argues that the Principle errs on the side of gullibility, since it only steers us away from claims that are similar to claims we know are false while ignoring the deeper question of the reliability of all the particular kinds of evidence on which conflicting claims are based, whether or not we can prove one of them false.

The conflicting claims that Jesus is Messiah and Mohammed is the greatest prophet bring into question the kind of evidence on which such claims are based, e.g., dreams or scripture. Confronting the same problem of justification that Creel did, Grover argues that it is especially difficult when we have no way of distinguishing either the causal origin of our belief or its impact on the belief. A dream prompted by indigestion or LSD may give rise to the same belief as one inspired by God, and the content of a dream under the influence of LSD may in fact be caused by God. Grover suggests that the "modest assumption" that "every kind of religious experience raises at least a few conflicting claims" should quickly cure the tendency to believe too much promoted by Swinburne. His conclusion tacitly implies that, given the distance between God and human beings, skepticism, not gullibility, should be our guide for plotting the course toward rationally justified religious belief.

Next, **Francis J. Beckwith**'s essay, "Hume's Evidential/Testimonial Epistemology, Probability, and Miracles," deals with an issue of religious belief that traditionally has been a target of skepticism: the occurrence of miracles and their role in justifying religious belief. Beckwith defines a miracle as "a divine intervention that occurs contrary to the regular course of nature" that is taken as having a specific meaning within a "historical-religious context." David Hume long ago concluded that a reasonable person should never believe a miracle has occurred, because the proof of the existence of a law of nature, being founded on the repeated experience of a conjunction of events, will always outweigh the "proof" of a miracle, which by its very definition is an improbable, unpredictable, singular occurrence.

Noting other scholars' criticisms of Hume's arguments, Beckwith reconsiders what questions Hume does and does not beg. He casts doubt on Hume's conception of laws of nature and replaces it with an analysis of them and their violation that is coherent with the practices and beliefs of contemporary science, fits our commonsense view of the world, and allows a place for miracles. In Beckwith's conception of such laws, "violations" may count as miracles, mere anomalies, or incentives to recast and refine our version of a particular law as scientists do in the face of repeated violations. He concludes with a discussion of the role of probability in the justification of knowledge claims in order to show that belief in miracles also depends on judgments about probabilities, as do beliefs in laws of nature, but ones concerning the reliability of the testimony of witnesses and the plausibility of alternative explanations.

Jesse Hobbs's "Religious and Scientific Uses of Anecdotal Evidence" focuses on a particular kind of testimonial evidence; but, as his title indicates, Hobbs, like Beckwith, compares its roles in justifying both scientific and religious beliefs. He admits anecdotal evidence supporting religious beliefs cannot answer the skeptic or provide a basis for consensus on dogma or practice, since the events it relates are unique, non-replicable, and uncontrollable, as Beckwith noted about miracles. He argues, though, that this does not mean it is without value in the justification of both religious and scientific beliefs.

Hobbs provides two main arguments for the value of anecdotal evidence. First, he argues that it is our only means of attributing "certain manifestations of intelligence" to both other human beings and God. A person impresses us with "a flash of brilliance that solves a puzzle," as did Solomon. But, Hobbs notes, "[E]vidence of God's intelligence is often found in events that are so serendipitous as to cry out for explanation." Not just any extraordinary or extremely improbable event is eligible for the status of a miracle, as we could see in Beckwith's discussion, but sometimes the appearance of a design or plan in our lives seems to massive, too richly detailed, to be attributable to mere coincidence and blind chance.

Second, Hobbs argues that even in some cases of purported natural phenomena, such as ball lightning, anecdotal evidence may be all we have. Since scientists cannot replicate the conditions that generate this unusual form of lightning or control its happening, they must rely on eyewitness testimony if they are to believe in its existence. Such is the case for our knowledge of Jesus' life, too. Hobbs justifies the practice of relying on a limited number of witnesses by invoking contemporary transcendental arguments against skepticism in general. Much of what we as individuals know is based on the testimony of others; we could not possibly verify all our beliefs ourselves. As Sessions points out in his paper, reliance on authority is the "life's blood" of our belief-forming practices. Hobbs con-

cludes that the uniqueness of anecdotal evidence and our inability to replicate it should not make us dismiss its importance
for understanding religious belief.

How does an authority in matters of religious belief come to
be regarded as an authority? Why do we trust some people's
judgment so much we appropriate it as our own? In "Intellectual Virtue in Religious Epistemology," **Linda Zagzebski**
provides an answer to these questions by giving us an overview
of the usefulness of a virtue-theory approach to ethics and
showing its parallel usefulness in epistemology. Pointing out
that epistemologists have long used ethical concepts such as
duty, responsibility, reliability, norms, and values in discussing
justified belief, the epistemic analogue of a right act, she notes
they tend to stick to the act-based model of evaluation prominent in deontological and consequentialist ethical theories.
Even Ernest Sosa, Lorraine Code, and James Montmarquet,
who see the usefulness of the concept of intellectual virtue in
epistemology, remain focused on justifying belief, even though
virtue is a characteristic of persons, not propositions.

Zagzebski argues our common evaluations of knowing do
not condemn a belief as unwarranted but a person as narrow-
minded, careless, prejudiced, rigid, obtuse, intellectually rash,
or cowardly, and so forth. Conversely, we admire people who
are insightful, sensitive to detail, able to think up explanations
of complex sets of data, open-minded, and aware of their own
fallibility; people who exhibit perseverance in the face of
opposition to their ideas and discretion in making judgments
and dealing with others' desire to know. Such talents of mind
are not a matter of "knowing that" but of "knowing how" and
must be learned by imitation and practice, as Aristotle suggests
the moral virtues are. Such modeling, of course, follows that of
the ethical dimension of religious life in which the believer tries
to imitate Christ. Affirming Hobbs's conclusion about the importance of anecdotal evidence while shifting the focus to the
knower rather than the belief, Zagzebski recommends that
epistemologists of religion turn to literature for examples of
excellent human functioning, as virtue ethicists have done. She
concludes by suggesting the virtue approach could enrich and
extend Plantinga's notion of properly functioning cognitive
capabilities.

The last two articles in our volume respond to the justifications of religious belief put forward in various works by Alvin Plantinga and William Alston. **James F. Sennett's** "Reformed Epistemology and Epistemic Duty" discusses Plantinga's claim that theistic beliefs are "properly basic," or foundational, and thus need no propositional evidence to justify them. A common reaction to Plantinga's claim, Sennett notes, is to reject it on the grounds that holding a religious belief without any evidence for it must violate some epistemic duty. Sennett revives an objection made by Philip Quinn that no belief is prima facie justified if one negligently ignores good reasons for thinking that it could be false or fails to rebut them. Since twentieth-century culture is "replete with atheistic testimony," the believer can hardly plead ignorance of such reasons.

Sennett finds Plantinga's responses to Quinn unconvincing. Not all theistic believers can even comprehend Plantinga's explanation of the existence of evil, so it hardly helps them meet their epistemic duty to reply to the arguments of atheism. In Plantinga's case of the purloined letter, the fictional protagonist can continue to insist he was walking in the woods when someone stole the letter from the dean's office that accused him of unprofessional conduct only if plausible doubts are not raised about the reliability of his memory, as they could be by either his wife or the dean pointing out that his memory has proven inaccurate previously when it got him out of trouble. Besides, Sennett argues, our almost universal acknowledgment of the reliability of memory as a source of properly basic beliefs hardly helps us in regard to the reliability of all theistic beliefs, although several of our authors have suggested interesting ways in which such beliefs are connected with personal memories. Sennett relies on Stephen Wykstra's distinction between an individual possessing evidence himself and his belief that someone in his epistemic community possesses it in order to reformulate Quinn's notion of epistemic duty so that we can rely on the authority of theologians, philosophers, and scientists to justify our beliefs and thus meet our epistemic duty in a way that keeps specific beliefs basic.

Michael A. Brown's "Skepticism, Religious Belief, and the Extent of Doxastic Reliability" serves as an appropriate cap-

stone for this collection of essays. It raises as an issue, worth pondering in its own right, the contrast that has been woven into the exchange among our authors. Do we attach reliability directly to the epistemic practices in which beliefs originate? Or do we only indirectly attribute reliability to them because they happen to produce beliefs which strike us as true or rational on other grounds, e.g., their coherence with other beliefs we hold? Furthermore, if we follow the latter course, is it for reasons having as much to do with our lifelong allegiance to a particular culture as to any attempt at a fair adjudication among competing claims of the sort that Alston's theory of "cognitive doxastic reliability" proposes?

This question of reliability has an "unnerving bite," Brown declares, when raised in the religious context in which the issue of truth is "decisively linked to the meaning of life" or, we might say in reference to the theme of our volume, when the truth of our beliefs is seen as vindicating our life of faith. Can faith as a social practice be justified if specific important beliefs which arise from it—for example, the belief in immortality—are false?

Brown argues that, seen simply as isolated beliefs, none of the following claims is obviously more bizarre than another: Jesus is God, the sun is a fusion reactor, and the sun is a white cockatoo. If we initially think otherwise, he suggests, it is a result of living in a post-Enlightenment culture deeply committed to the practices and beliefs of modern science and to ways of interpreting Christian belief that, as Nietzsche points out, conceal the oddity of thinking that God became man and died on a cross. If we are baffled by the aborigines' belief that the sun is a white cockatoo, this may be because we haven't lived up to the modern ideal of cultural fair play, which Brown suggests would require us to enter into their social practices to understand what the claim really means to them.

Brown notes that Alston's application of his theory of doxastic reliabilism seems to rule out religions whose beliefs are incompatible with those of experimental science. Natural religions, for instance, that connect deities with natural phenomena (e.g., rain) or geographical locales (e.g., volcanos) tread on territory we moderns long ago turned over to science—and Hebraic religions abandoned even earlier. Yet why accept the

practices and resulting beliefs of science as our epistemic touchstone? Brown quotes Alston's comment that a practice would not have "persisted over large segments of the population unless it was putting people into effective touch with some aspect(s) of reality and proving itself by its fruits." But, as we saw earlier in this introduction, Darwin's Doubt recognized effectiveness, or survival value, as one thing and contact with reality as another. Similarly, perhaps the "fruits" of Christianity simply may be those practices that produce the characteristics of love, trust, openness, serenity, joy, and so forth, which we not surprisingly find valuable after almost 2,000 years of Christian culture, whether or not the beliefs for which they provide evidence are true.

Readers new to the discussion of the justification of religious belief may want to begin with general discussions of the nature of this belief and thus should start with Creel's analysis of faith as a type of knowledge and work their way through Zagzebski's essay on intellectual virtue. This route leaves the reading of Alston's and Plantinga's essays, along with those of their two critics, Brown and Sennett, for last. Proceeding in this order gives one a general overview of the debates in the field before tackling the more specific discussions situated in and stimulated by the work of Alston and Plantinga.

The Fulfillment of Promises as Evidence for Religious Belief

William P. Alston

ABSTRACT

Among the grounds Christian (and other religious) believers have for their beliefs are what they take to be fulfillments of divine promises in their lives. Christianity represents God as promising various things upon the satisfaction of certain conditions. I concentrate on promises that have to do with one's moral and spiritual development and with one's relations with God and with one's fellow creatures. If we may take it that such promised fulfillments are forthcoming significantly often, to a significant extent, it looks as if this can count as some positive evidence for the system of belief that includes the claim that such promises have been made. I consider three reasons for denying this: (1) problems about determining that the outcomes in question have actually occurred, (2) the impossibility of making effective use of control groups, and (3) the existence of alternative explanations of the evidence. In each case I argue that the difficulties do not succeed in dissipating the evidential force of the phenomena.

I

The epistemology of religious belief is a complex and often bewildering subject. First, the territory of religious belief is enormously varied. In Christianity, which I will be using throughout as my example, there are historical beliefs about events in "salvation history" and theological beliefs about the nature of God, the persons of the Trinity, the church, the sacraments, and the scriptures. There are beliefs of a given individual as to just how she fits into God's master plan and as to what God's current attitude is toward her, beliefs about moral standards and their applications to various social issues, and so on. The epistemology of beliefs in one of these groups may not be the same as the epistemology of beliefs in another.

Second, there is a plurality of different sorts of grounds for beliefs of a given sort. To illustrate this point, I will focus on the basic theological beliefs that articulate the central Christian scheme: beliefs about the nature, purposes, and activities of God; about human nature and its vicissitudes; about the conditions of salvation; about God's incarnation in Jesus Christ as the central event in God's salvific activity; and about the work of the Holy Spirit in the world. My present point is that there are a variety of supports for this belief system, and that the strength of the case for it cannot be appreciated unless we take this diversity into account.[1] The grounds include (1) the arguments for the existence of God that have been prominent in natural theology; (2) the record of God's revelation to us, in messages communicated to selected persons and in the events of history; (3) the experience of God at work in individual lives throughout Christian history.

Third, different persons, and the same person at different times, will enjoy different degrees of access to different grounds. Many people have never thought deeply about the arguments of natural theology, and some are incapable of following such arguments.[2] It is notorious that people, including believers, differ widely in the extent to which they experience the presence of God in their lives.[3] Some believers are more knowledgeable about the traditions of their religion and about the scriptures, doctrines, and forms of worship. Some believers have thought more deeply about all this than others. And these variations hold across different stages of one person's life as well as across persons.

II

All this is a prolegomenon to my main concern in this paper, a particular ground of Christian belief that has not received the attention I believe it deserves. This ground, as the title indicates, has to do with the fulfillment of promises. A central feature of the Christian scheme is the way in which promises are held out to the believer by God, either in the person of Christ or through selected messengers. This is a prominent feature of the Biblical record, from the original compact with

Abraham down through the epistolatory literature of the early Christian church. God promises Abraham to give the land of Canaan to his descendants and to make the latter as "countless as the dust of the earth". Before entering Canaan the Israelites are told by God through Moses that they will enjoy prosperity and uninterrupted tenure of the land if they will keep His commandments. The Old Testament record is filled with such promises. However, it is not promises of this sort on which I want to concentrate. One may, indeed, take the fulfillment of promises like the ones to Abraham as reasons for crediting the Biblical record. Such appeals have often figured in expositions of the "evidences of Christianity". But this ensnares us in prickly historical questions, and I don't want to get involved in that here. Instead, I will focus on promises the fulfillment of which is to be found in the lives of believers. To tell that such a promise is being fulfilled in my case I don't have to rely on historical records; I only have to be alive to what is happening in my life.

More specifically, I will concentrate on promises that have to do with the moral and spiritual development of the individual and with the individual's relations with God and with fellow creatures. Thus, I will be trespassing on theological territory traditionally labled 'sanctification'. I shall further narrow my sights to promises that have to do with our spiritual condition in this life, as distinct from the life of the world to come. Such promises are not hard to find. A rich Biblical source is the farewell discourses of Jesus in the Fourth Gospel. There Jesus is represented as making a number of promises to his disciples concerning their spiritual life after He has left them.

> He who has faith in me will do what I am doing; and he will do greater things still because I am going to the Father. Indeed anything you ask in my name I will do, so that the Father may be glorified in the Son. If you ask anything in my name I will do it. (14: 12–14)

> If you love me you will obey my commands; and I will ask the Father, and he will give you another to be your Advocate, who will be with you for ever—the Spirit of truth. (14: 15–16)

> Anyone who loves me will heed what I say; then my Father will love him, and we will come to him and make our dwelling with him. . . . (14: 23)

I have told you all this while I am still here with you; but your Advocate, the Holy Spirt whom the Father will send in my name, will teach you everything, and will call to mind all that I have told you. (14: 25–26)

I am the real vine, and my Father is the gardener. Every barren branch of mine he cuts away; and every fruiting branch he cleans, to make it more fruitful still.... Dwell in me, as I in you. No branch can bear fruit by itself, but only if it remains united with the vine; no more can you bear fruit, unless you remain united with me. I am the vine, and you the branches. He who dwells in me, as I dwell in him, bears much fruit; for apart from me you can do nothing. (15: 1–5)

Before continuing, let me set aside one possible source of trouble. The Fourth Gospel is widely regarded by contemporary New Testament scholars as not presenting us with a historically accurate picture of Jesus—His words and deeds—but rather with a theological interpretation of what God was up to in the life and work of Jesus. I am not contesting that here. I quote these passages, not to show, or even to opine, that Jesus made these promises at the Last Supper. My point is, rather, that the Christian belief system contains beliefs to the effect that God has held out such prospects to us if we will satisfy certain conditions. In this section of the Fourth Gospel, the expression of that conviction takes the form of utterances attributed to Jesus. My concern is with the fact that the Christian faith contains divine promises like these and with the way in which that can provide a possible ground for accepting that faith.

I also want to disavow any suggestion that the Fourth Gospel is the only source in the Christian tradition for such promises. But it is a particularly rich source and will furnish us with at least as good a starting point as any other.

The passages cited do not wear their interpretation on their sleeve. What fruit is it that we cannot bear unless we remain united with Christ and dwell in Him? And what is it to be so united and to "dwell in Him"? What is it to receive the Holy Spirit and for Him to teach us? What is it for the Father and the Son to "make their dwelling with us"? We need clues from other parts of the Bible, from theological reflection, and from Christian experience to interpret these passages. I won't try to go into all that. I will suggest one way of reading these passages in which they have to do with the ground of Christian belief I want to explore. If you feel that the promises suggested to me by the above passages and by much else in the Christian record do not represent authentic Christianity, you may simply take what I am saying as having to do with an imaginary religion I call 'Christianity'. That will serve my purpose almost as well. For in this paper I seek only to consider whether certain developments in one's spiritual life would constitute some basis for accepting a religious belief system that implies that such developments are to be expected under certain conditions.

My suggestion, then, is that passages like the above represent God as promising the faithful a "payoff" in the form of a different mode of life, a "new life in the spirit", a life imbued with the divine spirit and manifesting that spirit to one's fellows. God has promised the faithful that they will receive spiritual fulfillment, a life of such spiritual quality as to constitute a realization of their deepest human potential. It is in this way that I understand the "fruit" spoken of in the famous vine-and-branches passage, and this new life of the spirit seems to me to be at least part of what is involved in the Father and Son "making their dwelling with us" and in the sending of the Holy Spirit. I will be a bit more explicit about this, both as to what is promised and as to the conditions that are laid down for the fulfillment of the promise. I begin with the former.

What is spirituality anyway? The term is used in many different ways. My usage here is tied to Christian ideas about the Holy Spirit, what He is and what He does. What are the marks of a "spiritual person" in this sense? I can't hope to give an adequate treatment of this, but here is a first shot.

1. Ordinary morality is presupposed. One can't be markedly spiritual if one is a wife-beater, a child-abuser, a libertine, a glutton, a liar and cheat, a person who can't be trusted, a grasper of the goods of this world who is prepared to run roughshod over others to get them. These are all preliminary conditions.

2. Nearer the heart of the matter are the contrasts between self-centeredness and other-centeredness, indifference and love, self-protectedness and openness to others, self-inflation and humility—contrasts that figure so heavily in the sayings of Jesus.

3. The spiritual person has a different scale of values, different priorities, in a number of respects: the contrasts between worldly and eternal values, getting and giving, security and commitment, demandingness of others, and trust.

4. Thus far I have been concentrating on one's relations to other human beings. But, obviously, relation to God comes into the picture as well. A spiritual person is devout. At the extreme of spiritual development, he lives his whole life in relation to God. Everything he does is done in the light of that relationship. Openness to God—to the promptings, direction, guidance, and inspiration of the Holy Spirit—is as good a single measure of spirituality as any.

5. The spiritual person is imbued by the Spirit, and this generates a variety of manifestations—power, calm, serenity, faith, trust in God, love of God and other human beings. Here I can bring in the famous passage in St. Paul's Letter to the Galatians, in which he enumerates the "fruits of the spirit".

> But the harvest of the Spirit is love, joy, peace, patience, kindness, goodness, fidelity, gentleness, and self-control. (Galatians 5: 22–23)

Let this suffice for an indication of some of the things that figure prominently in that spirituality growth in which is promised to the believer.[4]

Now what about the conditions for the reception of these gifts? My aspiration level here is even lower than for the account of what is promised. Various things are said in various texts. In the farewell discourses in the Fourth Gospel, Jesus speaks of "loving me and obeying my commands", "heeding what I say", and "dwelling in me". Paul often emphasizes accepting Christ as one's savior and having faith in Christ. Notoriously, different Christian groups differ in the emphasis placed on one or another of these requirements. Traditional Protestants tend to stress faith and acceptance of Christ as savior, while Catholics have tended to emphasize being a faithful communicant of the church, receiving the sacraments, and trying to lead a life in accordance with God's commandments. There is massive agreement that the new life in the Spirit, sanctification, is not to be construed as a reward for good behavior but, rather, as something that will itself issue in good behavior; though there is also general agreement that gross immorality is incompatible with openness to the reception of these gifts. There is, I believe, general agreement that there must be a readiness to respond to the divine initiative—to abandon one's old ways, so far as that is possible at a given stage, and to embark on a course indicated by God; but there is disagreement on just what is most crucially involved or required for such readiness. Let me cut through all this by simply speaking in terms of receptivity or openness as the basic condition, leaving it up in the air to a certain extent just what this comes to.

One final point about this. Even this sketchy discussion makes it clear that to satisfy the requirements for getting what is promised is to make at least a start on the realization of the promised development. Obedience to God, faith and trust in God and Christ, openness to the Holy Spirit, which are among the preconditions for the promised fulfillment, are themselves among the promised gifts of the Spirit. This indicates that the conditions and the payoff cannot be as cleanly separated as my exposition might suggest. What is required by us to trigger the sanctifying work of the Spirit is a beginning of the very spiritual development the full flowering of which through the Spirit is precisely what has been promised.

III

My central epistemological claim, as already hinted, is that the fulfillment of (alleged) divine promises of spiritual development by a large number of persons provides us with a significant reason for accepting the Christian belief system that involves the claim that such promises have been made.[5] More specifically, if many people have satisfied, to a significant extent, the conditions laid down for the availability of the fruits of the Spirit, and if they, or a large proportion of them, then receive those fruits to a significant extent,[6] this provides us with evidence for the truth of the claim that those promises were indeed made by a being with the wherewithal and the will to make good on them. Hence, it provides one with evidence for the truth of the religious belief system within which the claim of those promises was generated. Though my specific thesis concerns Christian belief, I am confident that it has general application to any religious belief system that promises fulfillment to its devotees, a condition that would seem to be universally satisfied. But I will not try to spell out that general application in this paper.

To be sure, the fulfillment of alleged divine promises provides us with positive evidence for Christian belief only if those promises have been fulfilled significantly often. I am not going to try to show that this is the case. I believe that Christian autobiographical literature through the centuries, plus my own experience and the oral testimony of others, gives me an adequate basis for this assumption. Obviously, the literary records, plus oral testimony available to me, cover only a tiny proportion of Christian believers. However, it seems reasonable to assume that here, as in other matters, the persons who communicate certain occurrences in writing, or who orally report them to a given observer, constitute a very small proportion of those who undergo such occurrences. Presumably, the people who write about having suffered from child abuse and those who have told me about it constitute a very small proportion of the victims. Similar remarks could be made for an appreciation for Mozart, a love of wine, and a disillusionment with the glamour of war. Hence, I think it eminently reasonable to suppose that the phenomena on which I am concentrating are widespread. If you are not convinced of this, let me ask you to simply suppose, for the sake of argument, that this is the case and to join me in considering what bearing this has on the epistemic status of Christian belief.

I should comment on three features of the above that may be worrying some of my readers.

1. Reflecting on one's spiritual development, as a fulfillment of divine promises, is not a possible way of coming to the faith. In order to satisfy the specified preconditions, in any meaningful way, one must already have faith. How could one obey God's commands (as God's commands) or "dwell in Christ" unless one already believed (at least the outlines of) the Christian story? One must already be a practicing and believing Christian to be in a position to reap the promised benefits. But this is not a difficulty for my position, for two reasons. First, I am not presenting the fulfillment of divine promises as a way of

acquiring Christian faith, but as a source of evidence for the truth of what is asserted in the faith. That evidence could very well be acquired after one had already assented to the system. In that case it would strengthen one's epistemic position but not, necessarily, make any difference to what one believes. Second, I take it that it is not only one's own experience of spiritual fulfillment but also that of others that provides one with significant positive evidence for the Christian scheme. And the spirituality of other people could contribute to moving me into a position of faith, as well as constitute support for what is believed.

2. In thinking of experienceable outcomes that are predicted by the Christian scheme as providing evidence for the scheme, am I not treating Christian belief as a *theory*, something that has been developed as an attempt to *explain* the world, human life, or whatever? Am I not supposing Christian belief to be most fundamentally playing a cognitive or intellectual role, as having originated and persisted because it meets cognitive needs? And isn't that palpably mistaken? Insofar as Christianity depends on human motivation, rather than on divine initiative, isn't it responding primarily to practical rather than to intellectual needs? Isn't it primarily an attempt to attain salvation or ultimate fulfillment, an attempt to escape from what otherwise looks like a hopeless human predicament? In short, in proceeding as I am, don't I have the wrong slant altogether on what Christianity and, more generally, religion is all about?

No. In defending my epistemological thesis I make no commitments as to the basic role, function, or aim of Christianity, or what gives it its continuing hold on people. I am, in fact, quite sympathetic with the idea that religion in general and Christianity in particular is at bottom a practical concern with human salvation. But it is consistent with that, and true to boot, that this concern leads us (with a lot of help from God, according to the Christian story) to develop a complex system of belief about God, humanity, and their interrelations. And hence the question inevitably arises as to why we should suppose this story to be true, or an approximation to the truth. *This question arises whether the deepest concerns of Christianity are practical or theoretical.* Hence, the claim that the fulfillment of divine promises provides evidence for the truth of the Christian scheme by no means implies that this scheme is, most fundamentally, an explanatory theory, though my thesis obviously does assume that it can be treated as such for purposes of epistemic assessment.

3. It looks as if I am supposing that it is part of the Christian system of belief that certain things we can do are a sufficient condition for sanctification, and perhaps necessary as well. Obviously, I am not assuming this in the crassest way, as if something in my control will lead directly to sanctification, apart from the activity of God. But are we not supposing that my satisfying moral, attitudinal, behavioral, and other conditions is a sufficient condition for God's exercising that sanctifying activity? And doesn't that compromise the freedom and sovereignty of God? No; we don't have to think of it in that way. We don't have to think of the satisfaction of these conditions as *determining* God's response in such a way that God has no free choice. A better model for the *satisfaction of preconditions-spiritual development* conditional than the deterministic cause-effect conditionals we have in physical science would be the conditionals we use to test hypotheses about the attitudinal, emotional, or cognitive state of other persons. Thus I suppose that if you like me, then if I ask you for a favor you will respond positively, and if I suggest spending time together you will respond favorably. But although checking these implications is obviously relevant for testing the hypothesis, no one would suppose that the hypothesis implies that my asking a favor is an unqualifiedly or deterministically sufficient condition for your responding positively; and hence no one would suppose that the positive evidential force of a favorable outcome of the test implies that you were not free to respond in one way or the other. The relation of the hypothesis to these conditionals is looser than that. The hypothesis implies that the specified behavior on my part will lead you to react positively *by and large* or *probably* or *normally* or *typically*. Obviously, many things could inhibit a positive response, even if you do like me. You may be too busy or emotionally upset or temporarily irritated by something I did, even though you basically like me. But even though the hypothesis implies only the weaker conditional, favorable outcomes can still support the hypothesis to

a significant extent. Otherwise, we would never get any pur-
chase at all on other peoples' attitudes.

But, it will be said, it is different with God. If God really did
promise certain kinds of fulfillment whenever certain conditions were satisfied, then there can be no question but that the
latter will be followed by the former. God would not go back on
His promises. Nor is the connection between antecedent and
consequent subject to the disruptions we have just seen with
human beings. God could not be too busy, emotionally upset,
or temporarily irritated. Hence, an unqualified *condition-
outcome* hypothetical really is implied here, unlike the human
case.

But even if that is so, we are not denying divine sovereignty
or free will in asserting such a hypothetical. For, according to
the paragraph before the last one, the unqualified connection
does not hold regardless of the divine will, but precisely because God has willed that it be so. God has freely made these
promises, and it is because He can be absolutely depended on
to carry them out that we can say unqualifiedly (if indeed we
can) that satisfying the specified conditions will lead to the
specified outcome.

But perhaps it is not really necessary, after all, to take the
precondition-outcome hypothetical so strictly; perhaps the situation is more similar than that to the attitudes-of-other-human-
beings case. It may be a misreading of the Biblical witness to
suppose that God has promised these outcomes if we obey His
commands or whatever, *no matter what*. Perhaps the promise
was meant to be interpreted more loosely. But even if it was
meant unqualifiedly, there is still a certain looseness in the relation between test results and the epistemic bearing on the hypothesis being tested. For there is the question of whether the
preconditions have been (sufficiently) satisfied and whether the
promised outcome has been forthcoming, in a given case. And
there is always room for doubt about this. For one thing, as we
saw earlier, it is not obvious how to interpret the conditionals,
especially the consequent. It is not obvious what is involved in
the presence of the Holy Spirit or in our dwelling in Christ. For
another thing, as we shall see in Section IV, even if these
concepts are unproblematic, we may not have the wherewithal
to be sure whether they have been exemplified in a given case.

The upshot of this discussion is that, however the fine print is spelled out, our central thesis does not have any negative implications for the freedom and sovereignty of God, nor does it necessarily imply any straightforward connection between the Christian scheme and unqualified *precondition-outcome* hypotheticals that make possible the most decisive kind of empirical test. While disavowing such implications, we can continue to maintain that empirical confirmation of the relevant conditionals will constitute significant positive evidence for the Christian scheme.

My thesis is a relatively modest one—that the phenomena in question provide *some evidence* for the truth of the Christian scheme. They could not be a *conclusive* reason for accepting that scheme, even if the specific objections I will consider shortly can be successfully answered. For one thing, what is directly supported—that such promises were made by a being with the wherewithal and the will to make good on them—is only one bit of the total system; even if we have a conclusive reason for accepting that bit, it doesn't definitively settle the question about the rest of the package, assuming, as seems clear, that the other parts of the system are not guaranteed by this one. Moreover, there is the familiar point that verifying particular consequences of a theory does not provide conclusive evidence for the theory, but at most renders it more or less probable, justified, warranted, or reasonable.

Thus, I claim only that the occurrence of promised outcomes in a considerable number of cases provides *a certain amount of evidence* for the truth of the Christian belief system. I will not even attempt to say how much evidence this is, how strong a support it provides, or to what degree it renders the system probable. I will not attempt to assess the strength of the evidence even in crude qualitative terms, except to say that it provides a *significant* amount of evidence, that it raises the probability of the system sufficiently to be worthy of notice. I will have my hands full defending even so weak a a claim as this.

The evidence I am discussing belongs to the general category of *empirical* or *experiential* evidence, as contrasted with, e.g., rational arguments for the existence of God or divine revelation. It consists of the experience of differences in one's life after opening oneself up to the Spirit, as well as other people's observations of one's greater spirituality. But this is quite different from more widely advertised modes of experiential evidence for Christian belief, particularly the direct awareness of the presence and activity of God. People sometimes take themselves to directly experience the presence of God and to directly experience God doing things vis-à-vis themselves—"speaking" to them, strengthening them, condemning them, forgiving them, pouring out His creative love into them, and so on. I have explored this kind of empirical support of religious belief in *Perceiving God*. But in this paper I am looking at another part of the forest. No doubt, a growth in spirituality can and often does involve a direct experience of God or, not to beg any questions here, involves what is taken as such. But I will leave that to one side and confine my attention to those aspects of spirituality that do not involve an awareness of God as present to one. This will include those aspects I briefly surveyed above—lovingness, humility, a delight in spiritual things, calm and serenity, a trust in God, living one's life in the light of one's relation to God, and so on. The empirical support of Christian belief provided by these phenomena is more indirect than the support provided by the direct experience of God. Here it is not that God or any other key element of the theological scheme is (taken to be) directly presented to one's experience. It is rather that one is experientially aware of developments that are *predicted* by the theological scheme. This reflects favorably on the epistemic status of the scheme.

IV

I am going to assume that my basic claim is plausible, on the face of it. It is surely prima facie plausible to suppose that the growth in spirituality on the part of a large number of persons who satisfy the relevant conditions provides significant positive support for the Christian belief system. Don't we have the same general pattern exhibited here that we can find in empirical testing of scientific theories? Empirically testable consequences are drawn from a theory; and to the extent that they are confirmed by observation, the theory gains in rational acceptability. But there are various features of this case that will be taken by many people to invalidate the analogy. There are differences between this case and the strongest cases of empirical testing of scientific theories, differences that will seem to many to override any prima facie plausibility that attaches to my thesis.

1. *Detecting the crucial variables.* "There are problems about the alleged empirical data. Are the concepts of these various modes of spirituality such that it can be conclusively settled by experience whether they are present? Has the concept of *agape*, the distinctively Christian form of love, been tied down enough to make it possible for one to make a reliable judgment as to when it is or is not exercised, in one's own case or in that of others? Can we really distinguish between *agape* and less exalted forms of friendliness, benevolence, amiability, or natural warmth in human relationships? What about openness to the Spirit? How can I tell whether that characterizes another person, even if I can discern it in myself? As for humility, it is a truism in the devotional literature that it is extremely difficult to discriminate true humility from 'spiritual pride' involving vainglory over one's own humility! And these problems apply equally to the satisfaction of the relevant conditions, since, as noted above, those conditions involve at least the beginnings of the promised spiritual developments. If we lack effective tests for the phenomena in question, we cannot determine when, if ever, they are forthcoming; hence, we are in no position to adduce them as evidence".

In response to this, I want, first, to point out that the situation is not nearly so desperate as this objection would have it. There are many aspects of spirituality that do not pose such problems. There is no special difficulty in determining whether success, position, prestige, wealth, or material possessions are high on a person's scale of values; or whether, on the contrary, such things as service to others, a right relationship to God, or the advancement of God's kingdom occupy that position. If you encounter a person who is markedly serene in the midst of vicissitudes, you can't miss it. If one regularly responds lovingly to interpersonal situations, even when other people are hostile, lacking in understanding, or otherwise difficult, this will be quite noticeable. An extreme self-centeredness, or, at the other extreme, a lack of attention to one's own rights, perquisites, and payoffs, will be sure to obtrude themselves on our attention.

The marked spirituality exhibited by such people as Mother Teresa is something that even the most callous and unfeeling can hardly fail to recognize. Thus we must balance the hard-to-spot aspects of spirituality with those that are hard to miss.

Nevertheless, it must be confessed that the components of spirituality are less reliably detected than observational data in the physical and biological sciences. But the uncertainties concerning their detection are not significantly greater than is the case with humanly important variables in the social and psychological sciences. To be sure, certain schools of psychology and sociology deliberately trim their aspirations and their subject matter for the sake of objectively detectable data. But when these disciplines confront issues of profound human interest, they have many of the same problems we encounter when we deal with spirituality. Detection and "measurement" are subject to analogous uncertainties when we deal with such things as repression and mechanisms of defense, strength and content of desire or attitude, belief systems, or emotional influences on behavior.

What are the epistemic implications of the fact that a given body of empirical evidence falls short of the highest standards for reliability and certainty of detection? Should we say that it has no evidential force whatever? Or should we say that although any uncertainty attaching to the report of the evidence must reduce the extent to which the (alleged) evidence supports the hypothesis or theory in question, a moderate degree of uncertainty will not reduce it to zero. Again, we cannot quantify all this, but the following would appear to be a reasonable judgment. Despite the problems noted, we have a considerable capacity to discern differences in various personal traits, capacities, and patterns of behavior that comprise spirituality. Though this is not one of our most reliable cognitive capacities—not up there with the ability to determine where a given pointer is on a dial—it is not one of the least reliable either—not down there with the ability to predict the stock market. Thus, it would seem that the degree of uncertainty that attaches to attributions of spirituality or components thereof, when made with as much care and attention as we can summon, will not reduce the prima facie evidential force of this phenomenon below a level at which it is significant.

V

2. *Absence of control groups.* "How can you claim that a mere survey of cases in which X (satisfaction of preconditions) was followed by Y (spiritual development) supports a theory that implies that X can be depended on to lead to Y, if you have no control groups to determine the extent to which we get Y without X or X without Y? It is notorious that the existence of cases, even numerous cases, of X's being followed by Y is of little or no worth as evidence for a causal connection between X and Y without a survey of a sufficient number and variety of other cases to determine the extent to which we get Y without X and X without Y. For if we are just as likely to get Y whether or not it is preceded by X and are just as likely to have X without its being followed by Y, no case can be made for the supposition that X and Y are linked causally. And when you take growth in spirituality, upon sincerely trying to lead the Christian life, as evidence for the Christian scheme, you are supposing that the former stems from the latter. You are, no doubt, not assuming the crassest sort of causal connection, according to which the satisfaction of preconditions itself causally determines the spiritual growth, without intermediaries. On the contrary, the idea is that the satisfaction of preconditions does its work by leading God to effect the sanctification. Nor do you have to think of this 'leading' on a crude causal model; you certainly would not want to think of it as causally determining God's behavior. Nevertheless, you are thinking of the satisfaction of preconditions as an essential part of what is (at least typically) *responsible* for the outcome, as *leading* to the outcome, and so, in an appropriately broad sense, as being *causally* connected with that outcome. And without appropriate control groups, mere anecdotal evidence of cases in which X is followed by Y is worthless as evidence for this. No one would take this sort of thing seriously as evidence for the medical efficacy of drugs. Why should it be taken any more seriously here?"

Before responding to this objection, I had better say something about the way in which it takes its target to be adversely affected by a significant number of cases of Y without X, as well as a significant number of cases of X without Y. Is the objector taking me to be committed to the view that satisfying the preconditions is a *necessary* as well as *sufficient* condition for the spiritual fruits (taking 'necessary' and 'sufficient' in the relaxed way just indicated, in which they have to do not with causal necessity but with what typically does or does not lead to what).[7] Obviously so, but I don't object to that. I could, of course, make it easier for myself by stripping down my thesis to the claim that the preconditions will typically lead to the spiritual development, leaving open what else might frequently lead to it. But since I believe that the Christian system of belief is committed to the stronger claim that the spiritual development in question will not typically (or perhaps ever) occur without the satisfaction of the preconditions, I will defend that stronger claim.

Some might answer the objection by denying the relevance of control groups in the epistemic assessment of religious belief, but I will not take that line. I readily concede that the evidence I am discussing would be stronger if it also included inductive evidence that we do not typically get Y without X or X without Y. But I deny that in the absence of control groups the evidence in question is worthless. To support that judgment, I will begin by considering the prospects of setting up control groups here.

Consider the objection made in Section IV—that we lack objective and decisive ways of detecting the presence of the crucial variables. This could pose problems for the effective deployment of control groups. But that point should not be overstated or we will fall victim to the first objection. As the discussion of that objection indicated, this disability affects some of the relevant variables much more than others. Openness and receptivity pose particular difficulties. It would seem that a person can mistakenly suppose that she is (sufficiently) receptive to the spirit. Defenses motivated by fear of the disruption of one's life that would result from the work of the Spirit can operate unconsciously. Nevertheless, we are not wholly without resources here. A person's testimony as to openness or the lack thereof is worth something. And other preconditions, especially those involving attitudes and patterns of behavior, are much more open to our discrimination. Therefore, we are not totally without the wherewithal to implement a control-group approach. To be sure, it is difficult to imagine a group of researchers on both sides of the theism-atheism divide or the Christian–non-Christian divide agreeing on procedures for identifying the crucial variables. But we must remember that the central thesis of this paper presupposes that we are, to some considerable extent, capable of identifying the satisfaction of preconditions and a growth in spirituality and sufficiently capable of this to enable us to compile evidence for the Christian scheme that consists of instances of the former followed by instances of the latter. Hence, we can hardly deny that it is possible in principle to identify cases that would be needed for control-group studies, at least well enough to provide a significant amount of evidence, whatever obstacles there may be to carrying this out in practice.

My next point is that there are good reasons for supposing that a careful study of control groups would not have an outcome unfavorable to my thesis. For there are good reasons for supposing that we do not, significantly often, get X without Y or vice versa. As for Y without X, it is true that some components of spirituality are found in varying degrees outside the Christian community. People in the population at large exhibit various degrees of calm and serenity under stress, a loving attitude toward others, and a transcendence of crass worldly values like prestige and wealth. Nevertheless, if we take into account the full breadth of the "spirituality profile", it would seem that it is not to be found (or very rarely found) except among those who are really "into" leading the Christian life. This can be seen from the fact that the kind of spirituality promised to the faithful, according to Christianity, prominently features distinctively Christian components, along with others that are more widely shared. I will develop this point in two stages, first comparing Christians with the non-religious and then comparing Christians with the devotees of other religions.

First, consider *agape*, the distinctively Christian form of love. In its full development it involves a loving attitude of acceptance, goodwill, benevolence, helpfulness, nurturance, and so on, that is directed to people in general without making discriminations in terms of the merit of the recipient, the claims the latter has on one, the established bonds between the two, natural attraction (affinity) or the lack thereof, and so on. It is loving others as God loves us (so far as in us lies). Needless to say, this is realized to different degrees among Christians, but it is what one is enjoined as a Christian to realize as far as possible. I make bold to say that such as attitude toward others is not cultivated and is rarely found in a secular context. Reacting to hostility in a thoroughly loving fashion is a virtue not prized there. Again, the degree of transcendence of self-centeredness that is characteristic of Christian spirituality is also something that does not figure among the prominent values of contemporary secular society. Finally, among the components of the promised spirituality enumerated earlier were some that clearly will not be found among the non-religious, such as living one's whole life in relation to God and being open to the promptings of the Holy Spirit. All this indicates that it will be rare, at most, to find our complete Y without our X outside religious circles.

But what about other religions? It would seem that something at least very similar to *agape* is found among Buddhists and Hindus. Self-transcendence is also a prominent feature of the spiritual norms of these religions. Do devout Buddhists and Hindus satisfy the preconditions of which I have been speaking? If not, they would seem to be cases of Y without X. As we will see, a thorough assault on this question will reveal further complexities of our problem.

Whether the preconditions laid down in Christianity are regularly satisfied by these other religionists depends on further details about those conditions. If they are construed in very neutral terms as something like "openness to the Ultimate" or "openness to the transcendent", then devout Hindus or Buddhists could be credited with their satisfaction. Our thesis would thereby escape disconfirmation, for these folk would not exemplify Y without X. On the other hand, perhaps the preconditions should be thought of in a more distinctively Christian fashion—not just openness to the Transcendent, whatever that is, but openness to the Holy Spirit; not just obedience to the Ultimate, but obedience to Christ, or to God as revealed in Christ. That would be a more precise reading of the Biblical exposition of the preconditions. But then our non-Christian religionists do exemplify Y without X, unless the Y itself contains essential components that are specifically Christian. Let's explore that possibility.

In the discussion thus far, I have been concentrating on aspects of spirituality that can be specified in terms that do not presuppose distinctively Christian doctrines—self-transcendence, love, humility, openness to others and to God, trust, living life in relation to God, the priority of eternal to worldly values, and such virtues and characteristics as serenity, gentleness, and self-control. But our exposition of the nature of spirituality contained other features that are more ineluctably Christian. These include being imbued with the Holy Spirit—having the Holy Spirit guiding, directing, and inspiring one, endowing one with love, power, and wisdom. They include "dwelling in Christ", realizing an intimate personal relationship with the risen Lord. To be sure, various manifestations of these "indwellings" and "relationships" with the several persons of the Trinity can be specified in more neutral terms, such as 'love', 'peace', and 'power'. But if we take the canonical formulations of Christian spiritual life sufficiently seriously, we will hold that one doesn't have the full package unless one is actually in the specified relationships with Christ and the Holy Spirit. Is this possible for non-Christians? That is a controversial matter. One can argue that persons in other religious traditions are actually imbued with the Holy Spirit and enjoy a personal relationship with Christ, even though they do not identify what is happening in those terms. Christianity has the correct account of what is happening, but the happenings are not restricted to Christians; just as Einstein has the correct account of gravitation, though one doesn't have to be an Einsteinian to be subject to gravitation. But this is highly questionable. I will not pursue that line here but will assume that the theologically specified components of Christian spirituality can, in the nature of the case, be realized only by those who have made a Christian commitment, or at least are in vital connection with the Christian community, through reception of the sacraments, faith, commitment, or whatever. In that case, although many aspects of the Christian spiritual life can be enjoyed by non-Christians, the full package can be found only in those who satisfy the distinctively Christian part of the preconditions as well as the other parts. That returns us once more to the conclusion that the full-blown Y is not forthcoming without the full-blown X.[8]

The above discussion puts us in a position to distinguish two possible arguments for Christian belief from the fulfillment of promises, depending on whether the content of the promises is articulated in terms of Christian theology. If they are not, the promise is something like (1) "If you are sufficiently receptive to divine influence, you will develop *agape*, peace, a shift in values, etc." If they are, then the promise is more like (2) "If you are obedient to Christ and open to the influence of the Holy Spirit, you will be imbued with the Spirit and live under the influence of the Spirit". (Needless to say, these are just stabs in the direction of adequate formulations. Fill them out in accordance with the above discussion.) Which way we are thinking of the matter will profoundly affect the content of our claim that the fulfillment of such promises provides evidence for the Christian belief system. And the two interpretations have different strengths and weaknesses. With (1) it is possible to carry out a more objective and decisive test of the satisfaction of the antecedent and consequent of the conditional promise. Since this is construed in terms of human attitudes, dispositions, and patterns of behavior, it is all recognizable by any qualified observer, and it should be possible, in principle, to reach general agreement on particular cases (within the limits that attach to any consideration of such matters). However, this construal leaves us vulnerable to a considerable incidence of Y without X, as we have been noting. On construal (2), on the other hand, we are in a much worse position to secure interpersonal agreement. There are no universally, or even generally, recognized procedures (usable by all qualified observers) for detecting the Holy Spirit at work, or Christ dwelling in the believer. Construed in these terms the argument is an "inside job"; it has to be carried out *within* the Christian community where there are accepted procedures (though they fall far short of being decisive) for determining one's spiritual condition vis-à-vis Christ and the Holy Spirit.[9] Construed in this second way, the argument is usable only within the Christian community, which means, for example, that it loses any promises of apologetic value it might have had. But it is not vulnerable to the Y without X objection, since, arguably, only those who satisfy the Christian preconditions have a chance of realizing the specifically Christian payoff.

Either interpretation of the promises can give rise to an argument from the fulfillment of those promises to the truth of the system of belief that implies that those promises were made. And, on either interpretation, if we get a suitable pattern of relationship of *satisfaction of the preconditions* and *occurrence of the payoff*, then this counts as evidence for the scheme.[10] But that is just the point—a suitable pattern. That requires the absence of numerous cases of X without Y and Y without X, as well as numerous cases of X with Y. And we have seen reason to doubt that that condition is satisfied with the more neutral interpretation. Hence, in the rest of this paper I will be thinking in terms of the second, specifically Christian interpretation. This does not imply, of course, that I cut myself off from the components of spirituality, and of the preconditions, that can be specified in more neutral terms. Love, joy, peace, trust, etc. are still essential features of Christian spirituality. It only means that the full package also contains more distinctively Christian components. As I have already pointed out, this leaves me more vulnerable to the first objection. But I have already argued that my thesis can adjust to less than ideal detectability of the relevant variables. As for the issue that led us into this long digression, whether we get a significant incidence of Y without X, this second construal is, as just noted, protected against that.

The other countercombination, a significant incidence of X without Y, may appear to be more of a live possibility. Don't we often encounter people who say that they have been trying to get with it, Christianwise, but just aren't making it? Nothing is happening. God doesn't seem to be responding. They aren't moving in the direction they would have expected to move, given their involvement in the process. Yes, this is not an uncommon pattern, but there are alternative readings of the situation. First, there is the oft-noted difficulty of determining that relevant preconditions have been met. Perhaps the person is putting up effective bars to the works of the Holy Spirit without realizing it; perhaps the person is kidding himself about the extent to which he has gotten beyond a thorough self-centeredness; and so on. Second, there is a timing problem. Perhaps God has good reasons for keeping the person on the hook for longer than is comfortable. Perhaps he gives up too soon. In the absence of a full understanding of God's program—something we are not likely to attain—that is always a real possibility. Third, it may be that the Holy Spirit is at work in ways that are not yet apparent to the individual. It may be that the person is actually on the road to spiritual development without realizing it. Again, this is a possibility we cannot dismiss in a given case without knowing a lot more than we can hope to know about God's ways with us. For these and other reasons it is not at all clear that there are a significant number of cases, or even any at all, in which divine conditions are satisfied but God withholds the promised consummation.

It may be alleged that the response just made to the apparent cases of X without Y amounts to ruling out a priori the possibility of such a combination and, hence, closing off the possibility of significant empirical evidence. If I am disposed to protect the claim that X leads to Y by ad hoc alternative readings of every apparent case of X without Y, there is no longer a genuine empirical issue as to the extent to which X is followed by Y; and so cases of that sequence can no longer provide empirical evidence for anything. But that would be a misreading of my procedure. I am by no means following a policy of rejecting every apparent case of X without Y, no matter what. The alternative readings I have suggested are themselves subject to investigation. In any particular case we could look into the question of whether the absence of Y is due to unconscious blocking by the subject or due to God's timetable for this person. It may be very difficult to settle these matters, especially those involving God's plans, but we are not wholly without resources. Hence, I am not rejecting a priori the possibility of X without Y. Indeed, I am making no assumptions at all as to what the outcome of a careful inquiry into this matter would be. My claim only concerns what it is reasonable to suppose, given the information we have at present. As applied to the question of whether we get a considerable incidence of X without Y, the point is that, so far as we can tell at present, all apparent cases of this sort might be explained in ways favorable to my thesis. It remains to be seen what a more thorough investigation would disclose.

So here is our situation. No careful investigation involving control groups has been set up, nor does there seem to be any considerable likelihood of such a development in the foreseeable future. In addition to the methodological problems involving the detection of crucial variables, this is hardly a top priority for researchers in the social sciences! That being the case, what should we say of the evidential force of the considerable body of *satisfaction of preconditions-spiritual growth* sequences we are supposing to obtain. I have already acknowledged that this evidence would be strengthened by a favorable outcome of a careful study involving control groups. But in the absence of such a study, now or in the foreseeable future, I take the most reasonable judgment to be that the phenomena cited provide significant evidence for the truth of the Christian scheme. After all, the scheme predicts that we would find such sequences, and so we do. This gives rise to a significant presumption that the sequences count as positive evidence, a presumption that has not been overridden by unfavorable results of control-group studies. This judgment is strengthened by the point that we presently have reason to suppose that the outcome of a control-group study would be favorable.

VI

3. *Alternative explanations of the evidence.* The other objection to which I will devote considerable attention has to do with alternative explanations of the *satisfaction of preconditions-growth in spirituality* connection. "In supposing that numerous cases of this connection constitute positive evidence for the Christian scheme, you are obviously supposing that these cases can be explained by the activity of God in fulfilling His promises. Since God has promised spiritual fruits if we will obey His commands, etc., He produces the spiritual fruits when we satisfy His conditions. This explains the fact that satisfaction of those conditions is followed by growth in spirituality. It is because the Christian story explains this sequence that it is supported by that *explanandum*, in the way any hypothesis is supported by the occurrence of what it serves to explain. But what if the sequences can be better explained in another way that doesn't involve God at all, a way that invokes only purely natural-world factors? In that case won't these phenomena lose their positive evidential force vis-à-vis the Christian scheme? If the water on the basement floor could conceivably be explained

by a leak in the walls, but then it turns out that what is really responsible is a leak in the hot water heater, doesn't this discovery of the correct explanation take away from the water on the floor whatever force it might earlier have had as evidence for leaky walls?"

This objection obviously supposes that some naturalistic explanation(s) of the phenomena is superior to the Christian explanation. If the objector were merely pointing to a possibility we hardly need take him seriously. And this supposition can be questioned. Before doing so, however, I want to consider what the situation would be if the supposition were correct. The crucial question here is this. Does the existence of a better explanation of *e* wipe out all the evidential force of *e* for the inferior explanation? That all depends on which of two types of explanatory superiority is involved.

The case of the water on the basement floor illustrates the type in which we have discovered what is really responsible for the phenomena. Here we have conclusively established that the water was due not to a leak in the walls but to a leak in the hot water heater. The former explanation is not just weaker but has been definitively eliminated. It is no longer a live possibility for being what is responsible for the *explanandum*. Hence, the water on the floor is no longer any evidence at all for a leak in the walls. That evidential relevance has been effectively neutralized.

But now consider a second type of case in which, in comparing two or more explanations of *e*, the best we can do is to judge one explanation to be superior to the others on some criterion like simplicity, economy, general plausibility, explanatory power, comprehensiveness, or systematic unity. Here we are in no position to make a definitive pronouncement on which is the *correct* or *true* explanation, the one that makes explicit what is really responsible for *e*. We have not "discovered" the true cause. In this case the weaker explanation, T, is not bereft of all evidential support. Since it is still a possible explanation of *e*, it cannot be claimed that the occurrence of *e* provides us *no* reason to accept it. Since it is still possible, so far as we can tell, that T is the correct explanation of *e*, then it remains true that *e* gives us some reason to suppose that T is correct. To be sure, if T', so far as we can tell, provides a better explanation of *e*, then *e* will give us an even better reason for accepting T', but that doesn't mean that it gives us no reason for accepting T. Remember, I do not claim that *preconditions-spiritual development* sequences give us a conclusive reason for accepting the Christian scheme or that they suffice to show that the Christian scheme is reasonably accepted, all things considered; but only that they give us some significant reason for believing it. Hence, if the supposed superiority of a naturalistic explanation is of the second sort, it does not rob the Christian scheme of evidential support from this quarter; however, if it is of the first sort, that does follow. So which is it?

It seems clear to me that the most that the objector could reasonably claim is an explanatory superiority of the second, weaker sort. To support this, I will concentrate on arguing that no one is capable of showing that some naturalistic explanation is the *correct* explanation, that it makes explicit what is really responsible for the phenomena. One reason for doubting this possibility is that there is a plethora of such explanations—from sociology, social psychology, psychoanalytic theory, and so on. If anyone has succeeded in showing that one such explanation gives the correct story as to what is responsible for spiritual development that news has not yet reached the intellectual world. But I don't want to rest my case merely on the plurality of candidates. Take one approach and consider what is to be said of it. Consider social imitation and social modeling processes. To the extent that a person is involved in a social group and the form of life it embodies, the person tends to internalize its values, norms, and standards, and to imitate and conform to the patterns of thought, feeling, attitude, and behavior that are normative for the group. I will assume (no doubt, too optimistically) that the effective operation of these mechanisms has been sufficiently demonstrated in other contexts, and so they *could* be responsible for our growth-in-spirituality phenomena. But are they? How could we tell? Assuming, as we are, that the mechanisms in question are "available" in the relevant situations, we would need to exclude the possibility that other factors—other natural-world factors, as well as supernatural factors—are responsible. And how could we do that? How could we exclude the possibility that it is the factors specified in the Christian scheme that are responsible? We can hardly set up situations in which the Holy Spirit is not at work but conditions are appropriate for the operation of the social psychological mechanisms in question and determine whether the results in question are forthcoming; for we have no effective procedures for determining where and when the Holy Spirit is engaged in sanctifying activity, except on the assumption that spiritual development is always due to that activity, precisely the point at issue. Nor is there any better prospect for considering situations that are not favorable for the operation of the social psychological mechanisms in question, but where the subjects satisfy the conditions required by Christianity; for presumably any example of the latter will be a case in which the social psychological mechanisms could be operative.

How about cases in which a person has not satisfied the Christian preconditions to any significant extent, but where there is enough involvement in and exposure to the Christian community to enable the social psychological factors to operate? But we are not likely to get a thorough enough involvement in the community to trigger a massive operation of social psychological mechanisms unless the person also satisfies to some considerable extent the (alleged) divine preconditions for the gifts of the spirit. Thus, it seems that we have no chance of showing that it is these social psychological processes that are really responsible for spiritual development. And this, in turn, means that both Christian and naturalistic candidates are still possible. Even if some naturalistic candidate(s) should be judged, on the basis of standard criteria for goodness-of-explanation, to be better than the Christian one, the Christian explanation is still a serious candidate. And hence the phenomena can still provide a significant degree of support for Christian belief.

Now let us look critically at the assumption that some naturalistic explanation(s) of our phenomena is superior to the Christian explanation. Why should we suppose that? One can appeal to economy. We all recognize social and psychological factors anyway; if they can do the whole job without bringing God into the picture, so much the better. This claim raises questions about the context of the discussion. In some circles God is recognized "anyway" just as much as social and psychological phenomena, and that would seem to leave us with a standoff. However, I have been restricting myself to considerations that are (or should be) recognized by all intelligent and thoughtful parties to the discussion. Hence, I will acknowledge the point that a naturalistic explanation that invokes factors only of a generally recognized sort is superior to the Christian explanation on grounds of economy.[11] But that is only one criterion, and an overall judgment of superiority has to take into account the full range of relevant criteria. How about explanatory adequacy? Let's say that an account of X is explanatorily adequate to the extent that the factors it cites *could* be responsible for the *explanandum* in question. Here I think that our rivals are at a standoff. So far as I can see, both introduce factors that could be responsible for the *explanandum*. What about other criteria? What about simplicity? Here the Christian explanation wins hands down. It is clearly simpler to suppose a personal agent produces the results to achieve certain purposes than to suppose the growth in spirituality results from the complicated processes proposed by social psychology. This brief sampling would suggest that overall we have a standoff. The competitors are equal in some respects; in others one has an advantage on one point and the other on another. Thus, I am not disposed to admit that a purely naturalistic social psychological explanation is superior to the Christian explanation.

This discussion has taken place on the assumption that the explanations are rivals, that they are incompatible and hence cannot both be accepted. I will now challenge that assumption. Why should we not suppose that growth in spirituality can be due both to social psychological processes and to the work of the Holy Spirit? There is more than one way in which two explanations of a given fact can both be accepted. For one thing, the factors cited by each might do part of the job but need supplementation by the factors cited by the other. Each explanation would provide only part of a sufficient condition. I will not suppose that is the case here. The work of the Holy Spirit could be wholly sufficient to bring about sanctification; and I will assume that the social psychological processes in question could, too. But there is another model according to which the factors cited in one explanation are working through, or by means of, the factors cited in the other. Was the boulder moved because of the force exerted by the crowbar or did the worker move it? Well, both. And it is not that each contributes only part of a sufficient condition. The force exerted by the crowbar was obviously sufficient to move the boulder, and so was the intentional act of the worker sufficient in the circumstances, though it does not bring about the result directly. And so it may be here. The Holy Spirit may bring about Jane's growth in spirituality not by a mere act of will, but by setting in motion just the social psychological processes cited by our envisaged naturalistic explanation. Indeed, this is part of the standard Christian story about the work of the Holy Spirit, who is supposed to work through the church and its activities, not independent of or alongside the church. To be sure, your typical social psychologist won't like this suggestion, for s/he typically supposes that the matters s/he investigates are causally determined by purely natural, this-worldly factors. But that is an extrascientific, philosophical assumption, and it forms no part of any social psychological explanation of spirituality. Such an explanation has the same explanatory force, and is in the same position with respect to the other explanatory virtues, whether or not the Holy Spirit acts at a certain point to push the processes in a direction they wouldn't have gone without that intervention. Nor does anyone have enough insight into the details of social and psychological phenomena to rule out the supposition that a divine contribution was involved. Thus, the most important point to make about the objection from naturalistic explanations is that any such explanation we have reason to take seriously is quite compatible with the Christian explanation and poses no threat to the thesis that the latter is to be taken seriously, and that the phenomena of growth in spirituality provide significant positive evidence for the Christian scheme.

4. *Religious diversity.* A final objection that I will barely mention concerns the diversity of religions with belief systems that are incompatible, at least in part. If the fulfillment of what Christianity claims to be divine promises is positive evidence for Christianity, how about other religions? Isn't it also the case that we can find significant fulfillment of what Islam, Judaism, and Hinduism claim to be divine promises in the lives of their devotees? And doesn't parity require that we recognize that these outcomes constitute positive evidence for the truth of

those belief systems as well? But how can this be? Don't these claims cancel each other, since at most one of these belief systems can be correct?

These queries can be answered briefly. If each system claimed the fulfillment of its promises to be a conclusive reason for its truth, those claims would cancel one another. But my thesis is only that fulfillment of divine promises constitutes *some* significant positive evidence for the truth of the Christian scheme. There is no difficulty at all in supposing that there can be significant positive evidence for each of a number of mutually incompatible systems of belief. This is a common phenomenon in any area in which there is a plurality of competitors for the status of the correct amount of something or the correct answer to a certain question—science, history, and the affairs of life. It would, no doubt, be desirable to find some neutral way of choosing between the conflicting claims of the major world religions. Some of the sources of evidence mentioned in Section VII may throw some light on this. But even in the absence of this desideratum, we can recognize that a number of conflicting belief systems can each enjoy a significant degree of positive support.

VII

I have pointed out repeatedly that my thesis is a relatively modest one. I claim only that the fulfillment of alleged divine promises provides *some* evidence for the truth of the Christian scheme. I have carefully refrained from claiming that it constitutes a conclusive reason for accepting that scheme, or that it suffices by itself to make it reasonable to accept the scheme. In what way, then, is the thesis designed to lend aid and comfort to the Christian believer? In just this way: a consideration of the fulfillment of promises can be combined with other considerations to make up a larger set of reasons that may suffice to make Christian belief reasonable, or even to provide a conclusive case for its truth. I will not undertake to argue here that the sum total of relevant considerations enjoys even the weaker of these two statuses. I only have time for a brief indication of how the evidence I have been discussing interacts with other sources of evidence in a total picture.[12]

In this quick survey I will confine myself to the additonal sources of evidence briefly mentioned at the beginning of the paper. These are

1. Arguments for the existence of God, as typified by various forms of the ontological, cosmological, teleological, and moral arguments
2. Putative communications from God, such as we have (in one way or another) in the Bible, according to the Christian tradition
3. The direct experience of God's presence or activity

The simplest point to make here is that these various sources of evidence add up to a total support that is weightier than any of them taken individually. This is an application of a general principle of confirmation. The more quarters from which we have indications of the truth of a theory, the more reason we have to accept it. Stated this baldly, the principle is subject to various qualifications. If we have only simple inductive evidence, there comes a point at which more favorable instances will not significantly raise the probability of the hypothesis. If the different bits of evidence are not independent—if, e.g., one presupposes the correctness of another or if one gets its status as evidence by explaining another—that will reduce the additive effect. But here, I assume, we are dealing with (relatively) independent sources of evidence.

There are also more complex interrelations between these bodies of evidence.[13] First, each of these supports is subject to question. It may be doubted that the alleged communications from God do have that status. Many objections have been leveled against the classic arguments for the existence of God. The supposition that people are directly aware of God has been repeatedly challenged. And this paper has been largely concerned with discussing objections to the supposition that Christian spiritual development provides evidence for Christian belief. Where a particular evidential source is faced with such doubts, the other sources can help to resolve them. As for the direct experience of the presence of God, if we have other reasons for believing in the existence of such a being and for supposing that He would want to enter into personal relations

with us, that will add credibility to claims to have been aware of
Him in a way that makes personal interaction possible. As for
claims by various people to be relaying messages from God, if
we have other reasons for supposing that God exists and that
He is interested in communicating with us, that will give us
reason to expect that such messages will be forthcoming,
though it is still a question as to whether a particular claim is
warranted. As for the evidence considered here, its force will
properly look stronger if we have other reasons to suppose that
there exists a God Who does, or might well, make such
promises and Who has the ability to make good on them. And
so it goes.

Second, the different sources of evidence supplement each
other by bearing on different stretches of the total system.
Arguments for the existence and essential nature of God have
to do, obviously, with that core component of the system. For
more detailed information on God's purposes, plans, requirements, and the like, we must look to God's messages to us.
Individual experience of the presence and activity of God, in
addition to shoring up the belief in God's existence and basic
nature, has the special function of providing information to
each individual concerning God's relations to that person—
God's dealings with him/her, the special tasks God has assigned
to him/her, and so on. The evidence dealt with in this paper
most directly connects with the beliefs that God is specially
interested in our spiritual development and will provide for that
if we cooperate. Though all these grounds support the total
system, they do so by impinging on it most directly at different
points.

I hope that this paper not only provides a defense of the
evidential force of one support for the Christian belief system,
but also, and more generally, serves as a model for the discussion of other sources of evidence.

Syracuse University

NOTES

1. This has often been put recently by talking of a "cumulative case" for

Christian (or more generally, theistic) belief. See, e.g., Basil Mitchell, *The Justification of Religious Belief* (New York: Oxford University Press, 1981); William J. Abraham, "Cumulative Case Arguments for Christian Theism", in W. J. Abraham and S. W. Holtzer, eds., *The Rationality of Religious Belief* (Oxford: Clarendon Press, 1987). I have taken a preliminary shot at discussing this diversity of grounds in *Perceiving God* (Ithaca, N.Y.: Cornell University Press, 1991), Ch. 8. The last section of this paper provides a capsule summary.

Let me make it explicit that I am focusing on grounds or bases for Christian belief that are accessible to the believer in question, that can be cited by the believer as providing support for the beliefs in question. I by no means suppose that grounds that satisfy this accessibility-usability condition are the whole story about the epistemology of religious, or other, belief. It may well be the whole story, or the central part of the story, for the *justification* of belief in at least one common sense of 'justification'. But knowledge, in my judgment, is a different matter altogether. If my Christian beliefs were reliably acquired, perhaps by the supernatural activity of God, or if they were acquired by a normal functioning of my cognitive faculties (a notion stressed recently by Plantinga), then, assuming they are true, they might well count as knowledge even though the believer is unable to specify grounds, reason, or bases that can be seen to be adequate support for the beliefs. In this paper I will have my eye on justification in the sense just indicated, not on knowledge.

2. This point is often stressed. See, e.g., St. Thomas Aquinas, *Summa Contra Gentiles*, Bk. I, Ch. 4.

3. A number of sociological surveys indicate that the direct experience of God is much more widespread today among Christians than is often supposed. See, e.g., Rodney Stark and Charles Y. Glock, *American Piety: The Nature of Religious Commitment* (Berkeley and Los Angeles: University of California Press, 1968). They report that in a survey of a wide variety of Christian denominations about 75 percent of the respondents take themselves to have been at some time aware of the presence of God.

4. I have said nothing about the gifts of the spirit that are given a prominent place in the charismatic movement—speaking in tongues, healing, prophecy, and the like. I certainly do not wish to deny their authenticity. They are recognized as such by St. Paul and other New Testament writers. I have not focused on them here because I do not wish to have my argument disrupted by controversy over such phenomena. By concentrating on aspects of spirituality that are more unanimously accorded a high value by Christians, I will avoid peripheral difficulties. It is also worthy to note that St. Paul, in his famous discussion in Chs. 12–14 of I Corinthians, does not put these "charismatic" gifts in the first rank.

5. This bears a strong family resemblance to the position put forward by Diogenes Allen in *The Reasonableness of Faith* (Washington-Cleveland:

Corpus Books, 1968) and, in a later form, in *Christian Belief in a Postmodern World: The Full Wealth of Conviction* (Louisville, Ken: Westminster/John Knox Press, 1989). Allen stresses the way in which Christian faith "satisfies our needs" and argues that this constitutes a reason for Christian belief. He does not present this as *evidence* for the truth of the Christian scheme, as I do, but there is a strong overlap in the emphasis on the fulfillment of promises and expectations.

　　6. The qualification 'to a significant extent' that is attached both to conditions and fulfillment reflects the obvious fact that both can be realized to various degrees. One can be more or less open to the Spirit. One can be more or less other-centered, loving, devout, trusting, serene, and so on.

　　7. Let me spell this out just a bit more. The preconditions are thought to be sufficient for the spiritual fruits in the sense that God's dispositions are such that the satisfaction of the specified preconditions will *typically* lead to the sanctifying work of the Holy Spirit (which is a strict necessary and sufficient condition of sanctification), and are thought to be necessary in the sense that His dispositions are such that this work of the Holy Spirit will not *typically* occur without the satisfaction of those preconditions.

　　8. By 'full-blown' I do not understand 'to the highest degree', something that is rarely if ever found anywhere in this life. I understand rather 'inclusive of all the essential components thereof'.

　　9. At least we can say that it is part of learning to be a Christian to recognize Christ and the Holy Spirit at work in one, or present to one.

　　10. It might be supposed that where the data are conceptualized in the language of the "theory", this loads the dice in favor of the latter. For the "data" in that case are bound to return a favorable verdict. Not so. The fact that the preconditions and consequences are specified in specifically Christian terms by no means ensures that those consequences will be forthcoming upon the satisfaction of those preconditions. That is a matter of how things in fact turn out. Hence, if they do turn out as predicted by the "theory", that can legitimately be reckoned to the credit of the theory.

　　11. This condition is not satisfied by all naturalistic explanations; it is not satisfied by, e.g., psychoanalytic explanations.

　　12. Let me once again remind you that I am confining myself to *grounds, reasons,* or *evidence* for Christian belief that could, in principle, be specified by a believer as his/her grounds, reasons, evidence, or support for his/her belief. I am leaving aside any other ways in which Christian belief might constitute *knowledge*, e.g., by being acquired in a *reliable* way or being acquired by the proper functioning of one's faculties—where this does not provide the believer with grounds that s/he might cite in support of his/her belief.

　　13. For a more extensive discussion of this, see my *Perceiving God*, Ch. 8.

An Evolutionary Argument Against Naturalism

Alvin Plantinga

ABSTRACT

The argument essentially depends upon the fact that the evolution of our cognitive faculties does not guarantee that they are reliable (produce mostly true or verisimilitudinous beliefs) but only, at most, that our *behavior* is adaptive in the circumstances in which our ancestors found themselves. Consider the objective conditional probability of our cognitive faculties' being reliable, given that they have arisen by way of the mechanisms sanctioned by contemporary evolutionary theory and given philosophical or metaphysical naturalism, according to which there is no such person as God. I argue that the reasonable attitude to take with respect to this probability is either to estimate it as low or to be agnostic with respect to it. Either way, I argue, one who accepts the conjunction of naturalism with the thesis that our cognitive faculties have developed in accordance with the mechanisms suggested by contemporary evolutionary theory, has a defeater for that conjunction—a defeater that can't be ultimately defeated. If so, however, evolutionary naturalism (or naturalistic evolutionism) is self-defeating and can't rationally be believed or accepted.

A. The Problem

Most of us think (or would think on reflection) that at least *one* function or purpose of our cognitive faculties is to provide us with true beliefs. Moreover, we go on to think that when they function properly, in accord with our design plan, then for the most part they do precisely that. Of course qualifications are necessary. There are various exceptions and special cases: visual illusions, mechanisms like forgetting the pain of childbirth, optimism about recovery not warranted by the relevant statistics, unintended conceptual by-products, and so on. There are also those areas of cognitive endeavor marked by enormous disagreement, wildly varying opinion: philosophy and Scripture scholarship come to mind. Here the sheer volume of disagreement and the great variety and contrariety of options proposed suggest that either not all of us are such that our cognitive faculties do function according to the design plan, in these areas, or that it is not the case that the relevant modules of the design plan are aimed at truth, or that the design plan for those areas is defective.

Nevertheless, over a vast area of cognitive terrain we take it both that the purpose (function) of our cognitive faculties is to provide us with true or verisimilitudinous beliefs, and that, for the most part, that is just what they do. We suppose, for example, that most of the deliverances of memory are at least approximately correct. True, if you ask five witnesses how the accident happened, you may get five different stories. Still, they will agree that there was indeed an *accident*, and that it was an *automobile* accident (as opposed, say, to a naval disaster or a volcanic eruption); there will usually be agreement as to the number of vehicles involved (particularly if it is a small number), as well as the rough location of the accident (Aberdeen, Scotland, as opposed to Aberdeen, South Dakota), and so on. And of course all this is against the background of massive and much deeper agreement: that there are automobiles; that they do not disappear when no one is looking; that if released from a helicopter they fall down rather than up; that they are driven by people who use them to go places; that they are seldom driven by three-year-olds; that their drivers have purposes, hold beliefs, and often act on those purposes and beliefs; that few of them (or their drivers) have been more than a few miles from the surface of the earth; that the world has existed for a good long time—much more than ten minutes, say—and a million more such Moorean truisms. (Of course there is the occasional dissenter—in the grip, perhaps, of cognitive malfunction or a cognitively crippling philosophical theory.)

We think our faculties much better adapted to reach the truth in some areas than others; we are good at elementary arithmetic and logic and the perception of middle-sized objects under ordinary conditions. We are also good at remembering certain sorts of things: I can easily remember what I had for breakfast this morning, where my office was located yesterday, and whether there was a large explosion in my house last night.

Things get more difficult, however, when it comes to an accurate reconstruction of what it was like to be, say, a fifth-century B.C. Greek (not to mention a bat), or whether the axiom of choice or the continuum hypothesis is true; things are even more difficult, perhaps, when it comes to figuring out how quantum mechanics is to be understood and what the subnuclear realm of quark and gluon is really like, if indeed there really is a subnuclear realm of quark and gluon. Still, there remains a vast portion of our cognitive terrain where we think that our cognitive faculties do furnish us with truth.

But isn't there a problem, here, for the naturalist? At any rate, for the naturalist who thinks that we and our cognitive capacities arrived upon the scene after some billions of years of evolution (by way of natural selection, genetic drift, and other blind processes working on such sources of genetic variation as random genetic mutation)? Richard Dawkins (according to Peter Medawar, "one of the most brilliant of the rising generation of biologists") once leaned over and remarked to A. J. Ayer at one of those elegant, candle-lit, bibulous Oxford college dinners that he couldn't imagine being an atheist before 1859 (the year Darwin's *Origin of Species* was published); "[A]lthough atheism might have been logically tenable before Darwin," said he, "Darwin made it possible to be an intellectually fulfilled atheist." Dawkins goes on:

> All appearances to the contrary, the only watchmaker in nature is the blind forces of physics, albeit deployed in a very special way. A true watchmaker has foresight: he designs his cogs and springs, and plans their interconnections, with a future purpose in his mind's eye. Natural selection, the blind, unconscious automatic process which Darwin discovered, and which we now know is the explanation for the existence and apparently purposeful form of all life, has no purpose in mind. It has no mind and no mind's eye. It does not plan for the future. It has no vision, no foresight, no sight at all. If it can be said to play the role of watchmaker in nature, it is the *blind* watchmaker.[1]

Now Dawkins thinks Darwin made it possible to be an intellectually fulfilled atheist, but perhaps Dawkins is dead wrong here. Perhaps the truth lies in the opposite direction. If our cognitive faculties have originated as Dawkins thinks, then their ultimate purpose or function (if they have a purpose or function) will be something like *survival* (of individual, species, gene, or genotype); but then it seems initially doubtful that among their functions—ultimate, proximate, or otherwise—would be the production of true beliefs. Taking up this theme, Patricia Churchland declares that the most important thing about the human brain is that it has evolved; hence, she says, its principal function is to enable the organism to *move* appropriately:

> Boiled down to essentials, a nervous system enables the organism to succeed in the four F's: feeding, fleeing, fighting and reproducing. The principal chore of nervous systems is to get the body parts where they should be in order that the organism may survive. . . . Improvements in sensorimotor control confer an evolutionary advantage: a fancier style of representing is advantageous *so long as it is geared to the organism's way of life and enhances the organism's chances of survival* [Churchland's emphasis]. Truth, whatever that is, definitely takes the hindmost.[2]

Her point, I think, is that (from a naturalistic perspective) what evolution guarantees is (at most) that we *behave* in certain ways—in such ways as to promote survival, or survival through childbearing age. The principal function or purpose, then (the "chore," says Churchland), of our cognitive faculties is not that of producing true or verisimilitudinous beliefs, but instead that of contributing to survival by getting the body parts in the right place. What evolution underwrites is only (at most) that our *behavior* be reasonably adaptive to the circumstances in which our ancestors found themselves; hence, it does not guarantee mostly true or verisimilitudinous beliefs. Of course, our beliefs *might* be mostly true or verisimilitudinous; but there is no particular reason to think they *would* be: natural selection is interested, not in truth, but in appropriate behavior. What Churchland says suggests, therefore, that naturalistic evolution—that is, the conjunction of naturalism with the view that we and our cognitive faculties have arisen by way of the mechanisms proposed by contemporary evolutionary theory—gives us reason to doubt two things: (1) that a *purpose* of our cognitive systems is that of serving us with true beliefs, and (2) that they *do*, in fact, furnish us with mostly true beliefs.

Willard Van Orman Quine and Karl Popper, however, apparently demur. Popper argues that since we have evolved and survived, we may be pretty sure that our hypotheses and guesses as to what the world is like are mostly correct.[3] And Quine says he finds encouragement in Darwin:

> What does make clear sense is this other part of the problem of induction: why does our innate subjective spacing of qualities accord so well with the functionally relevant groupings in nature as to make our inductions tend to come out right? Why should our subjective spacing of qualities have a special purchase on nature and a lien on the future?
>
> There is some encouragement in Darwin. If people's innate spacing of qualities is a gene-linked trait, then the spacing that has made for the most successful inductions will have tended to predominate through natural selection. Creatures inveterately wrong in their inductions have a pathetic but praiseworthy tendency to die before reproducing their kind.[4]

Indeed, Quine finds a great deal more encouragement in Darwin than Darwin himself did: "With me," says Darwin,

> the horrid doubt always arises whether the convictions of man's mind, which has been developed from the mind of the lower animals, are of any value or at all trustworthy. Would any one trust in the convictions of a monkey's mind, if there are any convictions in such a mind?[5]

So here we appear to have Quine and Popper on one side and Darwin and Churchland on the other. Who is right? But a prior question: what, precisely, is the issue? Darwin and Churchland seem to believe that (naturalistic) evolution gives one a reason to doubt that human cognitive faculties produce for the most part true or verisimilitudinous beliefs: call this Darwin's Doubt. Quine and Popper, on the other hand, apparently hold that evolution gives us reason to believe that human cognitive faculties *do* produce for the most part true or verisimilitudinous beliefs. How shall we understand this opposition?

B. Darwin's Doubt

Perhaps Darwin and Churchland mean to propose that a certain objective conditional probability is relatively low: the probability of human cognitive faculties' being reliable (producing mostly true or verisimilitudinous beliefs), given that human beings *have* cognitive faculties (of the sort we have) and given that these faculties have been produced by evolution (Dawkins's blind evolution, unguided by the hand of God or any other person). If (naturalistic) evolution is true, then our cognitive faculties will have resulted from blind mechanisms like natural selection, working on sources of genetic variation such as random genetic mutation. And the ultimate purpose or function (Churchland's "chore") of our cognitive faculties, if indeed they *have* a purpose or function, will be survival—of individual, species, gene, or genotype. But then it is unlikely that they have the production of true beliefs as a proximate or any other function. So the probability of our faculties' being reliable, given naturalistic evolution, would be fairly low. Popper and Quine, on the other side, judge that probability fairly high.

What is at issue, then, is the value of a certain conditional probability: P(R/N&E&C).[6] Here N is metaphysical naturalism. It isn't easy to say precisely what naturalism *is*, but perhaps that isn't necessary in this context; prominent examples would be the views of (say) David Armstrong, the later Darwin, Quine, and Bertrand Russell. (Crucial to metaphysical naturalism, of course, is the view that there is no such person as the God of traditional theism.) E is the proposition that human cognitive faculties have arisen by way of the mechanisms to which contemporary evolutionary thought directs our attention; and C is a complex proposition whose precise formulation is both difficult and unnecessary, but which states what cognitive faculties we have—memory, perception, reason, Thomas Reid's sympathy—and what sorts of beliefs they produce. R, on the other hand, is the claim that our cognitive faculties are reliable (on the whole, and with the qualifications mentioned above), in the sense that they produce mostly true or verisimilitudinous beliefs in the sorts of environments that are normal for them. And the question is: what is the probability of R on N&E&C? Alternatively, perhaps the interest of *that* question lies in its bearing on *this* question: what is the probability that a belief produced by human cognitive faculties is true, given N&E&C? And if we construe the dispute in this way, then what Darwin and

Churchland propose is that this probability is relatively low, while Quine and Popper think it fairly high.

1. Stich vs. Dr. Pangloss

Well, what considerations would be relevant to this question? Consider the sort of argument implicit in the passage from Quine: "Creatures inveterately wrong in their inductions have a pathetic but praiseworthy tendency to die before reproducing their kind," he says. Humankind, happily enough, has not died before reproducing its kind; so probably we human beings are not inveterately wrong in our inductions. This claim is specified to inductions, of course; but presumably the same would hold for all or some of our other characteristic beliefs. (According to J. Fodor, "Darwinian selection guarantees that organisms either know the elements of logic or become posthumous."[7]) The claim seems to be that the selection processes involved in evolution are likely to produce cognitive faculties that are reliable, given that they produce cognitive faculties at all.

Stephen Stich attempts to set out the argument implicit in Quine's and Popper's brief and cryptic remarks. (He notes that versions of this argument circulate widely in the oral tradition, but are seldom if ever developed in any detail.) As he sees it, this argument essentially involves two premises: (1) that "evolution produces organisms with good approximations to optimally well-designed characteristics or systems,"[8] and (2) that "an optimally well-designed cognitive system is a rational cognitive system," where (on one of the two understandings of 'rational' he considers) a *rational* cognitive system, in turn, is a *reliable* cognitive system, one that produces a preponderance of true or verisimilitudinous beliefs. Stich proposes "to make it clear that there are major problems to be overcome by those who think that evolutionary considerations impose interesting limits on irrationality";[9] what he shows, I think, is that the denials of (1) and (2) are wholly compatible with contemporary evolutionary theory and not implausible with respect to it.

By way of attack on (1) he points out that natural selection isn't the only process at work in evolution; there is also (among others) random genetic drift, which "can lead to the elimination of a more fit gene and the fixation of a less fit one."[10] For example, a genetically based and adaptively favorable trait might arise within a population of sea gulls; perhaps six members of the flock enjoy it. Being birds of a feather, they flock together—sadly enough, at the site of a natural disaster, so that all are killed in a tidal wave or volcanic eruption or by a large meteorite. The more fit gene thus gets eliminated from the population. (There is also the way in which a gene can be fixed, in a small population, by way of random walk.) He points out further, with respect to (1), that there is no reason to think it inevitable that natural selection will have the *opportunity* to select for optimal design. For example, an adaptively positive trait might be linked with an adaptively negative trait by pleiotropy (where one gene codes for more than one trait or system); then it could happen that the gene gets selected and perpetuated by virtue of its link with the positive trait, and the negative trait gets perpetuated by way of its link with the gene. A truly optimal system—one with the positive trait but without the negative—may never show up, or may show up too late to fit in with the current development of the organism.[11]

With respect to (2), the claim that an optimally designed cognitive system is rational (i.e., reliable), Stich observes, first, that optimal design, presumably, is to be understood in terms of fitness: "From the point of view of natural selection, it is plausible to say that one system is better designed than a second if an organism having the first would be more fit—that is, more likely to survive and reproduce successfully—than a conspecific having the second. A system is optimally well designed if it enhances biological fitness more than any alternative."[12] He then argues that reliable cognitive systems aren't necessarily more fitness-enhancing than unreliable ones; that is, he argues that it is not the case, for any two cognitive systems S_1 and S_2, that if S_1 is more reliable than S_2, then S_1 is more fitness-enhancing than S_2. S_1, for example, might cost too much by way of energy or memory capacity; alternatively, the less reliable S_2 might produce more by way of false beliefs but nonetheless contribute more to survival.[13]

So Stich's point is this: so far as contemporary evolutionary theory is concerned, there is little reason to endorse either (1) or (2). But has he correctly identified the conclusions (or the premises) of those he sets out to refute?[14] "We now have a pair of arguments," he says, "for the claim that evolution and natural selection *guarantee* at least a close approximation to full rationality in normal organisms, ourselves included"[15] and "An essential component in both arguments . . . , aimed at showing that evolution will *insure* rationality, is . . . ."[16] If his aim is to cast doubt on these arguments, taken as arguments for the claim that evolution and natural selection *guarantee* or *insure* rationality, then he has certainly accomplished it. But perhaps Quine and Popper and their allies do not mean to argue anything quite so strong as that evolution guarantees or insures this result. Perhaps what they mean to argue is only that it is fairly or highly *probable*, given that we and our cognitive faculties have evolved according to the processes endorsed by contemporary evolutionary theory, that those faculties are reliable; perhaps they mean to argue only that P(R/N&E&C) is fairly high. What Stich shows is that it is perfectly possible both that we and our cognitive faculties have evolved in the ways approved by current evolutionary theory, and that those cognitive faculties are not reliable. But that doesn't address Quine's argument taken as an implicit argument for the claim that P(R/N&E&C) is fairly high, and *a fortiori* it doesn't serve as an argument for Darwin's Doubt—i.e., for the claim that P(R/N&E&C) is fairly low.

2. The Doubt Developed

Can we assemble an argument for Darwin's Doubt from (among other things) the materials Stich presents? In order to avoid irrelevant distractions, suppose we think, first, not about ourselves and our ancestors, but about a hypothetical population of creatures much like ourselves on a planet similar to Earth. (Darwin proposed that we think about another species, such as monkeys.) Suppose these creatures have cognitive faculties, hold beliefs, change beliefs, make inferences, and so on; and suppose these creatures have arisen by way of the selection processes endorsed by contemporary evolutionary thought. That is the probability that their faculties are reliable? What is P(R/N&E&C), specified, not to us, but to them? According to Quine and Popper, the probability in question would be rather high: belief is connected with action in such a way that extensive false belief would lead to maladaptive behavior, in which case it is likely that the ancestors of those creatures would have displayed that pathetic but praiseworthy tendency Quine mentions.

But now for the contrary argument. First, perhaps it is likely that their *behavior* is adaptive; but nothing follows about their *beliefs*. We aren't given, after all, that their beliefs are so much as causally connected with their behavior; for we aren't given that their beliefs are more than mere epiphenomena, not causally involved with behavior at all. Perhaps their beliefs neither figure into the causes of their behavior, nor are caused by that behavior. (No doubt beliefs would be caused by *something* in or about these creatures, but it needn't be by their *behavior*.) You may object that as *you* use 'belief,' beliefs just *are* among the processes (neural structures, perhaps) that (together with desire, fear, and the like) *are* causally efficacious. Fair enough (you have a right to use that word as you please); but then my point can be put as follows: in *that* use of 'belief,' it may be that the things with propositional content are not beliefs— i.e., do not have causal efficacy. It can't be a matter of definition (or use) that there are neural structures or processes displaying both propositional content and causal efficacy with respect to behavior; and perhaps the things that display causal efficacy do not display the sort of relation to content (to a proposition) that a belief of the proposition **p** must display toward **p**. You say that in that case the things, if any, that stand in that relation to a proposition wouldn't be beliefs (because, as you see it, beliefs must have causal efficacy). Well, there is no sense in arguing about words: I'll give you the term 'belief' and state my case using other terms. What I say is possible is that the things (mental acts, perhaps) that stand in that relation to content (to propositions) do not also enjoy causal efficacy. Call those things whatever you like: *they* are the things that are true or false, and it is about the likelihood of *their* truth or falsehood that we are asking. If these things, whatever we call them, are not causally connected with behavior, then they would be, so to speak, *invisible* to evolution; and then the fact that they arose during the evolutionary history of these beings would confer no probability on the idea that they are mostly true, or most nearly true, rather than wildly false. Indeed, the probability of their being for the most part true would have to be estimated as fairly low.

A second possibility is that the beliefs of these creatures are not among the *causes* of their behavior, but are *effects* of that behavior, or effects of causes that also cause behavior. Their beliefs might be like a sort of decoration that isn't involved in the causal chain leading to action. Their waking beliefs might be no more causally efficacious, with respect to their behavior, than our dream beliefs are with respect to ours. This could go by way of pleiotropy: genes that code for traits important to survival also code for consciousness and belief; but the latter don't figure into the etiology of action. Under these conditions, of course, their beliefs could be wildly false. It *could* be that one of these creatures believes that he is at that elegant, bibulous Oxford dinner, when in fact he is slogging his way through some primeval swamp, desperately fighting off hungry crocodiles. Under this possibility, as under the first, beliefs wouldn't have (or needn't have) any purpose or function; they would be more like unintended by-products, and the likelihood that they are mostly true would be low.

A third possibility is that beliefs do indeed have causal efficacy with respect to behavior, but not by virtue of their *content*; put in currently fashionable jargon, this would be the suggestion that although indeed beliefs are causally efficacious, it is only by virtue of their *syntax*, not by virtue of their *semantics*. Indeed precisely this is part of a popular contemporary view: the computational theory of mind.[17] I read a poem very loudly, so loudly as to break a glass; the sounds I utter have meaning, but their meaning is causally irrelevant to the breaking of the glass. In the same way it might be that these creatures' beliefs have causal efficacy, but not by way of the content of those beliefs. Some probability must be reserved for each of these options; and under each, the likelihood that the beliefs of these creatures would be for the most part true or verisimilitudinous would be low.

A fourth possibility: it could be that belief is causally efficacious—'semantically' as well as 'syntactically'—with respect to behavior, but *maladaptive*. As Stich points out, it is quite possible (and quite in accord with current evolutionary theory) that a system or trait that is in fact maladaptive—at any rate less adaptive than available alternatives—should nonetheless become fixed and survive. Perhaps the belief systems of these creatures are like the albinism found in many arctic animals, or like sickle-cell anemia: maladaptive, but connected with genes coding for behavior or traits conducive to survival. These beliefs could be maladaptive in two ways. First, perhaps they are a sort of energy-expensive distraction, causing these creatures to engage in survival-enhancing behavior, but in a way less efficient and economic than if the causal connections bypassed belief altogether. And second, it could be that beliefs in fact produce maladaptive behavior. Perhaps a mildly maladaptive belief-behavior structure is coded for by the same genetic structure that produces some adaptive behavior. Suppose these creatures' beliefs do not for the most part produce adaptive behavior: the mechanisms that produce them might nonetheless survive. Perhaps on balance their behavior is sufficiently adaptive, even if not every segment of it is. Some probability, then, must be reserved for the possibility that these creatures have cognitive faculties that are maladaptive, but nonetheless survive; and on this possibility, once more, the probability that their beliefs would be for the most part true is fairly low.

A fifth (and final) possibility is that the beliefs of our hypothetical creatures are indeed both causally connected with their behavior and also adaptive. Assume, then, that our creatures have belief systems and that these systems are adaptive: they produce adaptive behavior at not too great a cost in terms of resources. What is the probability (on this assumption together with N&E&C) that their cognitive faculties are reliable; and what is the probability that a belief produced by those faculties will be true?

Not as high as you might think. For of course beliefs don't causally produce behavior *by themselves;* it is beliefs, desires, and other factors that do so together. Suppose we oversimplify a bit and say that my behavior is a causal product just of my beliefs and desires. Then the problem is that clearly there will be any number of *different* patterns of belief and desire that would issue in the same action; and among those there will be many in which the beliefs are wildly false. Paul is a prehistoric hominid; the exigencies of survival call for him to display tiger-avoidance behavior. There will be many appropriate behaviors: for example, fleeing, or climbing a steep rock face, or crawling into a hole too small to admit the tiger, or leaping into a handy lake. Pick any such appropriately specific behavior **B**. Paul engages in **B**, we think, because, sensible fellow that he is, he has an aversion to being eaten and believes that **B** is a good means of thwarting the tiger's intentions.

But clearly this avoidance behavior could result from a thousand other belief-desire combinations; indefinitely many other belief-desire systems fit **B** equally well. (Here let me ignore the complication arising from the fact that belief comes in degrees.) Perhaps Paul very much *likes* the idea of being eaten; but when he sees a tiger, he always runs off looking for a better prospect, because he thinks it unlikely that the tiger he sees will eat him. This will get his body parts in the right place so far as survival is concerned, without involving much by way of true belief. (Of course, we must postulate other changes in Paul's ways of reasoning, including how he changes belief in response to experience, to maintain coherence.) Or perhaps he thinks the tiger is a large, friendly, cuddly pussycat and wants to pet it; but he also believes that the best way to pet it is to run away from it. Or perhaps he confuses running *toward* it with running *away* from it, believing of the action that is really running away from it, that it is running toward it; or perhaps he thinks the tiger is a regularly reoccurring illusion and, hoping to keep his weight down, has formed the resolution to run a mile at top speed whenever presented with such an illusion; or perhaps he thinks he is about to take part in a 1600-meter race, wants to win, and believes the appearance of the tiger is the starting signal; or perhaps.... Clearly, there are any number of belief-cum-desire systems that equally fit a given bit of behavior. Indeed, even if we fix desire, there will still be any number of belief systems that will produce a given bit of behavior: perhaps Paul doesn't want to be eaten but (1) thinks the best way to avoid being eaten is to run toward the tiger and (2) mistakenly believes that he is running toward it when in fact he is running away.

But these possibilities are wholly preposterous, you say. Following Richard Grandy, you point out that when we ascribe systems of belief and desire to persons, we make use of "principles of humanity," whereby we see others as resembling what we take ourselves to be.[18] You go on to endorse David Lewis's suggestion that a theory of content requires these "principles of humanity" in order to rule out as "deeply irrational" those nonstandard belief-desire systems; their contents involved are "unthinkable" and are hence disqualified as candidates for someone's belief-desire structure.[19] Surely you (and Grandy and Lewis) are right: in ascribing beliefs to others we do think of them as like what we think we are. (This involves, among other things, thinking that a purpose or function of their cognitive systems, like that of ours, is the production of true beliefs.) And a theory of content ascription does indeed require more than just the claim that the content of my beliefs must fit my behavior and desires; that leaves entirely too much latitude as to what that content, on a given occasion, might in fact be. These principles of humanity will exclude vast hordes of logically possible belief-desire systems as systems (given human limitations) no human being *could* have; thus such principles will exclude my attributing logical omniscience (or probabilistic coherence) to Paul, or even a system involving the *de re* belief, with respect to each real number in the (open) unit interval, that it is indeed greater than 0. These principles will also exclude some systems as systems we think no properly functioning human being *would* have: accordingly, I will not attribute to Paul the view that emeralds are grue, or the belief that it would be good to have a nice saucer of mud for lunch.[20]

These points are quite correct, but they do not bear on the present question. It is true that a decent theory of content ascription must require more than that the belief fit the behavior; for a decent theory of content ascription must also respect or take for granted what we ordinarily think about our desires, beliefs, and circumstances and the relations between these items. But in the case of our hypothetical population, these "principles of humanity" aren't relevant. For we aren't given that they are human; more important, we aren't given that those principles of humanity, those commonsense beliefs about how their behavior, belief, and desire are related, are true of them. We can't assume that their beliefs, for given circumstances, would be similar to what we take it *we* would believe in those circumstances. We must ask what belief-desire systems are *possible* for these creatures, given only that they have evolved according to the principles of contemporary evolutionary theory; clearly, the above gerrymanders, gruesome as they no doubt are, are perfectly possible. So perhaps their behavior has been adaptive, and their systems of belief and desire such as to fit that adaptive behavior; those beliefs could nonetheless be wildly wrong. There are indefinitely many belief-desire systems that fit adaptive behavior, but where the beliefs involved are not for the most part true. A share of probability has to be reserved for these possibilities as well.

Our question was this: given our hypothetical population along with N&E&C, what is the probability that the cognitive systems of beliefs these creatures display are reliable? Suppose we briefly review. First, on the condition in question, there is some probability that their beliefs are not causally connected with behavior at all. It would be reasonable to suppose, on that condition, that the probability of a given belief's being true wouldn't be far from one-half, and hence reasonable to suppose that the probability that their cognitive faculties are reliable (produce a preponderance of verisimilitudinous beliefs) is very low. Second, there is some probability that their beliefs are causally connected with behavior, but only as epiphenomenal effect of causes that also cause behavior; in that case too, it would be reasonable to suppose that the probability of their cognitive systems' being reliable is very low. Third, there is the possibility that belief is only 'syntactically,' not 'semantically,' connected with behavior; on this possibility too, there would be a low probability that their cognitive faculites are reliable. Fourth, there is the possibility that their beliefs are causally connected ('semantically' as well as 'syntactically') with their behavior, but maladaptive; again, in this case it would be reasonable to suppose that the probability of R is low. Fifth, there is also some probability that their beliefs are causally connected with their behavior, and are adaptive; as we saw, however, there are indefinitely many belief-desire systems that would yield adaptive behavior, but are unreliable. Here one doesn't quite know what to say about the probability that their cognitive systems would produce mainly true beliefs, but perhaps it would be reasonable to estimate it as somewhat more than one-half.[21] These possibilities are mutually exclusive and jointly exhaustive; if we had definite probabilities for each of the four cases and definite probabilities for R on each of the four, then the probability of R would be the weighted average of the probabilities for R on each of the four possibilities—weighted by the probabilities of those possibilities. (Of course, we don't have definite probabilities here, but only vague estimates; it imparts a spurious appearance of precision to so much as mention the relevant formula.)

Trying to combine these probabilities in an appropriate way, then, it would be reasonable to suppose that the probability of R, of these creatures' cognitive systems being reliable, is relatively low, somewhat less than one-half. More exactly, a reasonable posture would be to think it very unlikely that the statistical probability of their belief-producing mechanisms' being reliable, given that they have been produced in the suggested way, is either very high or very low; and fairly likely that (on N&E&C) R is less probable than its denial.

Now return to Darwin's Doubt. The reasoning that applies to these hypothetical creatures, of course, also applies to *us*; so if we think the probability of R with respect to *them* is relatively low on N&E&C, we should think the same thing about the probability of R with respect to *us*. Something like this reasoning, perhaps, is what underlay Darwin's Doubt—although of course Darwin did not have the benefit of pleiotropy, random genetic drift, gene fixation by random walk, and the other bells and whistles that adorn current evolutionary theory. So taken, his claim is that P(R/N&E&C) (specified to us) is rather low, perhaps somewhat less than one-half. Of course arguments of this sort are less than coercive; but it would be perfectly sensible to estimate these probabilities in this way.

C. A Preliminary Argument Against Naturalism

Suppose you do estimate these probabilities in roughly this way: suppose you concur in Darwin's Doubt, taking P(R/N&E&C) to be fairly low. But suppose you also think, as most of us do, that in fact our cognitive faculties *are* reliable (with the qualifications and nuances introduced above). Then you have a straightforward probabilistic argument against naturalism—

and for traditional theism, if you think these two are the significant alternatives. According to Bayes's Theorem,

$$P(N\&E\&C/R) = \frac{P(N\&E\&C) \times P(R/N\&E\&C)}{P(R)}$$

where P(N&E&C) is your estimate of the probability for N&E&C independent of the consideration of R. You believe R, so you assign it a probability of 1 (or nearly so); and you take P(R/N&E&C) to be no more than one-half. Then P(N&E&C/R) will be no greater than one-half times P(N&E&C), and will thus be fairly low. You believe C (the proposition specifying the sorts of cognitive faculties we have); so you assign it a very high probability; accordingly, P(N&E/R) will also be low. No doubt you will also assign a very high probability to the conditional *if naturalism is true, then our faculties have arisen by way of evolution;* then you will judge that P(N/R) is also low.

The same argument won't hold, of course, for traditional theism; the probability that our cognitive faculties are reliable will be much higher, on traditional theism, than one-half; for, according to traditional (Jewish, Christian, Moslem) theism, God created us in his image, a part of which involves our having knowledge over a wide range of topics and areas.[22] So (provided that for you the prior probabilities of traditional theism and naturalism are comparable), P(traditional theism/R) will be considerably greater than P(N/R).

D. The Main Argument Against Naturalism

1. *The Doubt Developed Again*

Of course, the argument for a low estimate of P(R/N&E&C) is by no means irresistible. In particular, our estimates of the various probabilities involved in estimating P(R/N&E&C) with respect to that hypothetical population were (of necessity) both extremely imprecise and also poorly grounded. You might reasonably hold, therefore, that the right course here is simple agnosticism. One just doesn't know (and has no good way of finding out) *what* P(R/N&E&C) might be. It could be very low; on the other hand, it could be rather high. With our

limited cognitive resources, you say, the proper course is to
hold no views about what that probability might be; the proper
course is agnosticism. This also seems sensible. Accordingly,
let's suppose, for the moment, that the proper course *is*
agnosticism about that probability. What would then be the
appropriate attitude toward R (specified to that hypothetical
population)? Someone who accepts N&E and also believes that
the proper attitude toward P(R/N&E&C) is one of agnosticism, clearly enough, has good reason for being agnostic
about R as well. She has no other source of information about
R (for that population); but the source of information she does
have gives her no reason to believe R and no reason to
disbelieve it. The proposition in question is the sort for which
one needs (propositional) evidence if one is to believe it
reasonably; since there is no evidence, the reasonable course is
to withhold belief.

But now suppose we again apply the same reasoning to
ourselves and our condition. Suppose we think N&E is true: we
ourselves have evolved according to the mechanisms suggested
by contemporary evolutionary theory, unguided and unorches-
trated by God or anyone else. Suppose we think, furthermore,
that there is no way to determine P(R/N&E&C) (specified to
us). What would be the right attitude to take to R? Well, if we
have no further information, then wouldn't the right attitude
here, just as with respect to that hypothetical population, be
agnosticism, withholding belief?

Compare the case of a believer in God, who, perhaps
through an injudicious reading of Freud, comes to think that
religious belief generally, and theistic belief in particular, is
almost always produced by wish fulfillment. Such beliefs, she
now thinks, are not produced by cognitive faculties functioning
properly in a congenial environment according to a design plan
successfully aimed at truth; instead they are produced by wish
fulfillment, which, while indeed it has a function, does not have
the function of producing true beliefs. Suppose she considers
the objective probability that wish fulfillment, as a belief-
producing mechanism, is reliable. She might quite properly
estimate this probability as relatively low; alternatively, however, she might think the proper course here is agnosticism; and
she might also be equally agnostic about the probability that a

belief should be true, given that it is produced by wish fulfillment.

But then in either case she has a defeater for any belief she takes to be produced by the mechanism in question. Consider the first case: she thinks the probability that wish fulfillment is reliable is low, and the probability that a belief should be true, given that it is produced by wish fulfillment not far from one-half. Then she has a straightforward defeater for any of her beliefs she takes to be produced by wish fulfillment. Her situation is like that of the person who comes into a factory, sees an assembly line carrying apparently red widgets, and is then told by the shop superintendent that these widgets are being irradiated by a variety of red light that makes it possible to detect otherwise undetectable hairline cracks. She should take it that the probability that a widget is red, given that it looks red, is fairly low; and she then has a reason, with respect to any particular widget coming down the line, to doubt that it is red, despite the fact that it looks red. To use John Pollock's terminology (and since I am already filching his example, why not?), she has an *undercutting* defeater (rather than a *rebutting* defeater). It isn't that she has acquired some evidence that the widget is nonred, thus rebutting the belief that it is red; it is rather that her grounds for thinking it red have been undercut. And, indeed, upon hearing (and believing) that the widgets are being thus irradiated, she will probably no longer believe that the widget in question is red.

Consider, on the other hand, a second case: here she doesn't come to believe that the probability of a widget's being red, given that it looks red, is low; instead, she is agnostic about that probability. As before, the shop superintendent tells her that those widgets are being irradiated by red light; but then a vice president comes along and tells her that the shop superintendent suffers from a highly resilient but fortunately specific hallucination, so that he is reliable on other topics even if totally unreliable on red lights and widgets. Still, the vice president himself doesn't look wholly reliable: there is a certain shiftiness about the eyes. . . . Then she doesn't know *what* to believe about those alleged red lights. What will she properly think about the color of the widgets? She will presumably be agnostic about the probability that a widget is red, given that it looks red; she won't know what that probability might be. For all she knows it could be very low; but also, for all she knows, it could be high. The rational course for her, therefore, is to be agnostic about the deliverances of her visual perception (so far as color detection is concerned) in this situation. But then she also has a good reason for being agnostic about the proposition *a is red*, where **a** is any of those red-appearing widgets coming down the assembly line. She has an undercutting defeater for the proposition *a is red*; this defeater gives her a reason to be agnostic with respect to that proposition. If she has no defeater for that defeater and no further evidence for the proposition, then on balance the right attitude for her to take toward it would be agnosticism.

By parity of reason, the same goes, I should think, for the believer in God described above. She too has an undercutting defeater for belief in God; if that defeater remains itself undefeated and if she has no other source of evidence, then the rational course would be to reject belief in God. That is not to say, of course, that she would in fact be *able* to do so; but it remains the rational course.

But now suppose we return to the person convinced of N&E who is agnostic about P(R/N&E&C): something similar goes for him. He is in the same position with respect to any belief **B** of his, as is the above believer in God. He is in the same condition, with respect to **B**, as the widget observer who didn't know what or who to believe about those red lights. So he too has a defeater for **B** and a good reason for being agnostic with respect to it. If he has no defeater for that defeater and no other source of evidence, the right attitude toward **B** would be agnosticism. That is not to say that he would in fact be able to reject **B**. Due to that animal faith noted by Hume, Reid, and Santayana (but so-called only by the latter), chances are he wouldn't; still, agnosticism is what reason requires. Here, then, we have another way of developing Darwin's Doubt, a way that does not depend upon estimating P(R/N&E&C) as low, but requires instead only agnosticism about that probability.

2. The Argument

By way of brief review: Darwin's Doubt can be taken as the claim that the probability of R on N&E&C is fairly low. As I argued above, that is plausible. But Darwin's Doubt can also be taken as the claim that the rational attitude to take here is agnosticism about that probability: that is more plausible. Still more plausible is the disjunction of these two claims: either the rational attitude to take toward this probability is the judgment that it is low, or the rational attitude is agnosticism with respect to it. Now the next thing to note is that **B** might be N&E itself; our devotee of N&E has an undercutting defeater for N&E, a reason to doubt it, a reason to be agnostic with respect to it. (Of course, this also holds if he isn't agnostic about P(R/N&E&C) but thinks it low, as in the preliminary argument; he has a defeater either way.) If he has no defeater for this defeater and no independent evidence—if his reason for doubting N&E remains undefeated—then the rational course would be to reject belief in N&E.

And here we must note something special about N&E. So far, we have been lumping together all our cognitive faculties, all our sources of belief, and all the beliefs they produce. But perhaps these different faculties should be treated differentially; clearly, the argument can be narrowed to specific faculties or powers or belief-producing mechanisms, with possibly different results for different cases. And surely the argument does apply more plausibly to some cognitive powers than to others. If there are such differences among those faculties or powers, presumably *perception* and *memory* would be at an advantage as compared to the cognitive mechanisms whereby we come to such beliefs as, say, that arithmetic is incomplete and the continuum hypothesis is independent of ordinary set theory. For even if we evaluated the probabilities differently from the way I suggested above and even if we thought it likely, on balance, that evolution would select for reliable cognitive faculties, this would be so only for cognitive mechanisms producing beliefs relevant to survival and reproduction. It would not hold, for example, for the mechanisms producing most of the beliefs involved in a logic or mathematics or set theory course. According to Fodor (as we saw above), "Darwinian selection guarantees that organisms either know the elements of logic or become posthumous"; but this would hold at most for the most elementary bits of logic.[23] It is only the occasional assistant professor of logic who needs to know even that first-order logic is complete in order to survive and reproduce.

Indeed, the same would hold generally for the more theoretical parts of science.[24]

> [E]volution suggests a status for the distinctions we naturally make, that removes them far from the role of fundamental categories in scientific description. Classification by colour, or currently stable animal-mating groups is crucial to our survival amidst the dangers of poison and fang. This story suggests that the ability to track directly certain classes and divisions in the world is not a factor that guides scientists in theory choice. For there is no such close connection between the jungle and the blackboard. The evolutionary story clearly entails that such abilities of discrimination were 'selected for', by a filtering process that has nothing to do with successful theory choice in general. Indeed, no faculty of spontaneous discrimination can plausibly be attributed a different status within the scientific account of our evolution. Even if successful theory choice will in the future aid survival of the human race, it cannot be a trait 'selected for' already in our biological history.[25]

So even if you think Darwinian selection would make it probable that certain belief-producing mechanisms—those involved in the production of beliefs relevant to survival—are reliable, that would not hold for the mechanisms involved in the production of the theoretical claims of science—such beliefs, for example, as E, the evolutionary story itself. And of course the same would be true for N.

What we have seen so far, therefore, is that the devotee of N&E has a defeater for any belief he holds, and a stronger defeater for N&E itself. If he has no defeater for this defeater and no independent evidence, then the rational attitude toward N&E would be one of agnosticism. But perhaps he will claim to have independent evidence. "True," he says, "if N&E were all I had to go on, then the right cognitive stance would be agnosticism about R and in fact about any proposition produced by my belief-producing faculties, including N&E itself. But why can't I reason inductively as follows? My cognitive faculties must indeed be reliable. For consider A_1, any of my beliefs. Naturally enough, I believe A_1; that is, I believe that A_1 is true. So A is one of my beliefs and A_1 is true; A_2 is one of my beliefs and A_2 is true, A_3 is one of my beliefs and A_3 is true, and so on. So by induction, all or nearly all of my beliefs are true; I therefore conclude that my faculties are probably reliable (or at any rate probably reliable *now*) because as a matter of fact each of the beliefs they have presently produced is true."

This argument ought to meet with less than universal acclaim. The friend of N&E does no better, arguing this way, than the theist who argues that wish fulfillment must be a reliable belief-producing mechanism by running a similar argument with respect to the beliefs he holds that he thinks are produced by wish fulfillment. He does no better than the widget observer who by virtue of a similar argument continues to believe that those widgets are red, even after having been told by the building superintendent that they are irradiated by red light. Clearly, this is not the method of true philosophy.

Accordingly, the friend of N&E can't argue in this way that he has independent evidence for R. Indeed, is there any sensible way at all in which he can argue for R (or N&E)? For consider any argument he might produce. This argument will have premises; and these premises, he claims, give him good reason to believe R (or N&E). But of course he has the very same defeater for each of those premises that he has for R and for N&E; and he has the same defeater for his belief that those premises constitute a good reason for R (or N&E). For that belief, and for each of the premises, he has a reason for doubting it, a reason for being agnostic with respect to it. This reason, obviously, cannot be defeated by an undefeated defeater. For every defeater of this reason he might have, he knows that he has a defeater-defeater: the very undercutting defeater that attached itself to R and to N&E in the first place.

We could also put it like this: any argument he offers for R is, in this context, delicately circular or question begging. It is not *formally* circular; its conclusion does not appear among its premises. It is instead (we might say) *pragmatically* circular in that it purports to give a reason for trusting our cognitive faculties, but is itself trustworthy only if those faculties (at

least the ones involved in its production) are indeed trustworthy. In following this procedure and giving this argument,
therefore, he subtly assumes the very proposition he proposes
to argue for. Once I come to doubt the reliability of my
cognitive faculties, I can't properly try to allay that doubt by
producing an *argument*; for in so doing I rely on the very
faculties I am doubting. Naturalistic evolution gives its adherents a reason for doubting that our beliefs are mostly true;
perhaps they are mostly wildly mistaken. But then it won't
help to *argue* that they can't be wildly mistaken; for the very
reason for mistrusting our cognitive faculties generally will be
a reason for mistrusting the faculties generating the beliefs
involved in the argument.

But (someone might say) isn't there a problem with this
argument for pragmatic circularity? The devotee of N&E
begins (naturally enough) by accepting N&E; upon being
apprised of the above argument (so I say), he comes to see that
he has an undefeated undercutting defeater for R and hence
an undefeated reason for doubting N&E. Hence (so I say) it is
irrational for him to accept N&E, unless he has other evidence; but any purported other evidence will be subject to the
same defeater as N&E. But now comes the rejoinder: as soon
as our devotee of N&E comes to doubt R, he should also
come to doubt his *defeater* for R; for that defeater, after all,
depends upon his beliefs, which are a product of his cognitive
faculties. So his defeater for R (and N&E) is also a defeater for
that defeater—i.e., for *itself*. But then when he notes that and
doubts his defeater for R, he no longer *has* a defeater (undefeated or otherwise) for N&E; so how is it irrational for him
to accept N&E?

What we really have here is one of those nasty dialectical
loops to which Hume calls our attention:

> [T]he skeptical reasonings, were it possible for them to exist, and were
> they not destroy'd by their subtlety, wou'd be successively both strong
> and weak, according to the successive dispositions of the mind. Reason
> first appears in possession of the throne, prescribing laws, and imposing
> maxims, with an absolute sway and authority. Her enemy, therefore, is
> oblig'd to take shelter under her protection, and by making use of
> rational arguments to prove the fallaciousness and imbecility of reason,
> produces in a matter, a patent under her hand and seal. This patent has

at first an authority, proportioned to the present and immediate authority of reason, from which it is deriv'd. But as it is suppos'd to be contradictory to reason, it gradually diminishes the force of that governing power, and its own at the same time; till at last they both vanish away into nothing by a regular and just diminution. . . . Tis happy, therefore, that nature breaks the force of all skeptical arguments in time, and keeps them from having any considerable influence on the understanding.[26]

When the devotee of N&E notes that he has a defeater for R, then at that stage he also notes (if apprised of the present argument) that he has a defeater for N&E; indeed, he notes that he has a defeater for anything he believes. Since, however, his having a defeater for N&E depends upon some of his beliefs, what he now notes is that he has a defeater for his defeater of R and N&E; so he now no longer *has* that defeater for R and N&E. So then his original condition of believing R and assuming N&E reasserts itself: at which point he again has a defeater for R and N&E. But then he notes that *that* defeater is also a defeater of the defeater of R and N&E; hence. . . . So goes the paralyzing dialectic. After a few trips around this loop, we may be excused for throwing up our hands in despair or disgust and joining Hume in a game of backgammon. The point remains, therefore: one who accepts N&E (and is apprised of the present argument) has a defeater for N&E, a defeater that cannot be defeated by an undefeated defeater. And isn't it irrational to accept a belief for which you know you couldn't have an undefeated defeater?

Hence the devotee of N&E has a defeater D for N&E—a defeater, furthermore, that can't be ultimately defeated; for obviously D attaches to any consideration one might bring forward in attempting to defeat it. If you accept N&E, you have an ultimately undefeated reason for rejecting N&E. But then the rational thing to do is to reject N&E. If, furthermore, one also accepts the conditional *if N is true, then so is E*, one has an ultimately undefeated defeater for N. One who contemplates accepting N and is torn, let's say, between N and theism, should reason as follows: if I were to accept N, I would have good and ultimately undefeated reason to be agnostic about N; so I shouldn't accept it. Unlike the preliminary argument, this is not an argument for the *falsehood* of naturalism and thus (given that naturalism and theism are the live options) for the truth of theism; for all this argument shows, naturalism might still be true. It is instead an argument for the conclusion that (for one who is aware of the present argument) accepting naturalism is irrational. It is like the self-referential argument against classical foundationalism: classical foundationalism is either false or such that I would be unjustified in accepting it; so (given that I am aware of this fact) I can't justifiably accept it. But of course it doesn't follow that classical foundationalism isn't *true*; for all this argument shows, it could be true, though not acceptable. Similarly here; the argument isn't for the falsehood of naturalism, but for the irrationality of accepting it.

The traditional theist, on the other hand, isn't forced into that appalling loop. On this point his set of beliefs is stable. He has no corresponding reason for doubting that it is a purpose of our cognitive systems to produce true beliefs, or any reason for thinking that P(R/N&E&C) is low, or any reason for thinking the probability that a belief is true, given that it is a product of his cognitive faculties, is no better than approximately one-half. He may indeed endorse some form of evolution; but if he does, it will be a form of evolution guided and orchestrated by God. And qua traditional theist—qua Jewish, Moslem, or Christian theist[27]—he believes that God is the premier knower and has created human beings in his image, an important part of which involves his endowing them with a reflection of his powers as a knower.[28]

Of course, he can't sensibly *argue* that in fact our beliefs are mostly true, from the premise that we have been created by God in his image. More precisely, he can't sensibly follow Descartes in starting from a condition of general doubt about whether our cognitive nature is reliable, and then use his theistic belief as a premise in an argument designed to resolve that doubt. Here Reid is surely right:

> Descartes certainly made a false step in this matter, for having suggested this doubt among others—that whatever evidence he might have from his consciousness, his senses, his memory, or his reason, yet possibly some malignant being had given him those faculties on purpose to impose upon him; and therefore, that they are not to be trusted without

a proper voucher. To remove this doubt, he endeavours to prove the being of a Deity who is no deceiver; whence he concludes, that the faculties he had given him are true and worthy to be trusted.

It is strange that so acute a reasoner did not perceive that in this reasoning there is evidently a begging of the question.

For, if our faculties be fallacious, why may they not deceive us in this reasoning as well as in others?[29]

Suppose, therefore, you find yourself doubting that our cognitive faculties produce truth: you can't properly quell that doubt by producing an argument about God and his veracity, or indeed, any argument at all; for the argument, of course, will be under as much suspicion as its source. Here there is no argument that will help you; here salvation will have to be by grace, not by works. But the theist has nothing impelling her in the direction of such skepticism in the first place; no element of her noetic system points in that direction; there are no propositions she already accepts just by being a theist that together with forms of reasoning (deductive, inductive, or abductive) she accepts lead to the conclusion that our cognitive faculties do not have apprehension of truth as their purpose—or to the doubt that they do.

The conclusion to be drawn, therefore, is that the conjunction of naturalism with evolutionary theory is self-defeating: it provides for itself an undefeated defeater. Evolution, therefore, presents naturalism with an undefeated defeater. But if naturalism is true, then, surely, so is evolution. Naturalism, therefore, is unacceptable.[30]

University of Notre Dame

NOTES

1. Richard Dawkins, *The Blind Watchmaker* (London and New York: W. W. Norton, 1986), pp. 5–7.

2. *Journal of Philosophy* 84 (October 1987): 548.

3. *Objective Knowledge: An Evolutionary Approach* (Oxford: Clarendon Press, 1972), p. 261.

4. Willard Van Orman Quine, "Natural Kinds," in *Ontological Relativity and Other Essays* (New York: Columbia University Press, 1969), p. 126.

5. Letter to William Graham Down, July 3, 1881, in Francis Darwin, ed., *The Life and Letters of Charles Darwin Including an Autobiographical Chapter* (London: John Murray, 1887), Vol. 1, pp. 315–16.

6. We could think of this probability in two ways: as a conditional *epistemic* probability, or as a conditional *objective* probability. Either will serve for my argument, but I should think the better way to think of it would be as objective probability; for in this sort of context epistemic probability, presumably, would follow known (or conjectured) objective probability.

7. J. Fodor, "Three Cheers for Propositional Attitudes," in *Representations* (Cambridge, Mass.: MIT Press, 1981), p. 121.

8. Here I assume that (1) is to be understood as "evolution *always* or *nearly always* produces organisms with good approximations. . . ."

9. Stephen Stich, *The Fragmentation of Reason* (Cambridge, Mass.: MIT Press, 1990), p. 56.

10. Ibid., p. 64.

11. Stich also makes more fanciful suggestions as to how it is that natural selection may never get to select for truly optimal systems: "Modern technology builds prosthetic limbs out of space age alloys and communications systems that transmit messages with the speed of light. It seems very likely indeed that certain organisms would have a real competitive edge if they were born with such limbs, or with nerves that conduct impulses at the speed of light. That fact that there are no such creatures surely does not indicate that the imagined changes would not enhance fitness. Rather, we can be pretty confident natural selection never had the chance to evaluate organisms that utilize such materials" (ibid., p. 65).

12. Ibid., p. 57.

13. "[A] very cautious, risk-aversive inferential strategy—one that leaps to the conclusion that danger is present on very slight evidence—will typically lead to false beliefs more often, and true ones less often, than a less hair-trigger one that waits for more evidence before rendering a judgment. Nonetheless, the unreliable, error-prone, risk-aversive strategy may well be favored by natural selection. For natural selection does not care about truth; it cares only about reproductive success" (ibid., p. 62). The point seems correct, but its relevance is not wholly obvious. The claim he proposes to refute is that an optimally fit system would also be reliable (and maybe even optimally reliable); but this claim is compatible with the existence of a pair of systems one of which is both more fitness-enhancing but less reliable than the other. By way of analogy, consider the ontological argument: maximal greatness, no doubt, would require, say, maximal excellence with respect to knowledge; but it doesn't follow that if **x** is greater than **y**, then **x** is more excellent with respect to knowledge than **y**.

14. Of course, it would be easy to misunderstand these arguments, given their authors' reluctance to state them explicitly.

15. Ibid., p. 59 (my emphasis).

16. Ibid., p. 63 (my emphasis).

17. See, for example, J. Fodor's "Methodological Solipsism Considered as a Research Strategy in Cognitive Psychology," *The Behavioral and Brain Sciences* 3 (1980): 68; see also Stephen Stich's *From Folk Psychology to Cognitive Science* (Cambridge, Mass.: MIT Press, 1983), Ch. 8 and elsewhere.

18. "Reference, Meaning and Belief," *Journal of Philosophy* 70 (1973): 443ff.

19. David K. Lewis, *On the Plurality of Worlds* (Oxford: Basil Blackwell, 1986), pp. 38ff., 107–8.

20. G. E. M. Anscombe, *Intention* (Oxford: Blackwell, 1957), Sec. 38.

21. Of course it might be, with respect to this fourth case, that the relevant probabilities differ with respect to different cognitive faculties. Perhaps the probabilities are highest with respect to, say, perception and other sources of belief coming into play in situations crucial to survival; perhaps the probabilities are considerably lower with respect to the sorts of intellectual pursuits often favored by people past their reproductive prime— such pursuits as philosophy, literary criticism, and set theory, not to mention evolutionary biology.

22. Thus, for example, Thomas Aquinas:

> Since human beings are said to be in the image of God in virtue of their having a nature that includes an intellect, such a nature is most in the image of God in virtue of being most able to imitate God (ST Ia Q. 93 a. 4);

and

> Only in rational creatures is there found a likeness of God which counts as an image. . . . As far as a likeness of the divine nature is concerned, rational creatures seem somehow to attain a representation of [that] type in virtue of imitating God not only in this, that he is and lives, but especially in this, that he understands (ST Ia Q. 93 a. 6).

23. "At most" because, as I argued above, if Darwinian selection guarantees anything, it is only that the organism's *behavior* is adaptive: there isn't anything in particular it needs to *believe* (or, *a fortiori*, to know).

24. This hasn't been lost on those who have thought about the matter. According to Erwin Schrodinger, the fact that we human beings can discover the laws of nature is "a miracle that may well be beyond human understanding" (*What Is Life?* [Cambridge: University of Cambridge Press, 1945], p. 31). According to Eugene Wigner, "The enormous usefulness of mathematics in the natural sciences is something bordering on the myste-

rious, and there is no rational explanation for it" ("The Unreasonable
Effectiveness of Mathematics in the Natural Sciences," *Communications on
Pure and Applied Mathematics* 13 [1960]:2); and "It is difficult to avoid the
impression that a miracle confronts us here, quite comparable in its striking
nature to the miracle that the human mind can string a thousand arguments
together without getting itself into contradictions, or to the two miracles of
the existence of laws of nature and of the human mind's capacity to divine
them" (p. 7). And Albert Einstein thought the intelligibility of the world is a
"miracle or an eternal mystery" (*Lettre à Maurice Solovine* [Paris: Gauthier-
Villars, 1956], p. 115).

25. Bas van Fraassen, *Laws and Symmetries* (Oxford: Clarendon Press,
1988), pp. 52–53.

26. *A Treatise of Human Nature*, edited with an analytical index by L. A.
Selby-Bigge (Oxford: Clarendon Press, 1888), Bk. I, Part IV, Sec. I, p. 187.

27. Things may stand differently with a *mere* theist—one who holds
only that there is an omnipotent, omniscient, and wholly good creator, but
does not add that God has created humankind in his own image.

28. Of course, God's knowledge is significantly different from human
knowledge: God has not been designed and does not have a design plan (in
the sense of that term in which it applies to human beings). When applied to
both God and human beings, such terms as 'design plan,' 'proper function,'
and 'knowledge,' as Aquinas pointed out, apply *analogously* rather than univocally. What precisely is the analogy in this case? Multifarious, of course
(for example, divine knowledge as well as human knowledge requires both
belief and truth); but perhaps the central analogy lies in the following
direction. God has not been designed; still, there is a way in which (if I may
say so) his cognitive or epistemic faculties work. This way is given by his
being essentially omniscient and necessarily existent: God is essentially
omniscient, but also a necessary being, so that it is a necessary truth that
God believes a proposition **A** if and only if **A** is true. Call that way of
working 'W.' W is something like an *ideal* for cognitive beings—beings
capable of holding beliefs, seeing connections between propositions, and
holding true beliefs. It is an ideal in the following sense. Say that a cognitive
design plan **P** is *more excellent than* a plan **P*** just if a being designed according to **P** would be epistemically or cognitively more excellent than one
designed according to **P***. (Of course, there will be environmental relativity
here; furthermore, one thing that will figure into the comparison between a
pair of design plans will be stability of its reliability under change of environment.) Add W to the set to be ordered. Then perhaps the resulting
ordering will not be connected; there may be elements that are incompara-
ble. But there will be a *maximal* element under the ordering: W. W, therefore, is an ideal for cognitive design plans, and it is (partly) in virtue of that
relation that the term 'knowledge' is analogically extended to apply to God.

29. "Essays on the Intellectual Powers of the Human Mind," in William Hamilton, ed., *The Works of Thomas Reid* (Edinburgh: James Thin, 1895), Essay VI 447b, p. 5.

30. Thanks are due to many for advice and criticism: in particular William Alston, Marian David, Michael DePaul, Peter Forrest, Richard Fumerton, Kenneth Konyndyk, Richard Otte, William Ramsey, Delvin Ratzsch, Victor Reppert, Leopold Stubenberg, Fred Suppe, and Stephen Wykstra. Victor Reppert reminded me that the argument of this paper bears a good deal of similarity to arguments to be found in Chapters III and XIII of C. S. Lewis's *Miracles*.

Faith as Imperfect Knowledge

3

Richard E. Creel

ABSTRACT

Propositional faith and propositional knowledge are often thought to be psychologically and perhaps logically incompatible: we cannot have faith that a proposition is true if we know that it is true, and we cannot know that a proposition is true if we have faith that it is true. However, on a causal interpretation of knowledge a distinction can be made between perfect knowledge and imperfect knowledge, and it can be demonstrated that it is possible for an instance of faith-that-p to also be an instance of knowledge-that-p, although it would be imperfect rather than perfect knowledge.

Thomas Aquinas claimed that faith is a form of knowledge.[1] Can that claim be defended stoutly? Yes, given Aquinas's assumption that faith is a gift from God and given the further assumption that knowledge consists of (1) p being true, (2) x thinking that p is true, and (3) x having been caused appropriately to think that p is true. Here is an example of knowledge in the preceding sense: you know that the earth has a moon if the earth has a moon, you think that the earth has a moon, and you think that the earth has a moon because you have seen the moon and your seeing the moon is what has caused you to think that there is a moon. In such a case you know there is a moon even if you cannot prove that there is, that is to say, even if you do not know that you know there is a moon. Another example: if you think that you are sitting down, and you are sitting down, and your thinking that you are sitting down is being caused by your awareness that you are sitting down, then you know that you are sitting down. Presumably, however, you do not know that you know it, as you cannot rule out the possibility that you are dreaming or hallucinating or hypnotized, and are really in another posture.

In the preceding sense of knowing that p, the relation between one's thinking that p and it being the case that p cannot

be mere coincidence; there must be an appropriate causal
relation between one's thinking and p and it being the case that
p.[2] For that reason, the following example of true belief is not
an example of knowledge: John thinks that there is life in
Orion, and there is life in Orion, but he thinks that there is life
in Orion solely because he has been hypnotized to think so by
someone who knows nothing about Orion except that it is the
galaxy nearest to our own. Neither would the following be
knowledge: Jean thinks that x, y, z is the combination to a
certain lock, and it is the combination to that lock; however, she
thinks it is the combination only because a friend, meaning to
play a practical joke on her, randomly picked three numbers
and told her that they were the combination. (By contrast, if she
thought that p, q, r was the combination to another lock, and it
was the combination to that lock, and she thought it was
because another friend who routinely opened it by that
combination had told her that it was, then she would know the
combination to that lock—even though before she opened it
herself she would not know that she knew it.)

Let's call knowing in the preceding sense that is, knowing
when we do not know whether we know, 'imperfect knowledge,' and knowing when we know that we know, 'perfect
knowledge.' This fits the terminology of St. Paul in I Corinthians 13:10, where he says, "Our knowledge is imperfect . . . but
when the perfect comes, the imperfect will pass away."[3] In
verse 8, St. Paul says, "As for knowledge, it will pass away."
However, verses 9–12 make it clear that St. Paul did not mean
that knowledge *simpliciter* will pass away; rather, he meant that
imperfect knowledge, our current kind of knowledge, will pass
away and be superseded by perfect knowledge. Now we know
but do not know whether we know. Then we will know that we
know. Then our knowledge will be perfected.[4]

There are two forms of imperfect knowledge: evidentially
grounded imperfect knowledge and non-evidentially grounded
imperfect knowledge. Evidentially grounded imperfect knowledge is a species of belief, rather than faith, because it is
conviction based on evidence. By contrast, non-evidentially
grounded imperfect knowledge is a species of faith, rather than
of belief, because it is a basic conviction.

In the preceding paragraph, I am implicitly making recommendations as to how we can best use the words 'knowledge,' 'belief,' and 'faith' so as to capture three distinct, complementary concepts. Much confusion in thought and communication has resulted from each of these words being used in more than one way. We will reduce the confusion, I think, if we use 'thought,' rather than 'belief,' to refer to the epistemically non-modal state of affirming or holding that something is the case. For example, if one says, "I think there is life on other planets," that says nothing about *why* one thinks it; that is, it says nothing about whether one thinks it because of direct experience, proof, probability, revelation, intuition, or something else.

If we use 'think' in the preceding way, then 'belief' and 'faith' can be used to refer, respectively, to affirming that something is the case because of evidence that one thinks shows that it is probably the case, as distinguished from affirming that something is the case simply because it seems to one to be the case. Consider, for example, the faith of Jean-Jacques Rousseau. He reported that his conviction that God exists was an "involuntary feeling." He identified some of the causes of his thinking that God exists—for example, the highly regulated system of the world and the emergence of living, sentient beings from passive, inert matter; but he made it clear that these phenomena functioned not as premises or data from which he inferred the existence of God but, rather, as media through which he experienced, or at least thought he experienced, the reality of God. Indeed, he spoke of these phenomena "revealing" God to him. After discussing these phenomena, he states, "I believe, then, that the world is governed by a powerful and wise will; I see it, or rather I feel it, and that is important for me to know."[5]

The preceding distinctions mean that a group of people who *think* that God exists might be divided along lines of epistemic modality into (1) those who think they *know for certain* that God exists, that is, those who think that God exists because they think they have a proof that God exists—for example, St. Anselm; (2) those who *believe* that God exists, that is, those who think that God exists because they think they have evidence which indicates that probably God exists—for example, Richard Swinburne; and (3) those who have *faith* that God exists, that is, those who have non-evidential

confidence that God exists—for example, Rousseau and Alvin
Plantinga.[6]

Faith taken as a general propositional attitude can, of
course, be true or false. False faith cannot be knowledge.
Veridical faith inappropriately caused cannot be knowledge.
For example, having faith because of hypnosis by an ignorant
hypnotist that there is life in Orion would not be knowledge
even if there is life in Orion. However, veridical faith appropriately caused would be non-evidentially grounded imperfect
knowledge. Therefore, because God is not a deceiver or
deceived, and causes nothing accidentally, God-given faith that
p would be propositional knowledge of the non-evidentially
grounded imperfect sort.[7]

It seems to follow that if you think there is a God because
there is a God who has appropriately caused you to think so,
then you know that there is a God, even if you do not know that
you know it, and even if it is impossible in principle for a finite
being to know that she knows that there is a God. Hence, the
person who has God-given faith that God exists knows that
there is a God, but she does not thereby know that she knows
it, as the propositional content of faith-knowledge of the
existence of God is to the person who has it neither self-
evidently true nor affirmed because of a balance of favorable
evidence. A subsequent state of propositional perfect knowledge that God exists would supersede faith-knowledge that
God exists, as we can have faith that a proposition is true only
when we do not know for certain that it is true.[8]

Because of the preceding analysis, I think it is a mistake to
distinguish, as James Muyskens does, between "trusting faith"
and "doubtful faith," as though they are different, incompatible forms of faith.[9] Insofar as we are speaking of faith as a gift
from God, we are speaking of a gift that by its nature excludes
doubt, at least emotional doubt. If it did not do this, it would
not be faith; it would be no different from evidential belief or
opinion. Hence, the only way in which gift faith can be doubtful
faith is insofar as the one who has it realizes that faith is neither
perfect knowledge nor evidentially grounded belief, and so
realizes that his faith might be mistaken—and that is how
Muyskens describes doubtful faith, namely, as "a state of mind
in which one is aware of the 'objective insufficiency' of the

grounds for believing that the object of faith obtains."[10] But then *all* propositional faith is or should be doubtful faith, as all faith as faith is grounded on something other than evidence or ratiocination and, so, is objectively insufficient from the evidential point of view.

No wedge can be driven, then, between doubtful faith and trusting faith. Propositional faith that understands itself correctly is always doubtful faith. The distinction should be between trusting-doubtful faith and untrusting-doubtful faith. The latter distinction, I submit, is the same as, or a species of, the distinction between faithfulness and unfaithfulness. But faith as faithfulness is an action, whereas faith as the divine gift of imperfect knowledge is a passion.[11] Obviously, then, the appropriate response to faith is faithfulness; that is, the appropriate response to the divine gift of imperfect knowledge is devotion to its contents and its giver.[12]

Ithaca College

NOTES

1. See St. Thomas's *Summa Contra Gentiles*, Book 1, Ch. 4.; also, Etienne Gilson, *Elements of Christian Philosophy* (New York: New American Library, 1960), p. 58. I have chosen to begin with the claim that according to St. Thomas, faith is a form of knowledge. I hope that anyone who has misgivings about whether St. Thomas thought that faith is a form of knowledge will not be distracted by that misgiving from the central issue of this paper—viz., whether God-given faith would be a form of knowledge.

2. There is a wide agreement that there must be such a causal relation. How to understand it is highly controversial.

3. For an examination of St. Paul's epistemology, see Paul Gooch, *Partial Knowledge: Philosophical Studies in Paul* (Notre Dame, Ind.: University of Notre Dame, 1987), esp. Chs. 2 and 7.

4. Thomas Aquinas's "scientific knowledge," in which "thinking-out (cogitation) causes the assent," as a result of which we know that we know, seems to me to be a species of, or identical with, perfect knowledge. See, for example, *De Veritate*, Question 14, Article 1. By carefully qualifying some knowledge as "scientific," Aquinas makes it clear that he believes in the possibility of knowledge that is not scientific. That opens the possibility of faith being a species of knowledge.

I do not mean to suggest that we cannot have perfect knowledge of anything in this life; neither, I think, did St. Paul or St. Thomas. Indeed, I am inclined to think that the following argument is sound: if we had in this life no perfect knowledge, we could not have in this life the concept of perfect knowledge; but we do have that concept, therefore we must have some perfect knowledge.

5. Jean-Jacques Rousseau, *The Creed of a Priest of Savoy*, 2nd enl. ed., Arthur H. Beattie, trans. (New York: Frederick Ungar, 1957), pp. 16–20.

6. Because of the sophistication of Plantinga's positions, I am uneasy identifying him as someone whose conviction that God exists is of the mode of faith, rather than of belief or certain-knowledge, in my senses; but for now he seems a perfect instance.

Certain-knowledge and belief are incompatible, as are certain-knowledge and propositional faith, but faith and belief are not incompatible with each other. Faith may *rejoice* if it becomes convinced that probability favors the existence of God, but it need not cease to exist because of that conviction; it can continue to exist alongside the individual's newly acquired state of *belief* that God exists. See Etienne Gilson's discussion of this point in *Elements of Christian Philosophy*, pp. 26 and 58–59.

7. I was alerted to the relation of faith to these two types of knowledge by James F. Ross's article, "Aquinas on Belief and Knowledge," in Wm. A. Frank and Girard J. Etzkorn, eds., *Essays Honoring Allan B. Wolter* (St. Bonaventure, N.Y.: The Franciscan Institute, 1985).

8. However, we must not confuse propositional faith that God exists, which is superseded by propositional perfect knowledge that God exists, with the personal awareness of God that can be granted by grace and is sometimes described as 'faith in God.' The latter is compatible with certain-knowledge; the former is not, because propositional faith, when it understands itself correctly, understands that it does not know that it knows. To know that one knows, one cannot merely have a proof that one's thought is true; one must also understand correctly that one's proof is a proof that one's thought is true. (See the reference in note 6 to Gilson's discussion of some of these points.)

9. See James Muyskens, "What Is Virtuous About Faith?" *Faith and Philosophy* 2, 1 (January 1985): 43–52. Muyskens deploys his distinction, adapted from Immanuel Kant, in response to Robert Adams, "The Virtue of Faith," *Faith and Philosophy* 1, 1 (January 1984): 3–15.

10. Muyskens, "What is Virtuous About Faith?" p. 44.

11. I point out in an unpublished paper that 'faith' is used to refer to both a passion and an action. I argue that it is less confusing and more illuminating to use 'faith' to refer to a passion, and especially to God's gift to us of non-evidentially grounded confidence in His reality and goodness, and to use 'faithfulness' to refer to an action, and especially to loyalty and devotion to

God—loyalty and devotion that are informed and guided by the content of faith.

12. I discuss the relations of faith, belief, and knowledge to hope and the rationality of religious devotion in my article, "Agatheism: A Justification of the Rationality of Devotion to God," *Faith and Philosophy* 10, 1 (January 1993): 33–48.

The Certainty of Faith

4

William Lad Sessions

ABSTRACT

Analyses of faith and certainty are required to ascertain how faith can be certain, if at all. On a view of faith as a kind of personal relationship, various kinds of certainty are required, prohibited, and permitted. A central worry of many philosophers concerns whether or not Christian faith is compatible with epistemic certainty and its requirement of adequate evidence. I argue for compatibility, but hold that it is by no means easy to make or to be certain that particular instances of faith are certain.

There are almost as many different views on the certainty of faith[1] as there are views—a veritable Babel of voices. The major divisions are these: some hold that faith is completely certain, a special kind of knowledge excluding all doubt. Others think that faith is entirely uncertain, a risky commitment that is anything but knowledge. Still others maintain that while faithful persons often *feel* certain they can never *be* certain, and so faith is invariably irrational. Such wide divergence of opinion on such an important issue is a good sign that the speakers are talking past one another, using different if not incompatible or even confused conceptions of faith and certainty. In this paper, I present one conception of faith and one analysis of certainty so that, at the risk of Babeling on, I can set forth a more subtle and nuanced view of the certainty of faith.

Faith

Adequately characterizing faith is a much larger task than is commonly realized. In part this is because *the* concept of faith encompasses a variety of conceptions that differ in many different ways. In this section, I will focus on a Christian conception of faith as a kind of *personal relationship*. This is not *every*

Christian's conception of faith, but it is familiar to most branches of Christian tradition, and it may well find comfortable lodging elsewhere. The following is a schematic statement:

> A person S has faith in another person A if and only if S is in a trusting personal relationship with A, S believes certain propositions about A ('articles of faith'), and S's coming to be in that relationship with A is (at least partially) caused by A.

On this view, faith is essentially a *personal* relationship, a relationship between two distinct existing persons qua persons; it requires at least minimal mutual understanding by each person of his or her own[2] and the other person's character and intentions and also an understanding of the nature of their relationship. Personal relationships are of course ongoing, dynamic, and complex, involving a host of subsidiary acts, attitudes, feelings, expectations, and the like; and they are reciprocal, involving give and take by both persons.

Faith is a *trusting* personal relationship. Of course there are *degrees* of trust, and faith probably requires a minimum *threshold* of trust; but faith also tends to have a fairly high level of acceptance, commitment, and love.

Acceptance. The faithful person accepts the other's authority, more or less. Such authority is not only epistemic, but also practical and axiological.

Commitment. The faithful person is deeply committed to the other. The commitment is intentional, voluntary, and responsible, but it is also enduring, lasting, and open-ended. It tends toward both *ultimacy* and *wholeheartedness*.

Love. The faithful person longs for a deep, lasting, and harmonious relationship with the other. This love involves recognition of the value of the beloved and of personal relationship to him, desire to achieve greater intimacy, deep feelings for the beloved, and powerful motivation to act in light of relationship to the beloved.

Faith includes, essentially but not centrally, *believing* certain propositions about the 'object'[3] of faith. Those propositions that a person *must* believe in order to have faith at all I will label *'general articles of faith';*[4] those necessary to have the faith some specific person has I will call *'specific articles of faith.'*[5] (Articles of faith need not be the *only* beliefs the faithful one has about her 'object' of faith.) Articles of faith must actually be *believed*, not merely presupposed, presumed, assumed, and so forth.

The articles of faith are believed on, and only on, the *ultimate authority* of the 'object' of faith; S's acceptance of A's authority is both sufficient and necessary for S to believe the articles of faith. This authority must in the end be *first-hand* (where S believes p about A on A's authority) and not *second-hand* (S believes p about A on B's authority, where B may or may not believe p about A on A's authority). But the belief may be either *explicit* (S actually believes p) or *implicit* (S would believe p if S should learn that p is authorized by A).

The 'object' of faith must be an *agent-cause* of a person's faith, in such ways as proposing articles of faith for belief, producing belief in such articles, awakening natural capacities to believe, bestowing new or even 'supernatural' capacities, and so forth.

Certainty

A complete account of certainty lies far beyond our scope here,[6] but the following points are most relevant.

Various locutions are commonly used to attribute certainty or being certain, but two are central for our purposes:[7]

1. S is certain that p, and
2. S feels certain that p.

One should distinguish between *not certain* and *uncertain: S* is not certain that p just when it is not the case that S is certain that p; whereas S is uncertain that p just when both S is not certain that p, and S is not certain that not-p. (Similarly, for the opposites of "S feels certain that p.")

Certainty differs from *clarity*. In general, clarity is either a matter of a proposition's precision, explicitness, straightforwardness, etc., or a matter of a person's understanding. But S may be certain about what is clear *or* unclear in either sense of 'clarity.' Many writers have urged, for example, that religious faith in God is certain but mysterious. (Propositions about God exceed human ability to understand them, but this infirmity does not prevent their justifiably confident affirmation.) Conversely, clarity doesn't entail certainty: the proposition that Aldebaran has exactly six planets larger than Earth is precise and straightforward, but someone who understands it may be uncertain of its truth-value.

Certainty also differs from *ultimacy* or *absoluteness*. It is no doubt tempting in a religious context to conflate these two, since religious faith is one's "ultimate concern,"[8] final allegiance, or absolute commitment.[9] But although certainty *is* absolute or ultimate with respect to epistemic appraisal—there is no higher term of epistemic commendation, and none as high—nevertheless certainty need not concern what is finally valuable or of ultimate concern. S may be absolutely certain of quite trivial things, and she may be quite uncertain of very important things.[10]

Nearly everyone notices the vital distinction between *feeling certain* and *being certain*, a distinction between what I will call the *psychological* and the *epistemic* senses of 'certain' and 'certainty.'[11]

To say that someone is psychologically certain is to affirm that she has or is in a particular state of mind, a state of being convinced of the truth of some proposition. Such conviction typically has a strong dispositional-behavioral component as well as a pervasive occurrent-passional component, although these are somewhat independent. Psychological certainty comes in degrees, and it does *not* imply that the proposition believed is true. The attribution of such certainty neither makes nor implies an evaluation of the person's state of mind; it merely describes a condition that may or may not be good, appropriate, desirable, and so forth.

By contrast, the epistemic sense of 'certainty' is implicitly evaluative: to hold that S is certain that p is to affirm that S is in the best possible epistemic position (for S, in that situation, all things considered, etc.) with respect to p. Here S's convictional state of mind is strictly irrelevant: S could be certain that p without feeling certain that p, and conversely; and S's certainty may lack either or both of the behavioral or the passional components of feeling certain.

Within the category of epistemic certainty, several independent distinctions need to be made.

First, there is a distinction regarding what is certain.[12]

In one sense, that *S* is certain that *p* implies both that *S* is rationally justified in believing that *p* and also that *p* is true. Here *S* is not merely beyond epistemic reproach but also "can't be wrong" since *S*'s evidence "guarantees" the truth of *p*.[13] Rather awkwardly, I will call this *truth-certainty*.

In another sense, that *S* is certain that *p* does *not* imply that *p* is true even though it *does* imply that *S* is rationally justified in believing that *p* is true. Here *S*'s believing may be beyond epistemic reproach without "guaranteeing" that *S*'s beliefs are true. I will call this *justification-certainty*.

Second, there is a distinction between the availability and the actuality of certainty.

The former, *proposition-certainty*, obtains when, given *S*'s epistemic situation, either *p* is true and *S* is rationally justified in believing that *p*, or *S* is rationally justified in believing that *p*. But *S* doesn't need to actually believe that *p*: certainty is available for *S*, such that *S* would be justified if *S* did so believe.

The latter, *belief-certainty*, adds to proposition-certainty the condition that *S* actually believes that *p*.[14] So *p* may be proposition-certain for *S* without *S* being belief-certain that *p*, though of course not conversely.

Third, there is a distinction concerning *S*'s certainty-maker, between what may be called *categorical* and *effective* certainty.[15]

For *S* to be categorically certain that *p*, *S*'s certainty-maker *e* must put *p* beyond all doubt for *S* in such a way that if *e* then *p* cannot be false: *e* (or *e*'s possession by *S*) logically entails *p*. Categorical certainty seems unattainable with respect to nearly every belief we possess, since it requires that we rule out every logically possible mistake.

For *S* to be effectively certain that *p*, however, *e* must exclude not every logically possible doubt but only every reasonable doubt. Effective certainty is "the certainty of life" and is often attained, since it amounts only to the assurance that everything rationally needful in that situation has been done to ascertain the proposition's truth; all real possibility of being mistaken has been ruled out.[16]

Although psychological certainty is *relative*—it comes in degrees, with no clear conceptual upper limit—epistemic certainty standardly is *absolute*, in either or both of two ways: (1) *S* either has epistemic certainty or *S* lacks it (*S* doesn't more or less have it); and (2) if *S* has it, then there is nothing more of it that *S* could have (there is no more or less of it for *S* to have).[17] In the former sense, there are no degrees of propositional truth and hence none of truth-certainty; in the latter sense, there is nothing more reasonable for *S* to believe and hence no degrees of truth- *or* justification-certainty. The phrase 'absolute certainty,' therefore, should be applied only to epistemic certainty; it has no clear sense when applied to psychological certainty.

The Certainty of Faith

Assuming these analyses of faith and certainty, we can now fashion a clearer view of the certainty of at least one form of faith. But this clearer view is also a more complicated view.

First, faith *must* be certain in the psychological-belief sense of 'certain,' and the more certain the better. In particular, *S* has faith in *A* only if *S feels certain*, to a considerable degree, about the articles of faith concerning *A*. (*S* feels certain about these only if *S* has a few if any doubts about them and believes them with a high degree of conviction.) As *S*'s conviction varies from moderate to extraordinary, one may perhaps grade *S*'s faith from "warm" to "fervent"; but if the level of confidence it too low, then faith is absent.

At least this is true of distinctively religious faith as personal relationship, for a *religious* personal relationship must be extraordinarily trusting, with a commitment tending toward ultimacy and wholeheartedness (see *Commitment*, above). Although ultimacy is distinct from certainty (as discussed above), nevertheless they are connected: to achieve the kind of overarching commitment required by religious faith, one must have a very high level of psychological certainty or else one will be assailed, undermined, and defeated by doubts.

Of course, *complete* psychological certainty cannot be achieved by anyone. Not only is there no conceptual upper limit to commitment, but also commitment beyond certain limits (varying from individual to individual) cannot often be sustained every moment of every day. But if no one can *completely* rid herself of doubts, still anyone seeking religious faith should strive to approximate to the tranquility born of single-minded loyalty.

Second, it is better than not, other things being equal, that faith also be certain epistemically.[18]

Psychological certainty, I just argued, is a necessary feature of faith; but it is also a desirable feature on its own. It is, after all, better to *feel* certain and unperturbed than to feel "bewitched, bothered, and bewildered" by rampant doubts. No one seeks the discomfort of dubiety for its own sake, and everyone desires peace of mind for its own sake. Religious commitment promises to maximize this great good and typically claims that there is no other way to maximize it.

Epistemic certainty is similarly desirable, *ceteris paribus*. It is better to *be* certain than to be its opposite, because being rationally justified is better than being unjustified or not being justified, and possessing the truth is better than being ignorant or in error. Therefore, since faith is not necessarily irrational or nonrational, epistemic certainty is desirable for faith, *if it can and may be obtained.*

One important objection may be noted here. Some, following John Hick, hold that being certain is undesirable for faith because it is "coercive" and thus incompatible with faith's epistemic freedom.[19] The view is that if S is certain that p, then S somehow cannot be free to accept, reject, or withhold that p, whereas faith requires free acceptance of p in a situation of evidential ambiguity, where there are no certainty-makers.

> Only when we ourselves *voluntarily* recognize God, desiring to enter into relationship with him, can our knowledge of him be compatible with our freedom, and so with our existence as personal beings. If God were to reveal himself to us in the coercive way in which the physical world is disclosed to us, he would thereby annihilate us as free and responsible persons.[20]

This is unconvincing. First, p may be certain for S (proposition-certainty) without S being certain that p (belief-certainty); the certainty-makers for p may be available to S but S may not be aware of them or S may not believe that p. Second, epistemic certainty does not entail psychological certainty and need not constrain S's state of mind; psychological certainty is independent of epistemic certainty, and the former has at least as much to do with the freedom or voluntariness of behavior as the latter. Third, epistemic certainty does not render action, including the "act" of faith, not voluntary (much less involuntary). Even though S is certain that p, she may still voluntarily act contrary to what she believes (or knows) about p.

So Hick's position doesn't show that epistemic certainty is not desirable from the standpoint of faith.

Third, faith *cannot* be certain in at least two senses.

1. Faith cannot achieve categorical epistemic certainty, since faith neither yields nor rests upon certainty-makers sufficient to remove all logically possible doubt. Although faith, for all that anyone has shown, may be effectively certain for someone (beyond all reasonable doubt) and the requisite strong psychological certainty of religious faith may quiet nearly all actual doubts, there is no way for faith to achieve categorical certainty (beyond all logically possible doubt). But this is hardly cause for alarm, since very few if any beliefs can scale the heights of categorical certainty; effective certainty suffices as much for religious faith as for daily life and science.[21]

2. Faith cannot be certain in the combined case, where psychological certainty is conjoined with epistemic certainty, *if* the degree of the former must be *exactly* proportional to the strength of the latter's support. To ask that it do so would collapse 'belief on faith' into purely 'rational belief.' Faith must have, or at least permit, a surplus of confidence beyond the evidence. Requiring that conviction be *strictly* proportioned to evidence is not the mark of a person of faith, save for an inordinate faith in one's evidential fortune.

Fourth, if feeling certain need not be proportioned to being certain, how *are* they related in faith? (1) Some think that psychological and epistemic certainty are completely independent: S should always feel certain that p to the highest possible degree, regardless (and perhaps heedless) of whether or not S is or could be certain that p. (2) Some go further, holding that S can feel certain that p only if S is not certain (or perhaps is uncertain) that p. (3) And some propound a perverse inversion: in faith, S can feel certain that p only if S is certain that not-p! The first view expresses the truth about what is *possible*, though not necessarily about what is *desirable:* faith (as personal relationship) does not logically tie psychological to epistemic certainty; one *can* feel certain that p whether or not one is certain that p (or that not-p). The second and third views are arguably false.

Fifth, we have seen that faith need not proportion feeling certain to being certain. But there is a prior question: *can* faith be epistemically certain at all? My contention is that although religious faith *need* not be epistemically belief-certain, there is no good reason to think that it *cannot* be certain in this sense. This is controversial, for "probably the majority of recent philosophical critics of religion have in mind a definition of faith as the believing of propositions upon insufficient evidence."[22] But the majority is mistaken; to discredit it, I shall consider five major reasons offered on its behalf and show how unpersuasive they are.

1. One common argument is that epistemic certainty requires, and faith lacks, conclusive evidence; hence, faith cannot be epistemically certain. The premises are supported by two quite different analyses of faith. In one, faith allows some evidence, but never enough to constitute certainty; faith precludes *conclusive* evidence. In the other, faith has nothing to do with evidence; faith precludes *any* evidence.

Perhaps some persons do use the word 'faith' with either of these meanings. But neither is a part of the personal relationship conception of faith. Some, perhaps most, instances of this conception doubtless lack evidence, and some may even lack all evidence (and are therefore irrational); but not all, and not necessarily. Conceptually speaking, faith as personal relationship makes *no* claims about evidence—one (but not the only) reason why there can be both rational and irrational faith.

2. Another argument is that although the psychological certainty of faith may transcend evidence, epistemic certainty of beliefs must be directly proportional to evidence. Hence, faith permits—or even encourages—gross disparity between conviction and epistemic certainty. But it is not rational for conviction to outstrip certainty. Hence, religious faith cannot be serious about epistemic certainty; its 'certainty' is *only* psychological and has nothing to do with evidence.

But although the psychological conviction of religious faith outstrips, or may outstrip, epistemic certainty, it doesn't follow either that faith has no epistemic certainty or that the disparity is irrational. It clearly is possible, and may be thoroughly rational, to feel more certain than one is certain. It may also be rational to seek psychological certitude when little or no epistemic certainty is available.

3. A third argument holds that faith unavoidably involves risk with regard to truth, while epistemic certainty eliminates such risk: if you are epistemically certain, you "can't be wrong," and what you believe must be true. Hence, faith cannot be epistemically certain.

But the conclusion doesn't follow, because the second premise conflates two kinds of certainty. If S is truth-certain that p, it follows that p, but not if S is merely justification-certain that p. In the latter, "S is certain that p" means only "S's believing p is beyond rational reproach," without implying that p is true; here "you can't be wrong" means "you can't be blamed," not "you can't be mistaken." So even if faith is "risky" in not implying truth, it may still be epistemically (i.e., justification-) certain.

4. A fourth argument notes that faith requires believing articles of faith on the authority of another. But, it claims, believing on authority is somehow rationally or noetically subpar and cannot deserve the accolade of 'certainty,' which should be reserved only for those beliefs whose truth we can somehow "find out for ourselves."

On the contrary. So far from being subpar, believing on authority is the very life-blood of our doxastic-noetic existence.[23] Certainty, like knowledge, both can and must be gained through trusting others, and accepting others' epistemic authority is neither deviant nor defective.

5. A fifth argument holds that there is a special infirmity in religious faith in a transcendent person. The articles of such faith must be believed on the first-hand authority of a transcendent person; but no one can be a first-hand authority for S unless S can directly experience him or her; since no human can directly experience a transcendent person, the latter cannot be a first-hand authority for us.[24]

The topic of religious experience is notoriously thorny, but

I see no reason why a human being cannot experience a transcendent being through or in mundane objects. No doubt religious experience involves interpretation, but so does all experience, including experience of physical objects.[25] So, it seems, a transcendent being could be a first-hand authority for a human being.

Perhaps there are other arguments to show that faith cannot be epistemically certain, but until they are produced it seems reasonable to hold that faith *can* be epistemically certain, although it *need not* be.

So much for possibilities. Now, what is permissible? *Should* faith be certain? I venture the following principles:

1. If *S* is certain that not-*p* (or *p*), then it is not permissible that *S* feel certain that *p* (or not-*p*).
2. If *S* is certain that *p*, then it is permissible that *S* feel certain that *p*.
3. If *S* is uncertain that *p*, then it is permissible that *S* feel certain that *p*.

These principles may be defended either from reason or from faith. Here I will address only the concerns of faith. For faith, (3) seems clearly acceptable, for faith sometimes *is* a venture "over 70,000 fathoms." But what about (1) and (2)? Why, according to faith, should or shouldn't one feel certain about *p* when one is certain about not-*p* or *p*? Here there seems to be no definitive answer. The faith of some may involve believing that their faith is rational; but the faith of others may equally involve a contrary belief. The personal-relationship conception of faith accommodates *both* views; and so, at the minimum, there is nothing contrary to faith as such in (1) and (2), even if they are not required by a particular person's faith.

Well then, *can* faith (as personal relationship) be certain? Our answer has been that it both can and can't be, in various ways: faith must be psychologically certain; it is better for it to be epistemically certain than the opposite; faith cannot be categorically epistemically certain and cannot exactly proportion psychological certainty to epistemic certainty; there is no good reason to think that faith cannot be epistemically belief-certain; and there are plausible restrictions on the relations of being certain and feeling certain.

But there is another question that lies beyond "can" and "can't": *is* faith (as personal relationship) certain? Is such faith *as it actually exists* certain in any of the ways we have identified? To answer this question adequately, one would have to explore particular instances of faith in considerable depth and detail. Clearly, we can't do this here. But we can take notice of some obstacles to the certainty of faith—obstacles that make it difficult to *realize* and to *recognize* the certainty of faith and are particularly formidable for religious faith in a transcendent person.

Despite the presence of so much fanaticism in the world, it is by no means easy to *feel* (psychologically) certain, due to the constant pressure of doubts, temptations, and distractions. Religions provide many aids, both social and psychological, toward alleviating or removing these pressures: inquisitions, propaganda, cloisters, purifications, pilgrimages, confessions, and sermons, as well as personal routines, meditation, prayer, inquiry, and self-denial. But the aids vary in propriety and effectiveness. Moreover, it is not easy to *make* certain that someone (especially oneself!) does in fact *feel* certain, because of hidden thoughts and unconscious motives, self-deception and wishful thinking, the opacity and inchoateness of intention, the elusiveness of feeling, and the conspiracy of others' silence.

Nor is it any easier to *be* (epistemically) certain, for again obstacles abound: certainty-makers may be available but not actually appropriated; acquiring the proper certainty-makers may require considerable effort, or fortuitous extraordinary experience, or uncontrollable and unpredictable external assistance; and faith in its quest for certitude may not provide—may even undercut—the motivation to avoid such obstacles. Once again, it is also hard to *make* certain that someone *is* indeed certain: becoming certain that someone is certain may be tedious, laborious, convoluted, uninteresting, or unprofitable; it may be unclear just what certainty-makers are available or actually employed; and again faith may provide little assistance in overcoming such obstacles.

All these obstacles are greatly compounded when faith is religious—when it is faith in a transcendent person. As religious faith engages the total personality, the range and difficulty of feeling certain expand without limit; and as religious faith requires articles of faith with all-encompassing implications transcending empirical settlement, it becomes extremely difficult to determine not only whether one is epistemically certain but also whether one is even *entitled* to be certain about such matters.

It doesn't follow, of course, that religious faith isn't certain, sometimes. Faith on the personal relationship conception *can* be certain for some persons. But no one should underestimate the difficulties of being or making certain that someone's faith *is* certain.

Washington and Lee University

NOTES

1. Although I speak of 'faith' generically, I am chiefly concerned with *religious* faith in general and with *Christian* faith in particular. The generic usage indicates that the issues extend far beyond the boundaries of Christian theism. When necessary, however, I will specify faith as "religious" or as "Christian."

2. Henceforth, in an attempt to avoid pronominal sexism, I will use only feminine pronouns in speaking about person S and only masculine ones for person A, but one should bear in mind that gender is strictly irrelevant; S and A could be of either, neither, or both genders.

3. The quotation marks signal that I do not mean to imply that a person, particularly a divine person, is reducible to a material object or 'thing' or to an object of thought.

4. See Aquinas, *Summa Theologiae*, 2a2ae. Q. 1, Art. 6. Some possible kinds of general articles of faith include that A is an actual person whose character warrants belief in A's authority; that S trusts A or has confidence in A's authority; that A must believe certain propositions if S is to have faith in A (a kind of 'meta-article'); and so forth.

5. All faithful persons must subscribe to the same general articles, but different persons will subscribe to different specific articles—not only because they have different 'objects' of faith but also because they conceive of their 'objects' differently (even when their objects are one and the same entity). Hence, there need be few if any specific articles of faith that all Christians share.

6. The major omissions concern (1) *criteria of certainty*, how one tells or tests that S is (or feels) certain that p; (2) *certainty-making*, what makes something epistemically certain and what is the certainty-making relation; (3)

paths to certainty, how both psychological and epistemic certainty can be gained or produced; (4) the *content of certainty*, what kinds of thing are or can be certain; and (5) the *scope of certainty*, how much certainty there actually is, for whom, and under what conditions.

7. Other forms, with one major exception, arguably imply or reduce to these two. The exception is "*S* feels certain." This non-propositional usage expresses *S*'s state of mind—one of confidence, assurance, serenity—without implying any propositional 'object,' or indeed any object at all. Such states of mind are peripheral to the personal relationship conception of faith, even though they are central to other conceptions of faith; see, e.g., Sung Bae Park, *Buddhist Faith and Sudden Enlightenment* (Albany: State University of New York Press, 1983).

8. "Faith is the state of being ultimately concerned. . . . If it [i.e., a "concern"] claims ultimacy it demands the total surrender of him who accepts this claim, and it promises total fulfillment even if all other claims have to be subjected to it or rejected in its name" (Paul Tillich, *Dynamics of Faith* [New York: Harper & Row, 1958], p. 1).

9. 'Ultimacy' incorporates ends, commitments, concerns, and so forth, which are either "paramount" ("dominant") *or* "comprehensive" ("inclusive"). See W. F. R. Hardie, *Aristotle's Ethical Theory* (Oxford: Clarendon Press, 1968), pp. 329–31, for this distinction as it is found in—or rather ignored by—Aristotle's treatment of *eudaimonía*.

10. Normally religious concerns are thought to be *both* supremely important *and* absolutely certain, but even so certainty remains distinct from ultimacy.

11. Terminology varies. Some distinguish between 'subjective' vs. 'objective' certainty, others between 'psychological' and 'epistemological' certainty. Perhaps one could speak of 'descriptive' vs. 'evaluative' or 'normative' certainty; or perhaps 'certainty' could be reserved for the epistemic sense, with 'certitude' or 'conviction' used for the psychological sense.

12. See Roderick Firth, "The Anatomy of Certainty," *Philosophical Review* 76 (1967): 3–27, for a distinction among "truth-evaluating," "warrant-evaluating," and "testability-evaluating" uses of 'certain.' Only the first two uses are important here; the third might be expressed by the locutions "*S* makes certain that *p*" or "*S* tells for certain that *p*."

13. Here the logic of 'certain' accords with the logic of 'know,' as standardly analyzed by philosophers. But I do not intend 'guarantee' in this sentence to mean 'logically entails'; see below and Robert Audi, *Belief, Justification, and Knowledge* (Belmont, Calif.: Wadsworth, 1988), p. 142.

14. Note that this condition is that *p* is certain for *S* and *S* believes that *p*, not that *S believes* that *p* is certain for *S* (or for herself).

15. The terminology is from Nicholas Rescher, *Scepticism: A Critical Reappraisal* (Totowa, N.J.: Rowman & Littlefield, 1980), p. 37. Rescher also

speaks of "real," "mundane," or "practical" certainty vs. "ideal," "rigid," "logical," or "transcendental" certainty.

16. Ibid., p. 42.

17. See Peter D. Klein, *Certainty: A Refutation of Scepticism* (Minneapolis: University of Minnesota Press, 1981), p. 132; and Peter Unger, *Ignorance: A Case for Scepticism* (Oxford: Clarendon Press, 1975), Ch. II, esp. pp. 54–62 and 66–68.

18. More formally: if *S* has faith in *A*, then it is better than not, *ceteris paribus*, that *S* be certain about *A*. The *ceteris paribus* clause is all-important. It is not necessarily good to feel certain while languishing in blissful error or ignorance, or bad to feel uncertain while entertaining honest doubts. Likewise, it is not clearly better to be rationally justified in holding the truth regarding something trivial while ignoring something vital than to secure something important at the cost of ignorance or error. So although it is desirable that religious faith be certain, both psychologically and epistemically, it is not clear that it can be both or, at any rate, the latter.

19. See John Hick, *Faith and Knowledge* (Ithaca, N.Y.: Cornell University Press, 1957), Ch. 6.

20. Ibid., p. 179.

21. See Rescher, *Scepticism*, Ch. III; Audi, *Belief, Justification, and Knowledge*, p. 148.

22. John Hick, *Philosophy of Religion*, 2nd ed. (Englewood Cliffs, N.J.: Prentice-Hall, 1973), p. 53.

23. See James F. Ross, *Introduction to the Philosophy of Religion* (New York: Macmillan, 1969), Ch. II.

24. A more cautious conclusion would be that there is no way for us to make certain, or to tell for certain, whether an alleged transcendent being is a first-person authority for us.

25. See Hick, *Faith and Knowledge*, Part III; Ross, *Introduction*, pp. 94–108; George Mavrodes, *Belief in God* (New York: Random House, 1970), Ch. III; William P. Alston, "Religious Experience as a Ground of Religious Belief," in Joseph Runzo, ed., *Religious Experience and Religious Belief* (Lanham, Md.: University Press of America, 1986), pp. 31–51, and "Perceiving God," *Journal of Philosophy* 83 (November 1986): 655–65.

On the Rationality of Being Religious

5

Joshua L. Golding

ABSTRACT

I pose the problem of whether it is rational to be a "God-oriented" religious person. I discuss the conditions involved in being this sort of religious person and argue that as long as certain constraints are met, it is in some respects rational and in some respects *internally* rational to fulfill those conditions. I also claim that these constraints can be met and include a brief discussion of my use of the notion of *internal* rationality.

A central issue in the epistemology of religious belief is the question of whether it is rational to believe that God exists. The standard arguments in support of the rationality of this belief fall into two categories: cognitive and pragmatic. Cognitive arguments seek to establish that God exists by a priori reasoning or by appeal to empirical evidence. Examples are the Ontological, Cosmological, and Teleological Arguments, as well as the Argument from Religious Experience. Pragmatic arguments seek to show that it is valuable or potentially valuable to adopt the belief that God exists. Examples include Pascal's Wager and, after its own fashion, James's "Will to Believe."

In this paper, I will address a different but related question, namely, whether it is rational to be what we might call a "God-oriented" religious person, that is, a person who pursues a way of life that is oriented toward attaining the best relationship with God. Indeed, one reason people are interested in whether it is rational to believe that God exists is because this belief seems to play an important role in the religious life. But surely, the question of whether it is rational to be a religious person is worth directly confronting; and, as I shall illustrate, this question raises different issues from those raised by the more traditional problem of whether it is rational to believe in God's existence.

I begin by articulating the notion of a God-oriented religious person. Basically, such a person pursues the goal of attaining what he or she regards as the best relationship with God. By 'God' I mean some being who is conceived by the religious person as the most perfect possible being, or in Anselm's words, "that than which none greater can be conceived." I leave open precisely what constitutes God's perfection, and what other traits God may conceivably have. In more detail, someone is a God-oriented religious person if and only if he fulfills the following five conditions:

1. He has some conception of God and some conception of what would constitute for him the best relationship with God.
2. He believes that there is some non-zero probability that *God exists* and that there is some non-zero probability that *he will attain that relationship.*
3. He believes that having that relationship with God would be more valuable for him than any other possible state.
4. He believes that certain actions are "religious," that is, that certain actions on his part *increase* the probability that he will attain that relationship.
5. He regularly *does* those actions that he believes are "religious."

Notably absent is any requirement that this person have a *full-blown* belief that God exists; he or she need only believe that the probability that God exists is greater than zero. Now there is no pressing need for me to defend the above as an account of what it means to be a God-oriented religious person. In what follows, I shall simply take this conception as given, and address the question of whether it is rational for a person to fulfill conditions 1 through 5.

Condition 1 is that the person has some conception of God and of what would constitute for him the best relationship with God. I presume it safe to say that a given conception is held rationally by a person if it is internally coherent and if it coheres with other related conceptions that person has, such as his conception of good and evil. Now there is nothing prima facie internally incoherent about the notion of a most perfect possible being, or about the notion of a "best relationship" with that being. Similarly, there is no prima facie reason to think that a person's conception of God will perforce conflict with that person's conception of such related matters as good and evil. Of course, different religious people have different conceptions of what God is like *in detail* and some of these versions may encounter logical trouble, such as, to give a well-known example, when God is conceived both as unchanging (as in ancient Greek philosophy) and also as interacting with human beings (as in the Bible). Moreover, *some* detailed conceptions of God are prima facie in conflict with some conceptions of such matters as good and evil, as for example, when God is conceived as the source of all moral values and when at the same time moral values are conceived as stemming from human autonomy. But conceptions of God and of what constitutes the best relationship with God *need not* be internally incoherent, and they *need not* conflict with other related conceptions held by that same person. So long as these constraints are met, it is rational for a person to fulfill condition 1.

Condition 2 is that the religious person believes there is some non-zero probability that *God exists* and that there is some non-zero probability that *he will attain the best relationship with God.* What constraints must be met in order for these beliefs to be rational? At the very least, each of these propositions must not be logically incompatible with any proposition the person knows for certain or assigns probability 1. Now this constraint is easily met, since very few things are known for certain, and, unless God is conceived in a rigid manner, none of these things need be logically incompatible with the propositions in condition 2. For example, the argument that the existence of an omnipotent and omnibenevolent God is logically incompatible with the existence of evil has few proponents, and, even if it worked, it would rule out only one particular conception of God. On some theories of probability, the fact that these propositions are not incompatible with any proposition known to that person would be sufficient to entitle him to assign some non-zero probability to each of them.

On a more demanding theory, it may be required that there be some *evidence* (however minimal) for these propositions. But again, this requirement is easily met. For example, depending on how God is conceived in detail, evidence for God's existence might include the existence of the world, the orderly operations of nature, the moral sense of mankind, putative religious experience, or even the mere fact that people have the idea of God. Similarly, depending on how that relationship is conceived, evidence for the proposition that a person will attain the best relationship with God might follow from the claim that there is some evidence (however minimal) that God exists, or from the claim that there is some evidence (however minimal) that some human beings have in the past attained such a relationship, or even from the known fact that some human beings have claimed to know (by purported divine revelation) that such a relationship is attainable by humans. Of course, a skeptic could (perhaps even correctly) claim that such data are better explained by non-theistic or atheistic hypotheses, such as the big bang theory, the theory of evolution, psychoanalytic theories of projection, and so forth. But on the probability theory under consideration, as long as a person has some evidence (however minimal) for each of the propositions in condition 2, he is rationally entitled to believe them with some non-zero probability. I venture to say that on any plausible theory of probability, the constraints required for those propositions to have some non-zero probability can be easily met.

Condition 3 is that the person believes that having (what he conceives as) the best relationship with God would be more valuable for him than any other possible state. Under what circumstances is it rational for a person to have this belief? This question brings up a classic philosophical problem, namely, how can we evaluate as rational or irrational beliefs about what states are valuable? Of course, I cannot hope to solve this problem here, but I would not be the first to suggest that, in a particular case, we can evaluate a person's belief about whether some state is valuable at least *internally*, that is, with respect to that person's *other* beliefs. Now, given a person who conceives of God as the most perfect possible being and conceives of *x* as the best relationship with God, it would seem to make perfectly good *internal* sense for him to believe that *x* would be more valuable for him than any other possible state. But whether or not it does make good *internal* sense depends on the details of his conceptions of God and this relationship, as well as his other beliefs about what is valuable. For example, if he conceives of that relationship as one in which he is constantly frightened of God, then, depending on what other sorts of states he regards as valuable, it might turn out that there is some internal irrationality in his believing that such a state is more valuable than any other possible state. On the other hand, if he conceives of that relationship as one in which he somehow partakes of God's perfection, the belief that that state is more valuable than any other possible state seems to make sense within such a framework. Thus, a full support of the *internal* rationality of the belief involved in condition 3 would require a detailed theology and axiology, explicating how one's conception of the best relationship with God interlinks with what one conceives as most valuable. Obviously, I cannot work all this out here, but in principle it seems that such a theology and axiology can be worked out in an internally coherent manner. So long as a person's conceptions of God and the best relationship with God fit together in the appropriate way with his conception of what is valuable, it is (at least) *internally* rational for him to have the belief described in condition 3.

Condition 4 is that the religious person believes that certain actions are "religious"; i.e., that certain actions on his part *increase* (even if only slightly) the probability that he will attain (what he conceives as) the best relationship with God. Now I submit that *if* there is some method for a person to *rationally estimate* which actions are religious, and *if* the person applies that method, then his belief that certain actions are religious is rationally held. I further claim that there are at least two methods by which a person can rationally estimate which actions are religious. I call these the 'conceptual' and the 'empirical' methods. For these methods to be used successfully, certain further conditions must hold, which I shall mention shortly.

In using the conceptual method, the person *reasons out* or *derives* which actions are religious directly from his conceptions of God and of the best relationship with God. For example, if he conceives of God as morally perfect, and he conceives of that relationship as one in which God loves the religious person, then he may reason that the probability that he will attain this relationship is increased if he does those things that (on his conception) God approves of, such as moral action. Or, if the best relationship with God is one in which the religious person is in some way similar to God, then he may reason that the probability that he will attain that relationship is increased if he strives to imitate God. This is one way whereby the religious person can rationally estimate which actions are religious. However, it must be noted that for this method to yield results, the person's conception of God and the best relationship with God must be sufficiently rich in detail. Otherwise, he will not be able to derive therefrom any consequences about which actions are religious.

In using the empirical method, the person undertakes an investigation to find *evidence* for which actions are religious. Thus, for example, she might take into account records of putative divine revelation (such as the Bible) purporting to report God's directives for those who pursue a good relationship with Him. Or, if she finds people (such as reputed saints or holy men) whom she believes are the most likely of all available candidates to have attained that relationship with God, she may estimate what actions those persons did in order to attain that relationship. In this manner, a person can rationally estimate which actions increase (even if only slightly) the probability that she will attain the best relationship with God. I hasten to emphasize that it need not be rational for her to believe that records such as the Bible have a probability greater than one-half of being divinely revealed, or that there is a probability greater than one-half that such reputed saints or holy men have attained any relationship with God. All one needs to do is find evidence (however minimal) for believing that one has a greater probability of attaining the best relationship with God if one does certain actions *rather than others.*

Now it must be noted that the success of this method depends, so to speak, on the contingent facts of the world. For one can attempt to draw lessons only from those sources whose conception of God accords with one's own. And it is a contingent matter of fact whether one will be able to find such sources. For example, it is a contingent fact that there are putative records of divine revelation and reputed saints and holy men. Thus, if one has a peculiar or highly idiosyncratic conception of God, these traditional sources may turn out to be irrelevant and therefore unhelpful in estimating which actions are religious.

Ideally, the religious person should use both the empirical and the conceptual methods. Indeed, they are interdependent. For one's conception of God and the best relationship with God will guide one's empirical investigations, and results gleaned from empirical investigations may reshape one's conception of God. Now, of course, different people using these same methods will obtain different results as to which actions are religious. This will be true even if they have similar conceptions of God and the best relationship with God. For the same methods applied by different people may yield different results. However, to the extent that a person has used these methods, it is rational for him to believe that certain actions on his part are religious.

Finally, we come to the question of whether it is rational for a person to fulfill condition 5, that is, to regularly *do* those actions that he believes are religious. This raises the general question, how can a policy or course of action be evaluated as rational or irrational? One standard way in which a policy may be evaluated as 'rational' is according to the Principle of Expected Value (PEV), which has clear application to decision problems in which one is able both to assess the probabilities of what results will occur on various actions and to rank the values of those results on some quantitative scale.

For example, in standard gambling situations, one can often determine both the probability as well as the monetary value of winning or losing a certain bet. Given such assessments, PEV says that the rational choice is that action that has the highest 'expect value' of all available options. To compute the expected value of a given action, one multiplies the value of each possible outcome by the probability of that outcome on that action, and then sums over all the possible outcomes of that action. Thus, for example, if on option O_1 I believe there is a 1/2 probability of winning 10 units and a 1/2 probability of losing 8 units, and on option O_2 I believe there is a 1/2 probability of winning 20 units and 1/2 probability of losing 14 units, the expected value of O_1 is 1 unit and that of O_2 is 3 units; and so PEV says that of the two options, O_2 is the rational choice.

Can we use PEV to evaluate whether it is rational for a person to regularly engage in religious action? Two problems confront us here. One general way in which PEV is limited as a criterion of rational choice is that it takes the beliefs about probabilities and value assignments involved in a given decision problem as *given* and determines a choice without concern for the rationality of those given beliefs. To overcome this problem, I suggest the following "beefed-up" criterion for rational choice; namely, a course of action is rational if and only if, given a person's beliefs about the probabilities and values of the outcomes of his actions, the 'expected value' of that action is higher than that of any other available option *and* the 'given' beliefs on the basis of which the expected value is computed are rational. We can also add a proviso stating that to the extent those beliefs are only *internally* rational, that course of action is only *internally* rational as well. Now I have already argued that—so long as certain methods are used—it is rational for a religious person to believe that certain actions are religious, i.e., increase the probability that he will attain the best relationship with God. I have also argued that—so long as certain constraints are met—it is *internally* rational for a person to believe that this relationship would be more valuable than any other possible state. Hence, if those constraints are met *and* given these beliefs as the basis for computation, the expected value of doing religious actions turns out to be higher than that of not doing them, we could conclude that it is to some extent rational and to some extent *internally* rational for a person to do those actions.

Yet, a second limitation of PEV is that it seems to have clear application only to decision problems in which one can rank on some quantitative scale the values of the possible outcomes of one's choices. Now, in fact, it is not necessary that one can make specific quantitative measurements in order to reason about decision making *along the lines* of PEV. If, for example, I believe that attaining some state S is "extremely more valuable" than some other state S', then (given that belief) it is obviously more rational to choose what I believe will lead to S rather than S'—even though I may not be able to quantitatively measure the values of S and S'. And if I believe that one option has a positive probability p of leading to S' (and no probability of leading to *S)* and a second option has a probability of a hairline below *p* of leading to *S* (and no probability of leading to *S'*), it is still more rational (given that belief) to choose the second option. One does not need specific quantitative measurements of the values of *S* and *S'* in order to realize that this is a rational way of making decisions. However, the problem is that unless one can make quantitative measurements of the values in question, one cannot know *precisely* at what probability to choose the option that leads to less valuable *S'* rather than more valuable *S*.

Now let us return to the problem of whether it is rational for a person to regularly engage in religious actions, i.e., those actions that she believes increase the probability of her attaining (what she conceives as) the best relationship with God. Such a person may also believe that other, non-religious actions are more likely to result in her attaining *other* valuable states. And, if she believes the probability that God exists is low, then she may very well be in the position of believing that by engaging in religious action she has a low chance of attaining the best relationship with God; whereas by engaging in non-religious actions she has an even lower chance of attaining the best relationship with God, but also a higher chance of attaining other valuable states. So according to PEV, the answer to our decision problem will then depend on *how* valuable she deems it to attain the best relationship with God. But now the problem confronts us that unless one can rank on some quantitative scale the value of attaining the best relationship with God and, for that matter, the values of the other possible outcomes of this decision, there seems to be no way of applying PEV to resolve this decision problem.

A Pascalian way of trying to circumvent this impasse might be to stipulate that the religious person conceives of attaining the relationship with God as having *infinite* value and conceives of all other goods as having only *finite* value. The suggestion would then be that application of PEV would yield the result that the expected value of engaging in religious action is infinitely high, whereas that of not doing so would be only finitely high. This yields the result that the rational choice is to engage in religious action. However, the attempt to use PEV in cases where an 'infinite value' is deemed to be at stake raises several problems, and there is no room here to discuss them all. But one major problem with this suggestion is that even if he conceives of the relationship with God as having infinite value, it still does not ensure that the expected value of engaging in religious action is highest. For it would be unreasonable for the religious person to believe that there is *absolutely zero* probability of attaining the best relationship with God if he chooses *not* to engage in religious action. Hence, the expected value of not engaging in religious action may also turn out to be infinite! So it does not seem that this Pascalian move will work. (This is a cousin of the well-known "other gods" objection to Pascal's Wager.)

Instead, I propose the following variation on Pascal in order to apply PEV to our decision problem. The religious person believes that of all available options, it is by regularly engaging in religious action that he has the highest probability of attaining the best relationship with God. Let us designate the value of this relationship as V. Now assuming that all other values deemed at stake in this decision problem are finite, there is some *finite* number F such that if V is greater than F, the expected value of engaging in religious action will be higher than that of any other option. Now the religious person also believes that the value of V is greater than any other possible state, including one that has value F! Hence, even though the religious person may not be able to assign a specific quantitative measurement to this state as well as to other possible outcomes at stake in the decision problem, it is assured that the value of attaining the best relationship with God is great enough so that the expected value of engaging in religious action is higher than that of not doing so. This holds true even if the religious person believes there is some small probability that he will attain the best relationship with God even if he does *not* engage in religious action.

Now I have already argued that—so long as certain constraints are met—it is rational for a person to believe that certain actions increase the probability that he will attain the best relationship with God, and it is *internally* rational for him to believe that attaining that relationship would be more valuable than any other possible state. I now conclude by application of PEV that, so long as those constraints are met, it is to some extent rational and to some extent *internally* rational for a person to fulfill condition 5—that is, to engage regularly in religious action. And with this I reach the overall conclusion of this paper; namely, that so long as the above-described constraints are met, it is rational for a person to fulfill conditions 1, 2, and 4; it is *internally* rational to fulfill condition 3; and, finally, it is to some extent rational and to some extent *internally* rational to fulfill condition 5. In sum, as long as the described constraints are met, it is in some respects rational and in other respects *internally* rational to be a God-oriented religious person.

Bellarmine College

Religious Experiences: Skepticism, Gullibility, or Credulity?

Stephen Grover

ABSTRACT

I argue that when conflicting religious perceptual claims are made on the basis of the same kind of religious experience this gives us reason to regard that kind of experience as an unreliable basis for making such claims. Because of the security of the inference from the existence of the conflict to the falsity of at least one of the claims, we can proceed just as we do when we know one of the claims is false. The existence of conflicting claims then constitutes grounds for regarding with suspicion all similar claims, whether in conflict with others or not. This yields a further restriction on the application of Swinburne's Principle of Credulity, and therefore the protection of the Principle has to be withdrawn from most religious perceptual claims as they stand. When reinterpreted so as to eliminate the conflict, religious perceptual claims can continue to enjoy the protection of the Principle of Credulity, but this will not preserve the immediacy of justification for religious belief that the Principle seemed at first to promise.

> Matilda told such Dreadful Lies,
> It made one Gasp and Stretch one's Eyes;
> Her Aunt, who from her Earliest Youth,
> Had kept a Strict Regard for Truth,
> Attempted to Believe Matilda:
> The effort very nearly killed her,
> And would have done so, had not she
> Discovered this Infirmity.[1]

The sad tale of Matilda, whose habit of telling lies engendered such widespread skepticism that her cries of "Fire!" were ignored even when true and who was thus burned to death (while her aunt was watching *The Second Mrs. Tanqueray* at the theater), is a cautionary tale for children, designed by Belloc to instill in them a "Strict Regard for Truth." As such, it is doubtless most instructive. But we can perhaps detect in it a lesson for Matilda's audience as well: the gullibility with which her first and false cry of "Fire!" was greeted, and the skepticism that her second and true alarm met, turned out to be equally inappropriate as epistemological responses. A little less willingness to believe in the one case, and a little more in the other, and Matilda might be with us still, which would, I suppose, be "a Good Thing."

These two reactions, of skepticism on the one hand and gullibility on the other, mark out the epistemological dangers that constantly beset us on either side. To plot a safe course between them is one of the tasks of a theory of rational belief. Whether it is cries of "Fire!" from little children or perceptual claims made by more reliable adults, we need some guidance on how to avoid the twin pitfalls of believing too little or believing too much. In the case of claims made on the basis of religious experiences, such guidance is particularly important, both because of the great significance that religious beliefs have for our lives if true and because of the thicket of claims made on behalf of the various and rival religions, at least some of which must be false. It is therefore not surprising that philosophers sympathetic to religious belief have sought to steer us away from the dangers of skepticism in relation to religious perceptual claims, while maintaining that we can avoid falling into gullibility.

One recent and influential proposal—Richard Swinburne's Principle of Credulity—promises to provide such a 'middle way' between believing too little and believing too much. In this paper, I will consider whether the Principle represents a suitable guide along the narrow path between skepticism and gullibility. My conclusion is that, as applied by Swinburne, it does not, because it grants credulity to many claims that we have some reason to believe are false and so errs on the side of gullibility. If the Principle is applied more strictly, however, it seems that relatively few religious perceptual claims are worthy of belief as they stand, and the attractiveness of the Principle of Credulity is much diminished, at least for those who hope to underwrite an immediate justification of religious belief on the basis of religious experience.[2] My reasons for this conclusion derive from the existence of conflicts among the various perceptual claims that are made on the basis of all kinds of religious experiences.[3]

The Principle of Credulity

The Principle of Credulity states that "(in the absence of special considerations) if it seems (epistemically) to a subject that x is present, then probably x is present; what one seems to perceive is probably so" (p. 254).[4] In support of this claim, Swinburne points out that many philosophers accept such a principle when discussing experiences other than religious ones and argues that failure to accept it as a general principle threatens to land us in a "sceptical bog" (p. 254, n. 1), in which, presumably, we end up believing little or nothing at all.[5] If many claims made on the basis of religious experience enjoy the protection of this Principle, it seems difficult to deny that, at least for those who enjoy such experience, religious belief is rationally justified.[6] On its own, the Principle of Credulity would seem obviously defective, rescuing us from the skeptical bog only at the cost of plunging us into the thicket of gullibility; but, as the quotation above implies, Swinburne allows a number of special considerations to limit the application of the Principle of Credulity. Just as the permission granted us to believe what we are inclined to believe preserves us from believing too little, these special considerations are designed to keep us from believing too much.

Swinburne lists four such special considerations (pp. 260–64). The last two involve the improbability either of x being present when it seems to us that it is so, or of x causing the experience of its seeming to be so, whether it is present or not. In the case of religious perceptual claims, these considerations would limit the application of the Principle of Credulity only if it was very improbable that the object of those perceptions— God or Vishnu, for example—existed; or if it was very probable that the perceptions had a cause other than the object that seemed to be perceived.[7] Let us assume that these considerations do not apply. What about Swinburne's first and second considerations? These both involve the availability of "good inductive grounds" for believing that a new perceptual claim is false, the grounds being past perceptual claims that are known to be false and are "of a kind" with the new perceptual claim (pp. 260–61). The suggestion is, presumably, that if we have found a certain kind of claim to be unreliable in the past, this fact then robs these kinds of claims of the presumption of epistemological innocence that the Principle of Credulity embodies in the future. And this seems right: initial credulity should be tempered by subsequent experience; and if we have been led astray by certain kinds of claims in the past, then we should suspend our credulity regarding such claims in the future. But this seems to present a general challenge to the reliability of religious perceptual claims; for, on the modest assumption that every kind of religious experience raises at least a few conflicting claims, all religious perceptual claims are of a kind with at least some false claims, and so should be regarded with suspicion.

In order to assess the validity of this challenge, we need to be clear about the ways in which past perceptual claims, which turned out to be unreliable, render future similar claims unreliable. Swinburne's full statement of the first two considerations limiting the application of the Principle of Credulity is as follows:

> First, one may show that the apparent perception was made under conditions or by a subject found in the past to be unreliable. Thus one may show that S's perceptual claims are generally false, or that perceptual claims are generally false when made under the influence of LSD, which is good inductive grounds for believing that a particular new perceptual claim made by S or made under the influence of LSD is false. Secondly, one may show that the perceptual claim was to have perceived an object of a certain kind in circumstances where similar perceptual claims have proved false. Thus if it seems to S that he has read ordinary-size print at a distance of a hundred yards, we can test him on a number of other occasions and see if he is able to read what is written at that distance; and if he is not we have good inductive evidence that the original claim was false. (pp. 260–61)

From this it is clear that the occurrence of a number of false claims can provide good inductive grounds for doubting all claims made under similar conditions, as in the case of LSD-influenced experiences. It is also clear that the occurrence of some false claims can render unreliable all similar claims made in similar circumstances. So it would seem obvious that the occurrence of conflicting claims could provide equally good grounds for doubting all claims made under the same conditions as the conflicting claims and can render all similar claims made in similar circumstances unreliable. We can simply substitute 'conflicting claims' for 'false claims' in Swinburne's account of the considerations limiting the application of the Principle of Credulity, this substitution being justified by the indisputable fact that at least one of two conflicting claims must be false. But Swinburne denies the availability of any such general challenge to the reliability of religious perceptual claims from the existence of a number of such claims that are in conflict with one another. On his view, claims that are known to be false can provide good inductive gounds for rejecting similar claims in the future, but conflicting claims provide a source of suspicion only for those particular claims that happen to be in conflict (p. 266). Are there any good reasons for this differential treatment?

Conflicting Religious Perceptual Claims

Clearly, of the two past perceptual claims made on the basis of religious experience that are in conflict,[8] both cannot be true. We know at least one of them is false as it stands, even if it can be in some way reinterpreted so as to eliminate the conflict. How does our ignorance about which one is false, or whether both are, affect our ability to build up good inductive grounds for believing that similar future claims are false as well? If the two conflicting claims are made under quite different conditions, then we cannot draw any significant conclusions. Unless we know which of the two conflicting past perceptual claims is false, we cannot know which conditions resulted in a false claim. And if we cannot know this, we cannot know which future claims resemble the false perceptual claim in terms of the conditions under which they were made, for we do not know which is the false perceptual claim. If many future claims resemble one of the conflicting claims in terms of the conditions under which they were made and many future claims resemble the other, we can know that one or the other group of future claims resembles a past perceptual claim, which must be false. This is surely enough to suggest that we might be wise to qualify our credulity with respect to the members of both groups. But it does not constitute the inductive grounds for rejecting future claims as unreliable of the sort demanded by Swinburne. Equally, if the two conflicting claims are of very different kinds, even though made in similar circumstances, we shall not be able to tell which kinds of claims made in such circumstances are to be regarded as unreliable in the future. Thus, many cases of conflicting claims can be distinguished from cases of past perceptual claims, which we know to be false, and which then provide grounds for regarding similar future claims as false as well.

But no such distinction can be made where two claims of a similar kind made in similar circumstances conflict; nor can it where the two conflicting claims are made under similar conditions. When the conflict is between claims that are the same in all relevant respects, we can proceed exactly as we do when a particular claim is known to be false. For example, let us suppose that I make a claim about Christ being the Messiah, and a Muslim makes a claim about Mohammed being the greatest prophet, and both claims are made on the basis of the same kind of religious experience—say, a dream. And let us suppose that these two claims are in conflict with each other, as they certainly seem to be. In this case, we know that all claims made on the basis of dreams, including these two claims themselves, are of a kind with at least one false claim. It would seem that here we would have at least the beginnings of the good inductive grounds required by Swinburne for regarding all future claims made on the basis of dreams as unreliable. Just because both claims are made under precisely the same conditions, we do not have to know which is false, or whether both are, before we can draw a conclusion about the general unreliability of dreams as a basis for making these kinds of perceptual claims.[9]

Swinburne is thus wrong to think that the existence of conflicting claims yields a source of challenge only to particular, detailed claims that happen to be in conflict with each other. If, as a result of the failure of past perceptual claims made under the influence of LSD, we have grounds for believing that a particular new perceptual claim made under the influence of LSD is unreliable, as Swinburne holds that we do (p. 261), then we also have grounds for believing that *any* perceptual claim made under the influence of LSD is unreliable. That is, we have a source of skepticism about the claims of LSD-induced experience in general, because we know that the conditions under which such claims are made in the past have given rise to false perceptual claims. Similarly, if we have grounds for believing that a new religious perceptual claim is not genuine because it is made under conditions found in the past to raise false claims, we have grounds for believing that all claims made under such conditions are not genuine. In my imagined case, we have grounds for believing that all religious perceptual claims made on the basis of dreams are false. Our ignorance about whether one or both of the two conflicting claims is false is irrelevant; for as long as we know that one of them is, we have a source of suspicion for all claims made under similar conditions, whether in conflict with others or not. The argument from the existence of particular conflicting claims to the unreliability of large numbers of those claims does not depend upon there being a large number of claims in conflict with each other, but upon there being a large number of claims made under conditions of a kind with those under which the claims that are in conflict are made. One way of showing that certain kinds of conditions give rise to unreliable claims is to show that they give rise to claims that are in conflict. We do not have to know which of the two conflicting claims is false, or whether both are, before we can conclude that conditions of these kinds are unsuitable for the making of perceptual claims.

The strength of this argument depends, of course, upon there being no way of discriminating between the experiences that produce the conflicting perceptual claims in terms of their conditions. If my dream about Christ follows a large and indigestible meal, of the kind known more generally to be followed by dreams of peculiar objects, while the Muslim's dream does not, then the existence of a conflict between the claims made on the basis of these two dreams is more akin to cases of two different kinds of experiences; but with the further feature that one of the experiences is known to be similar to experiences that have, in the past, produced false perceptual claims. Here we employ Swinburne's fourth consideration limiting the application of the Principle of Credulity, by which the claim to have perceived x may be challenged on the grounds that whether or not x was there, x was probably not a cause of the experience of its seeming that x was there: my dream about Christ was probably the result of gastronomic overindulgence rather than the real presence of Christ. In the absence of conditions warranting the employment of this consideration, and where the existence of conflict provides our only grounds for regarding certain kinds of experiences as unreliable sources of perceptions, we need to reassure ourselves that the conflict is ineliminable and that the two conflicting claims are based upon experiences that are the same in all relevant respects. Once we have done this, it seem undeniable that we have a case in which certain conditions have generated at least one false claim, and therefore have good reason for regarding all claims made under such conditions with suspicion.

The major problem with this result is that it seems altogether too strong. As Swinburne points out, the existence of conflicting perceptual claims does not constitute grounds for doubting the reliability of such perceptual claims in general. When two people offer different descriptions of the objects of their perception, that does not imply that there is nothing that they are perceiving, but only that further evidence is required to settle which description is correct or whether both are incorrect. In Swinburne's own example, the conflict between Babylonian and Greek astronomers over the nature of the stars and the planets does not imply that there are no "specks in the sky" of which they offer further and conflicting descriptions (p. 266). In this case, both parties can retreat to a narrower perceptual claim and so resolve the conflict between them; for both can agree to the description of the objects they perceive as "specks in the sky," even if they refuse to grant that this is in any sense a better description of what they perceive than "holes in the firmament" or "physical bodies in the heavens." This shows, as Swinburne himself notes, that further arguments are required to adjudicate between the two descriptions of the nature of these specks in the sky. In other words, it shows that observation with the naked eye is an unreliable source for perceptual claims about the *nature* of specks in the sky, though not an unreliable source for claims about the *existence* of such specks. The conflict between the Babylonians and the Greeks thus does constitute a general challenge to claims about the *nature* of specks in the sky made on the basis of the observations of the human eye unaided by telescopes and unbuttressed by arguments. It does not constitute a challenge to claims about the *existence* of those specks.

In the religious case, we can suppose something similar: each of the religious dreamers retracts her claim about Christ or Mohammed in favor of some less specific claim about a figure of divine authority, a figure whose identity is not settled by the contents of the dream but which requires further evidence for its determination. Dreams are then treated as an unreliable basis for making claims about the identity of figures of religious authority, but can be regarded as a reliable source of claims about the existence of some such figure or figures. But this assumes that there is some description of the common contents of my dream about Christ and the Muslim's dream about Mohammed equivalent to the description of the objects of astronomical observations as "specks in the sky." It assumes that the conflict between the claims made on the basis of the two dreams is eliminable, whereas it is the existence of in-eliminable conflicts that is under consideration here. The example of the Babylonian and Greek astronomers is not an ineliminable conflict just because we can imagine both parties retreating to some less committed description of the contents of their observations, and because we can imagine other evidence that can be brought to bear on the question of which, if any, of the more committed descriptions is the correct one. We withdraw the protection of the Principle of Credulity from the conflicting claims about "holes in the firmament" or "physical bodies in the heavens," but retain that protection for the non-conflicting claim about the existence of specks in the sky. But if the conflict between the Greeks and the Babylonians was indeed ineliminable, because there was no less committed description to which both parties could retreat or because one party asserted while the other denied the existence of specks in the sky, then we should surely withdraw the protection of the Principle from the claims made by both sides. We would conclude that the observations of the naked eye were an unreliable source for claims about the existence of specks in the sky or for claims about holes or physical bodies that could not be reduced to claims about such specks.

Conclusion

As Swinburne interprets the Principle of Credulity, claims in conflict with each other are treated quite differently from claims we know to be false. The latter can generate a general skepticism about the reliability of claims made under certain conditions, or of claims of particular kinds, whereas the former cannot. But given the straightforward inference of the falsity of at least one of two conflicting beliefs from the mere existence of that conflict, Swinburne's application of the Principle of Credulity seems odd. If initial credulity is to be tempered only by induction from past perceptual claims we know to be false, it will hardly be tempered at all. For surely it is the existence of conflict between particular claims that often provides us with grounds for believing certain kinds of claims to be generally unreliable: when a number of witnesses give contradictory accounts of a road accident, we treat the reports of other, similarly situated witnesses with suspicion as well. The existence of the conflict is taken as evidence that the conditions under which the observations were made were less than ideal.[10] Again, we do not regard drug-induced experience as unreliable solely because it gives rise to claims we know to be false, but also because it has other hallmarks of unreliable conditions for making perceptual claims, including a tendency to generate sets of claims not all of which can be true because of the conflicts between them.[11]

The general challenge to the reliability of religious perceptual claims from the existence of conflicts among those claims seems too strong only if we assume that most of these conflicts are ineliminable. Provided there is available a less committed description of the contents of religious experiences that eliminates the apparent conflict, there do not seem to be any grounds for withdrawing the protection of the Principle of Credulity that derive from the existence of that apparent conflict. But it is important to note that the protection of the Principle only extends to religious perceptual claims under their less committed description and to remember that suspicion about claims under more committed descriptions should extend even to those claims where there is no apparent conflict.[12] Insofar as a particular kind of experience gives rise to conflicting claims, it should be regarded generally as an unreliable source of such claims, whether they happen to be in conflict with others or not. If I dream of Christ, and another of Mohammed, then any claim about the identity of figures of religious authority based on a dream should be treated with suspicion rather than credulity. For it is as much a hallmark of unreliable conditions for the making of perceptual claims that they give rise to conflicting claims as it is that they give rise to claims that we know are false.

The moral I drew from the tale of Matilda was that we need a guide to lead us along the narrow path between skepticism and gullibility. The Principle of Credulity, as applied by Swinburne, saves us from the former only by nudging us too far in the direction of the latter. I propose that we further qualify the Principle by allowing the existence of conflicting claims to constitute grounds for suspicion concerning all relevantly similar claims, whether they happen to be in conflict with others or not. This means that most religious perceptual claims will not enjoy the protection of the Principle as they stand. Because of the conflicts between them, we shall not be able to take them as evidence of the way things are. But this is to the good, for not all of them can be true. We should not be so scared of falling into the skeptical bog that we plunge headlong into the thicket of gullibility.

All Souls College, Oxford University

NOTES

1. From Hilaire Belloc, *Cautionary Verses*, "Matilda, Who Told Lies, and Was Burned to Death" (London: Gerald Duckworth, 1940), pp. 17ff.

2. Although I do not consider views other than Swinburne's here, I anticipate that similar remarks could be made about any attempt to provide a justification for particular, detailed religious beliefs directly upon the basis of religious experiences.

3. If follows from this that if there are any kinds of religious experience that do not give rise to conflicting perceptual claims, they will continue to enjoy the protection of the Principle of Credulity. For example, if mystical experiences occurred only within one Christian tradition, there could be no grounds for regarding this kind of experience with suspicion, which derives

from the existence of conflicting claims. But it seems that each of Swinburne's five kinds of religious experience is represented in more than one religious tradition, and so it seems likely that each kind of religious experience gives rise to at least some conflicting claims.

4. Text references are to Richard Swinburne, *The Existence of God* (Oxford: Clarendon Press, 1979).

5. The presumption here is that the main route to skepticism is through doubt. This is certainly true of much modern skepticism, but skeptics such as Montaigne, following Classical examples, typically argued for skeptical conclusions by producing contradictions, each term of which was securely established. This route to skepticism proceeds not by doubt but by credulity.

6. Swinburne extends the evidential force of religious experiences to persons other than those who actually enjoy such experiences by appeal to the Principle of Testimony: "the principle that (in the absence of special considerations) the experiences of others are (probably) as they report them" (p. 272).

7. Swinburne argues that this latter consideration cannot apply in the case of experiences of God, for God is among the causes of all experiences. This has the peculiar result that God may be no more the cause of an experience of Him than He is the cause of an experience of the Devil.

8. By "in conflict," I mean that the conflict persists even when due allowance has been made for the fact that different perceivers may describe their perceptions in different ways because they belong to different religious traditions. Doubtless, many apparent conflicts disappear when the subjects of the experiences involved are willing to retreat to some less committed description of that experience; I assume only that not all apparent conflicts can be made to disappear in this way.

9. Of course, there is one difference between the two dream-based claims that might be relevant: one is made by me while the other is made by someone else. But unless I have some reason to think that I am generally a more reliable claim-maker than my Muslim counterpart, this difference cannot justify treating the two claims as of different kinds and so as incapable of providing inductive grounds for judgments about the reliability of dreams as a basis for the making of religious perceptual claims.

10. It is important to recognize that this more widespread suspicion of the reports of all witnesses is grounded in the fact that they all observed the accident under the same conditions. We do not suspend our credulity concerning claims about slow-moving objects observed at close quarters in good light because claims about fast-moving objects seen from a distance at night often result in conflicting reports.

11. Another example, suggested by Joseph Runzo in discussion, is provided by disputes between umpires in sporting events. It is true that the

existence of some conflicting calls by line-judges in lawn-tennis should not lead us to treat all calls, whether in conflict with others or not, with suspicion. But it can quite properly encourage us to treat all *close* calls with suspicion, as the introduction of electronic 'judges' at the major tournaments shows. In cases where we are required to resolve disputes one way or the other so that play may continue, we must have a decision-procedure of some kind, even if it is the arbitrary *fiat* of the umpire; this does not affect the general point that the epistemologically responsible spectator should suspend judgment about which call is correct in cases of conflict and have a healthy suspicion about all close calls, whether in conflict or not.

12. This is the conclusion of Caroline Franks Davis, who regards "highly ramified religious beliefs" of the kind typically held by most religious believers as requiring grounds other than those deriving from religious experience if they are to be justified. See Caroline Franks Davis, *The Evidential Force of Religious Experience* (Oxford: Oxford University Press, 1989), pp. 248–50. Franks Davis believes that the conflicts between the various kinds of religious experiences are generally eliminable through being subsumed within a "broad theism" (pp. 190–92). If this is right, then such experiences may provide some grounds for believing in a theism of this broad kind. But this restriction of the scope of justification provided by religious experience is considerable and seems altogether at odds with the kind of straightforward and immediate justification of detailed religious claims that the Principle of Credulity seemed at first to promise.

Hume's Evidential/Testimonial Epistemology, Probability, and Miracles

`7`

Francis J. Beckwith

ABSTRACT

In this paper I will critically analyze the first part of David Hume's argument against miracles, which has been traditionally referred to as the in-principle argument. However, unlike most critiques of Hume's argument, I will (1) present a view of evidential epistemology and probability that will take into consideration Hume's accurate observation that miracles are highly improbable events while (2) arguing that one can be within one's epistemic rights in believing that a miracle has occurred.

As for the proper definition of a miracle, I offer the following, which I believe most religious people generally mean when they call an event miraculous: *A miracle is a divine intervention that occurs contrary to the regular course of nature within a significant historical-religious context.* Although I am fully aware that this definition has its detractors, it will merely function in this paper as a working definition so that we can come to grips with Hume's argument. This definition has been defended in detail elsewhere.[1]

Presentation of Hume's In-Principle Argument

Hume begins this section of *An Enquiry Concerning Human Understanding* with a comparison of his work on miracles with John Tillotson's[2] argument against the Roman Catholic doctrine of transubstantiation. Hume writes that Tillotson's argument "is as concise, and elegant, and strong as any argument can possibly be supposed against a doctrine so little worthy of a serious refutation."[3] Tillotson puts forth his argument in the following way:

> Every man hath as great evidence that transubstantiation is false as he hath that the Christian religion is true. Suppose then transubstantiation

to be part of the Christian doctrine, it must then have the same confirmation with the whole, and that is miracles: but, of all the doctrines in
the world, it is peculiarly incapable of being proved by a miracle. For if a
miracle were wrought for the proof of it, the very same assurance which
any man hath of the truth of the miracle, he hath of the falsehood of the
doctrine; that is, the clear evidence of his senses. For that there is a
miracle wrought to prove that what he sees in the sacrament, is not bread,
but the body of Christ, there is only the evidence of sense; and there is the
very same evidence to prove, that what he sees in the sacrament, is not the
body of Christ, but bread.[4]

Hume's argument is similar in this regard: Tillotson argues
that if the truth of the unobservable phenomenon of transubstantiation were dependent on an observable miracle, the
evidence for transubstantiation (the observability of the miracle) would actually count against transubstantiation; that is, the
reason you believe the miracle (it can be observed) is the same
reason why you reject transubstantiation (it cannot be
observed). In like manner, Hume argues that the reason why
you believe an event is miraculous—that it violates natural
law—is the same reason why you reject the miraculous: the
proof of natural law outweighs the proof of any miracle (as to
the possible ways to interpret what Hume means by this, see the
following critique). Comparing his argument to Tillotson's,
Hume writes:

> I flatter myself, that I have discovered an argument of a like nature, which,
> if just, will, with the wise and learned, be an everlasting check to all kinds
> of superstitious delusion, and consequently, will be useful as long as the
> world endures. For so long, I presume, will the accounts of miracles and
> prodigies be found in all history, sacred and profane.[5]

Reiterating the epistemological framework set forth earlier
in the *Enquiry*, Hume continues that experience is "our only
guide in reasoning concerning matters of fact," although "this
guide is not altogether infallible, but in some cases is apt to lead
us into errors." Admitting that "in our reasonings concerning
matter of fact, there are all imaginable degrees of assurance,"
he asserts that "a wise man," nevertheless, "proportions his
belief to the evidence." In some cases, a belief may be founded
on infallible experience, and the wise man therefore "regards

his past experience as a full *proof* of the future existence of that event." However, "in other cases, he proceeds with more caution: He weighs the opposite experiments: He considers which side is supported by the greater number of experiments: to that side he inclines, with doubt and hesitation; and when at last he fixes his judgment, the evidence exceeds not what we properly call *probability*."[6]

Hume then applies this reasoning to the reports of eyewitnesses in general (not only to the alleged eyewitnesses of miracles). He writes that when it comes to human testimony we should not ignore the epistemological principle set forth in the earlier part of the *Enquiry:* "It being a general maxim, that no objects have any discernible connexion together, and that all the inferences, which we can draw from one to another, are founded merely on our experience of their constant and regular conjunction." Since human testimony "is founded on past experience, so it varies with experience, and is regarded either as a *proof* or a *probability*, according as the conjunction between a particular kind of report and any kind of object has been found to be constant and variable."[7]

According to Hume, whenever we are judging human testimony, "we balance the opposite circumstances, which cause any doubt or uncertainty; and when we discover a superiority on any side, we incline to it; but still with a diminution of assurance, in proportion to the force of its antagonist."[8] What he means by this is simply that the human testimony of a particular event may be opposed by a contrariety of evidence (for example, contradictory testimony, too few witnesses of doubtful character, and so forth), "which may diminish or destroy the force of any argument, derived from human testimony."[9] Therefore, an event having strong evidence in its favor and little or no contrary evidence possesses a very high degree of probability.

Prior to applying the above to the miraculous, Hume first applies it to those witnesses who have claimed to have partaken in what he calls "the extraordinary and the marvellous." (Today we put in the classification of extraordinary or marvellous such alleged events as visitations by UFO occupants.) Hume writes that "the evidence, resulting from the testimony, admits of a diminution, greater or less, in proportion as the fact is more or less unusual." That is to say, "when the fact attested is such a one as has seldom fallen under our observation, here is a contest of two opposite experiences; of which one destroys the other, as far as its force goes, and the superior can only operate on the mind by the force, which remains."[10] Hume is saying that the extraordinary nature of the event counts as contrary evidence against the event having actually happened. For example, our overwhelming experience tells us that elephants do not have wings and therefore cannot fly. Suppose, however, that two airplane pilots on a rainy, lightning-filled, winter night observe from the cockpit what they perceive to be a flying elephant. According to Hume, we should weigh the pilots' testimony against the contrary evidence of our overwhelming experience of never having observed a flying elephant, not to mention the bad weather conditions, and conclude that it is more likely that the pilots were somehow deceived than that a flying elephant was actually observed. "The very same principle of experience, which gives us a certain degree of assurance in the testimony of witnesses [i.e., pilots are trained observers and often accurate], gives us also, in this case, another degree of assurance against the fact, which they endeavor to establish [i.e., flying elephants have never been a part of our experience, bad weather can alter one's perceptions, and pilots have been mistaken]."[11]

Hume now moves from the marvellous to the miraculous. He asks us to imagine that there is testimony for an alleged miracle that "amounts to an entire proof." He is arguing that *even if* there is good evidence for the miraculous we still should not believe that it has occurred. For the regularity of natural law is itself a "proof." Therefore, we weigh proof against proof; and since "a miracle is a violation of the laws of nature" and "a firm and unalterable experience has established these laws, the proof against a miracle, from the very nature of the fact, is as entire as any argument can be imagined."[12] Hume goes on to assert:

There must, therefore, be a uniform experience against every miraculous event, otherwise the event would not merit that appellation. And as a uniform experience amounts to a proof, there is here a direct and full *proof*, from the nature of the fact, against the existence of any miracle; nor can such a proof be destroyed, or the miracle rendered credible, but by an opposite proof, which is superior.[13]

Take, for example, the story in the Book of Joshua when the sun stood still for one day while the Amorites were conquered by Israel (Joshua 10:13). According to Hume, Newton's laws of planetary motion (which include the law that the sun never remains motionless), having been substantiated by a countless number of observations, would serve as contrary evidence to what allegedly happened in the Book of Joshua.[14]

Hume recognizes that one of the consequences of his argument is that in principle no testimony is sufficient to establish the veracity of any miraculous event.[15] For example, he tells us that if someone approached him claiming to have witnessed a dead man resurrected to life, Hume would ask himself whether it is more probable that this witness "should either deceive or be deceived, or that the fact, which he relates, should really have happened."[16] And, of course, since it is more probable that the witness is involved in some sort of deception than that a resurrection had actually occurred, Hume would reject the miracle. As he puts it: "If the falsehood of his [the witness'] testimony would be more miraculous, than the event which he relates; then, and not till then, can he pretend to command my belief or opinion."[17] Therefore, "since the wise man . . . proportions his belief to the evidence,"[18] one should not believe that a miracle has occurred. Hume's in-principle argument can be summarized as follows:

1. Natural laws are built on uniform experience (which, according to Hume, is what makes something a "proof").
2. Miracles are alleged violations of natural law (and are, therefore, rare).
3. Therefore, the "proof" of natural laws always outweighs the "proof" of any particular miracle.
4. The wise person should always choose to believe that which has the greater weight of evidence.
5. Therefore, miracles can never be believed by a wise person.

Critique of Hume's In-Principle Argument

I believe there are at least two problems with Hume's in-principle argument: (1) it begs the question, and (2) it confuses evidence and probability.

A Question-Begging Argument

A number of thinkers have made the observation that Hume's argument begs the question.[19] It is my contention that the degree to which Hume begs the question is contingent upon how one interprets his argument. For instance, if Hume defines nature as that which is by definition uniform, he clearly begs the question in favor of naturalism. This has been aptly pointed out by C. S. Lewis:

> Now of course we must agree with Hume that if there is absolutely "uniform experience" against miracles, if in other words they have never happened, why then they never have. Unfortunately, we know the experience against them to be uniform only if we know that all the reports of them are false. And we can know all the reports to be false only if we know already that miracles have never occurred. In fact, we are arguing in a circle.[20]

Is Lewis correct in his assessment of Hume's argument? Is Hume *really* arguing that nature is uniform? The answer to both questions is no. Given Hume's rejection of necessary connection[21] and his reliance on an empiricist epistemology, it would stretch credibility to the limit to claim that Hume is arguing for the uniformity of nature. I think it is safe to say, however, that Hume is arguing that our *formulations* of natural law, if they are to be considered lawful appraisals of our perceptions, must be based on uniform *experience* or they cease to be natural law. According to David Fate Norton's interpretation, the following is the crux of Hume's argument:

> If our experience of X's has been "firm and unalterable" or "infallible," then we have, in Hume's scheme, a "proof" and are in a position to formulate a law of nature, or a summation of uniform experience. Correlatively, the moment we fail to have a proof, or perfect empirical support for any summation, we fail to have a law of nature.[22]

Hence, given that a law of nature must be what Hume calls a "proof," and proofs are by definition built on uniform and infallible experience, a violation of natural law would automatically disqualify the alleged law and would relegate it to the status of a probability. Norton continues:

> It is in this context that Hume grants (for the sake of argument, no doubt) that the evidence for a particular (alleged) miracle may be perfect of its kind. But even given this concession, he points out, there would be insufficient grounds for concluding that the event was a miracle, for there would be, contra this evidence, equally perfect evidence that the event has not taken place—the evidence of the uniform experience that is summarized by the (allegedly) violated law of nature. . . . A miracle is a violation of the laws of nature; a law of nature is established by a firm and unalterable experience. The champion of miracles is arguing, however, that this experience is not firm and unalterable; at least, one exception is, he claims, known. From this exception it follows, Hume reminds us, that there is no violation of a law of nature because there is no law of nature, and hence, there is no miracle.[23]

What Norton is saying is simply this: a miracle is an event that is, by definition, a violation of natural law, but a violated law (because a natural law, by definition, is only such if based on uniform experience, i.e., a proof) is no longer a law. Hence, "the proof against a miracle, from the very nature of the fact, is as entire as any argument can possibly be established."[24]

Although this interpretation is much truer to the text than Lewis's interpretation, one could still argue that Hume begs the question in favor of naturalism (although the circle is certainly not as vicious as the one pointed out by Lewis). For the question can be asked, why must one accept that a natural law cannot be a natural law if it has been violated? If the reply is that natural law cannot be otherwise, then the question has been begged, or Hume's argument against miracles is strictly tautological. Asserting that a natural law can only remain a natural law if it has not been violated is to assume that a violation can *count against* a natural law. In terms of Hume's own epistemology, this is entirely consistent; for this reason, I believe that Norton is correct in his interpretation. It should be noted, however, that Hume understood natural law in the sense that it was understood in his day: strictly determined and mechanistic. And it was against this version that he reacted, arguing that necessary connection could not be philosophically validated (hence, his appeal to unalterable *experience*). He thus rejected natural law as then understood, or at least he argued that one could not justify it philosophically.

However, I think that one can question Hume's view of natural law by showing that it is possible, and hence perfectly coherent and in accord with both contemporary science and our experience of the world, to speak of a natural law and its violation. As Swinburne points out, in order to combat Hume's view of natural law "one must distinguish between a formula being a law [i.e., a law that can be violated and still remain a law] *and* a formula being (universally) true or being a law which holds without exception [i.e., Hume's view]."[25]

Before examining natural law, it is well worth pointing out George Mavrodes's observation that this interpretation of Hume's argument "need not be greatly disturbing to any religious person or any 'friend of miracles.'"[26] After all, writes Mavrodes, the fact that these "violations" have undermined "natural law" does not mean they did not really occur. As he puts it:

> Nothing that the objector has said tends to show at all, or make it in any way probable, that Jesus did not turn water into wine, that he did not calm a storm with a word or raise Lazarus from the dead, and so on. Nor does it tend to show that these events did not have a profound religious significance. It does not even tend to show that these things, if they happened, were not miracles. At most (for better or worse) it tends to show that they are not *Humean* miracles.[27]

No doubt there is considerable debate among philosophers of science as to the precise technical meaning of the term *natural law*. However, R. S. Walters writes that there is "agreement that a minimum necessary condition of a scientific statement proposed as lawlike is that it be a universal generalization."[28] Swinburne defines what scientists generally mean by natural law when he writes that a natural law is that which describes "what happens in a *regular* and *predictable* way" (emphasis mine).[29] Contrary to Hume's appeal to constant conjunction and proof (an unvaried constant conjunction), a natural law does *not* only describe what happens in the actual course of events, but explains the actual course of events in terms of hypothetical universal formulas (regular and predictable); for example, if X has a certain mass, it will have a certain weight in Earth's gravity. For if a natural law were merely descriptive of what regularly occurs and nothing more, the term 'natural law' would be devoid of any cognitive content, similar to such assertions as "whatever will be will be." After all, scientists do revise laws because of recurring anomalies, but rarely if ever on the basis of a *single* non-recurring anomaly that is nevertheless recognized as an anomaly (which obviously does not *count against* the law violated). Hence, natural laws must be cognitively significant assertions in which a true counterfactual is possible, whether it be a violation (a singular non-analogous anomaly) or a recurring anomaly. For this reason, if "what happens is entirely irregular and unpredictable [i.e., a violation], its occurrence is not something describable by natural laws." In other words, to "say that a certain such formula is a law is to say that in general its predictions are true and that any exceptions to its operations cannot be accounted for by another formula which could be taken as a law. . . ."[30] Furthermore, a violation of natural law is non-analogous; that is, it should not be confused with an anomaly that occurs regularly under like natural circumstances, which is usually a good indication that the law in question should be revised, replaced, or altered in some fashion so as to account for this anomaly under these particular circumstances.

Consider the following example. Suppose we have a natural law, L, which states that when a human being has been dead for 24 hours it is physically impossible for this corpse to become alive again. L is so intertwined with what has been well established by years of anatomical, physiological, and biological study that no one doubts its status as a law; it is regular and predictable (i.e., given these circumstances, X, P will remain dead). Every epitaph testifies to this reality.

Suppose that on one Sunday afternoon a certain human being, H (let us say, a recognized holy person), who has been dead for more than 24 hours, gets up and walks out of the coroner's office. If this counterinstance to L, E, cannot be subsumed under either L or a more comprehensive law and it is a non-recurring anomaly, I do not see why it is incorrect to call E a legitimate violation of natural law without saying that L is no longer a natural law.

Let us say, however, that prior to his death H had drunk a yet-undiscovered serum that has a natural chemical ability to restore life. Furthermore, let us say that the scientists studying this serum conclude that its chemical composition fits perfectly with what we already know about life, but yet takes us far beyond this knowledge. We are then forced to alter (although not completely change) some of our natural laws in light of this new discovery confirmed by repeatable experiment and observation (i.e., if P drinks the serum prior to his death, P will resurrect within 36 hours of his death): L will be replaced by a new law, L_2.

But if E cannot be subsumed under a more comprehensive law such as L_2 and we have good reason to believe that E would not occur again under similar circumstances (that is, it is a non-repeatable counterinstance), it is perfectly coherent to say that E is a violation of natural law without saying that E counts against L. For E to be able to count against L, it would have to be an anomaly repeatable under similar circumstances (such as in the case of the serum and L_2). "For these latter reasons it seems not unnatural to describe E as a non-repeatable counterinstance to a law of nature L. . . ."[31]

Suppose the naturalist responds by saying that it is possible that any alleged miracle has a natural explanation.[32] But to simply say that one should treat an alleged miraculous event as a mere scientific oddity ad infinitum is to be guilty of special pleading. For if the "natural" is compatible with everything and anything that may occur in the natural world, then the term *natural* has lost any significant meaning. This is not to say that we should resort to the interpretation of miracle whenever an anomalous event occurs. Rather, I am asserting that the non-theist should take seriously the strength of well-established natural law, especially if science's problem-solving capacity has been completely impotent in explaining an alleged miracle in terms of any known law (and is not even remotely close in a forthcoming explanation), as in the case of the primary law-violating miracles of the Christian tradition (e.g., resurrections, changing water into wine, multiplying fishes and loaves, instantaneously healing lepers, walking on water, and so on). Although it is certainly *possible* that scientific explanations of these events will some day be discovered, the fact that the possibility is currently remote, and that science has been incapable of finding *any* explanations, should count for something. Hence, we do have natural, albeit corrigible, grounds to assert what is and is not beyond the scope of nature's capacities.

In summary, to argue that natural law is based on 'uniform experience,' and that this epistemologically forbids one from asserting that a violation of natural law has occurred, is to beg the question in favor of naturalism (whether you take Lewis's or Norton's interpretation of Hume), for it is possible to be perfectly coherent in speaking of a violation of natural law without undermining the law's status as a law.

Proof, Probability, and Evidence

There are some scholars who acknowledge that it is possible to interpret Hume's in-principle argument to be "softer" than Norton interprets it to be.[33] This interpretation emphasizes Hume's rejection of miracles as a weighing of probabilities. Hume is arguing that the "proof" of the way nature generally functions (i.e., violations do not generally occur) outweighs the "proof" of the extremely rare occurrences of the miraculous. As Antony Flew explains it: "But now, clearly, the evidence for the subsistence of such a strong order of Nature will have to be put on the side of the balance opposite to that containing the evidence for the occurrence of the exceptional overriding."[34] And for this reason, Flew asserts that Hume was *not* trying to establish "that miracles do not occur . . . ; but that, whether or not they did or had, this is not something we can any of us ever be in a position positively to know."[35] In contrast to Norton, who views Hume's argument as demonstrating the logical inconsistency in holding to both the miraculous and natural law, Flew sees Hume's argument as a precursor to critical history.[36] Of course, it is possible to view these interpretations as two sides of the same coin. That is,

Hume is showing both the logical (Norton's interpretation) and the testimonial (Flew's interpretation) problems of asserting that a violation of natural law has occurred. Since we have already shown that it is perfectly coherent to speak of violations of natural law, it is only the latter that remains an obstacle to be hurdled.

Hume's weighing of probabilities in his miracles argument is entirely consistent with his epistemological foundation. All knowledge is derived from experience, and "a wise man . . . proportions his belief to the evidence."[37] For Hume, we are unable to know *the necessary connection* between any two events, but can only *believe* what we *customarily* infer from a constant conjunction. Consequently, when particular events continue to occur together, our *belief* that there is a causal connection present is given greater credibility. So in actuality what Hume means by "greater evidence" are events of greater repetition. This is why a miracle (which is a rare event) can never be believed for Hume: it is, by definition, evidentially weaker than the laws of nature it is being weighed against.

Now the problem with this argument is that Hume confuses evidence with probability. He asserts that we should always believe what is more probable, and whatever has occurred more often has greater probability in its favor and hence greater evidence. One must weigh as evidence the antecedent improbability of a miraculous event occurring against the particular evidence for the alleged event. Of course, based on this reasoning, it is never reasonable to believe that a miracle has occurred. Hume's assertion can be put this way:

1. If E is a highly improbable event, no evidence is sufficient to warrant our belief that it has occurred.

This is certainly not a correct form of reasoning. Is it not the case that on the basis of sufficient evidence it is perfectly reasonable to believe that which is improbable has in fact occurred? A number of examples should help demonstrate this.[38] Take for instance the following well-documented case:

> *Life* magazine once reported that all 15 people scheduled to attend a rehearsal of a church choir in Beatrice, Neb., were late for practice on March 1, 1950, and each had a different reason: a car wouldn't start, a

radio program wasn't over, ironing wasn't finished, a conversation dragged on. It was fortunate that none arrived on schedule at 7:15 p.m.—the church was destroyed by an explosion at 7:25. The choir members wondered whether their mutual delays were an act of God.... Weaver estimated there was a one-in-a-million chance that all 15 would be late the same evening.[39]

According to Hume's view of probability and evidence, it seems that a wise man should reject the reliable testimony and circumstantial evidence that has substantiated the fact of this occurrence, even though we know that no reasonable person would reject it.

It is highly improbable that my friend will be dealt a royal flush in a Las Vegas poker room; i.e., it is much more probable that he will be dealt a less promising hand (in fact, the probability of being dealt a royal flush is $0.15 \cdot 10^{-5}$).[40] But according to Hume's reasoning, if my friend is dealt a royal flush, which is a highly improbable occurrence, I should not believe the testimony of several reliable witnesses who claim to have seen the hand.

Finally, suppose a man, who had never murdered anyone in his life, is accused of murder and brought to trial. Five responsible and upstanding citizens, with no reason to lie about what they had witnessed, testify on the witness stand that they had seen the accused commit an act of murder. However, the defense attorney, a follower of Hume, calls 925 people to the witness stand to testify that they had known the accused for a good part of their lives and they had never seen him murder anybody. After this long parade of witnesses, the defense attorney argues: "Let us weigh the 'evidence' of all the people who have seen my client not murdering against the evidence of the five people who say that they had seen my client commit murder at one single moment. Since the 'evidence' ('proof') of non-murdering is greater than the evidence of murdering and the intelligent person always sides with what has greater evidence, my client is *not* guilty." If the jury in this case is any jury at all, it would see through the clever charade this defense attorney is trying to pull; for they know that what is most probable (i.e., that which occurs most often, like non-murdering) can never be weighed as irrefutable 'evidence' against the evidence of a rare occurrence (like murdering).

Now it may be the case that we have misunderstood Hume. After all, the above are examples of improbable, yet *natural*, events. Maybe he is saying that we should only disbelieve the testimonial and circumstantial evidence for violations of natural law, not just any improbable event. I think this is closer to what Hume is saying, for in one place Hume makes the following interesting comment:

> I beg the limitations here made may be remarked, when I say, that a miracle can never be proved, so as to be the foundation of a system of religion. For I own, that otherwise, there may possibly be miracles, or violations of the usual course of nature, of such a kind as to admit the proof of human testimony; though, perhaps, it will be impossible to find any such in all the records of history. Thus, suppose, all authors, in all languages, agree, that, from the first of January 1600, there was a total darkness over the whole earth for eight days: suppose that the tradition of this extraordinary event is still strong and lively among the people: that all travellers, who return from foreign countries, bring us accounts of the same tradition, without the least variation or contradiction: it is evident, that our present philosophers, instead of doubting the fact, ought to receive it as certain, and ought to search for the causes whence it might be derived. The decay, corruption, and dissolution of nature, is an event rendered probable by so many analogies, that any phenomenon, which seems to have a tendency toward catastrophe, comes within the reach of human testimony, if that testimony be very extensive and uniform.[41]

Apparently Hume is saying that one can know that an improbable event has occurred, but that there is no reason to suppose that it does not have a natural explanation. Although he calls the above event a "miracle," it seems Hume is using it in a different way than he did earlier in the text (i.e., in the sense of a bizarre or apparently law-violating event). This seems clear enough when Hume presents another example in which Queen Elizabeth dies (and the witnesses of her death are many and above reproach) and returns to claim her throne a month after her successor assumes it (and the same witnesses of her death are sure it is the same queen who has returned to her throne). Despite this apparently strong evidence for the queen's resurrection, Hume declares: "I would still reply, that the knavery and folly of men are such common phenomena, that I should rather believe the most extraordinary events to arise from their occurrence, than admit of so signal a violation of the laws of nature."[42] Hume goes on to make two important points. First, even if the above event is ascribed to God, it does not make it any more probable, since we know only of God's attributes and actions in what we observe in the usual course of nature (i.e., nature is uniform). And from this, Hume's second point follows: since in the usual course of nature it is more likely that a person not tell the truth about a religious miracle than the laws of nature be violated, it is more probable that the miracle did not occur.[43] The problems that lurk behind both these points—whether one can ascribe a divine source to a miraculous event and whether religious people tend to exaggerate—have been discussed elsewhere and for the sake of brevity must be shelved for another time.[44] However, resolution of these problems is not germane to this paper.

But let us first confront the claim implied in what Hume asserts in the employment of the above two stories. It seems Hume is saying that if apparent violations of natural law occur, they either have a natural cause (and hence, they would not be *real* violations of natural law) or they did not really occur as the witnesses have described them. Hume's assertion can now be put this way:

2. If E is a *real* violation of natural law, no evidence is sufficient to warrant our belief that it has occurred.

But since we have already seen that it is possible to be perfectly coherent in speaking of a violation of natural law, which is an improbable event, and sufficient testimony and evidence can make it reasonable to believe that an improbable event has occurred, to say that no testimony or evidence is sufficient to warrant our belief that a violation of natural law has occurred is to beg the question in favor of naturalism.

For the only way Hume could rightfully argue that no evidence is sufficient to warrant our belief that a violation of natural law has occurred is if violations of natural law are maximally improbable if one already *knows* they could or have never occurred. But as Alvin Plantinga points out, " . . . why should a theist think that such a proposition [i.e., *E has occurred and E is a violation of a law of nature]* is maximally improbable? (Indeed, why should anyone think so? We aren't given a priori that nature is seldom interfered with.) Even if a theist thinks of miracles as a violation of laws of nature . . . she needn't think it improbable *in excelsis* that a miracle occur; so why couldn't she perfectly sensibly believe, on the basis of sufficient testimony, that some particular miraculous event has occurred?"[45] Therefore, the defender of Hume's argument cannot say that violations of natural law are maximally improbable unless he begs the question.

This is not to say that a wise person should not be skeptical of the testimony of an individual who claims to have witnessed a violation of natural law (or any highly improbable event for that matter). However, as J. C. A. Gaskin has pointed out: "There is an uncomfortable sense that by means of it [Hume's argument] one may well justify disbelieving reports of things which did in fact happen—like your disbelief in my report of seeing water turned into wine if my report had also been vouched by numerous other good and impartial witnesses."[46] He continues:

> While it is certainly true that when something altogether extraordinary is reported, the wise man will require more evidence than usual and will check and re-check the evidence very carefully, nevertheless at some stage in his accumulation of respectable evidence the wise man would be in danger of becoming dogmatic and obscurantist if he did *not* believe the evidence.[47]

For example, suppose someone tells you that he has just seen his father, who has been dead for the past two days, alive and walking the streets of New York City. You would be perfectly reasonable if you thought like Hume: "When someone tells me, that he saw a dead man restored to life, I immediately consider with myself, whether this person should either deceive or be deceived, or that the fact, which he relates, should really have happened."[48] That is, it is more probable that deception is involved than that the testimony is accurate. After all, you would have no problem believing the testimony if this man's father had never died. This is because your expectations and judgments hinge on your previous experience: dead men do not come back to life. However, let us say that there are a number of reliable witnesses who corroborate this testimony. Furthermore, the mortuary, which had embalmed the body, reports that it is missing, and police confirm that the fingerprints of the living man (which they found on a glass he had touched) correspond perfectly to the fingerprints of the dead man. Moreover, the man in question was very religious and had prayed prior to his death asking God to resurrect him in order to demonstrate to his atheistic relatives the truth of his religious convictions.

In light of this example, it becomes apparent that Hume's weighing of probabilities is highly artificial, not to mention woefully inadequate. In this case it is not a weighing of *a* probability, L (a law of nature), against a probability, T (a testimony claiming to have witnessed a violation of L), but a weighing of L against what Cardinal Newman called a "convergence of independent probabilities,"[49] T, T_1, T_2, ... T_n (i.e., diverse and reliable testimonies, fingerprints, circumstantial evidence such as the missing embalmed body and his prayer to God, and so on).

As some have pointed out, just as our formulations of natural law are based on certain regularities, our standards of evaluating testimony and evidence are also based on certain regularities (e.g., "Witnesses in such-and-such a situation are more apt to tell the truth").[50] Because these standards do not have the same individual probative strength as a natural law, a single piece, or even several pieces, of testimonial evidence in most cases is insufficient to warrant our belief that a violation of natural law has occurred (although a single testimony is usually sufficient to warrant belief in most everyday situations, such as "Honey, get the checkbook, the paper boy is here"). However, if the testimonial evidence is multiplied and reinforced by circumstantial considerations (as in the above example), and the explanation of the event as a violation connects the data in a simple and coherent fashion (just as we expect a natural law to do),[51] and a denial of the event's occurrence becomes an ad hoc naturalism-of-the-gaps,[52] I do not see why it would not be entirely reasonable to believe that this event has occurred (based on a convergence of independent probabilities). I believe that this approach retains a healthy Humean skepticism by taking into consideration the improbability of a miraculous event, but I also believe that it resists a dogmatic skepticism by taking seriously the possibility that one may have evidence for a miracle.

This in no way denies Hume's point that we make our judgments on the basis of uniformity, regularity, and probability. Rather, the point is being made that Hume incorrectly assumed that, because we *base* our knowledge of the past on regularities (constant conjunction), the *object* of our knowledge must therefore be a regular event and not one that is either singular or highly improbable. Therefore, since we base both evidential and natural law judgments on regularities, it is certainly possible that we can have sufficient evidence to believe that an event highly improbable in terms of natural law has occurred. For if the question of a miracle's occurrence is relegated exclusively to whether the event is improbable in terms of our general experience, then we would be forced to the absurd conclusion that we can never know that an improbable event has occurred; but we do in fact know that some improbable events have occurred. Hence, the question of the event's probability of having occurred must be answered in terms of the evidence for its occurrence on this single occasion, not exclusively on its antecedent improbability. That is why it is entirely reasonable to believe that the above examples of improbable events have in fact occurred: evidential considerations, based on certain regularities, were able to "outweigh" the antecedent improbability of the event occurring.[53]

As to what standards or criteria would be employed in judging the adequacy of the evidence of any alleged violation of natural law that is a miracle, the evidential criteria employed in legal reasoning have been suggested.[54] For the purposes of this paper, however, it is only necessary to justify the possibility that sufficient testimony and evidence can warrant our belief that a violation of natural law has occurred. I believe that this task has been accomplished. In summary, Hume has failed to realize that the wise and intelligent person bases his or her convictions on *evidence*, not on Humean "probability." That is, an event's occurrence may be very improbable in terms of past experience and observation, but current observation and testimony may lead one to believe that the evidence for the event is good. In this way, Hume confuses evidence with probability.

University of Nevada, Las Vegas

NOTES

1. See Francis J. Beckwith, *David Hume's Argument Against Miracles: A Critical Analysis* (Lanham, Md.: University Press of America, 1989), pp. 7–18.

2. Tillotson (1630–1694), a Presbyterian theologian and archbishop of Canterbury (1691–1694), argued in both his *Rule of Faith* (1676) and *A Discourse Against Transubstantiation* (1684) that it is not possible to establish transubstantiation as part of Christian doctrine.

3. David Hume, *An Enquiry Concerning Human Understanding*, 3rd ed., text revised and notes P. H. Nidditch, introduction and analytic index L. A. Selby-Bigge (Oxford: Clarendon Press, 1975; reprinted 1777 edition), p. 109. It should be noted that John Passmore writes that the tenth section of the *Enquiry*, "Of Miracles," "was originally meant to form part of the *Treatise [on Human Nature*, 1739–1740]; and without it the *Treatise* is incomplete" (*Hume's Intentions*, rev. ed. [New York: Basic Books, 1952], p. 32). Concerning this point, Hume writes in a letter to Henry Home: "Having a frankt [*sic*] letter, I was resolved to make use of it; and accordingly inclose some *Reasonings Concerning Miracles*, which I once thought of publishing with the rest, but which I am afraid will give too much offence, even as the world is disposed at present" (J. Y. T. Greig, ed., *The Letters of David Hume*, 2 vols. [Oxford: Clarendon Press, 1932], Vol. I, p. 24). See also John O. Nelson, "The Burial and Resurrection of Hume's Essay 'Of Miracles'," *Hume Studies* 12 (April 1986): 57–76.

4. Tillotson, *A Discourse Against Transubstantiation*, Vol. II, p. 448, as quoted in Antony Flew, *Hume's Philosophy of Belief* (London: Routledge & Kegan Paul, 1961), p. 172. For an extended discussion of Tillotson's argument and how Hume applies it, see Dennis M. Ahern, "Hume on the Evidential Impossibility of Miracles," in Nicholas Rescher, ed., *Studies in Epistemology*, *APQ* Monograph No. 9 (Oxford: Basil Blackwell, 1975), pp. 14–30. Ahern writes in detail of the possible ways one can interpret Hume's use of Tillotson and concludes that a similar interpretation to mine possesses independent plausibility and is a viable interpretation of Hume's

argument. Although the interpretation of Tillotson's argument and how it relates to Hume's argument are worthy topics, for both the sake of brevity and the importance of dealing exclusively with the specific content of Hume's argument, I refer the reader to Ahern's excellent work.

5. Hume, *Enquiry*, p. 110.

6. Ibid., pp. 110–11.

7. Ibid., p. 112.

8. Ibid.

9. Ibid., p. 113.

10. Ibid.

11. Ibid.

12. Ibid., p. 114. Concerning Hume's use of the term 'unalterable,' J. C. A. Gaskin's comments are worth noting: "Even here there is an incipient mistake. The word 'unalterable,' although justifiable on some account of the laws of nature, is not justifiable on Hume's. What he should have written is something like 'unvaried'" (*Hume's Philosophy of Religion* [London: Macmillan, 1978], p. 122).

13. Hume, ibid., p. 115.

14. This is an example used by Richard Swinburne, *The Concept of Miracle* (New York: Macmillan, 1970), p. 14.

15. Hume, *Enquiry*, pp. 115–16.

16. Ibid., p. 116.

17. Ibid.

18. Ibid., p. 110.

19. For example, see C. S. Lewis, *Miracles* (London: Fontana Books, 1947), pp. 104–7.

James Noxon writes: "If Hume really intended his critique 'Of Miracles' to 'establish it is a maxim, that no human testimony can have such a force as to prove a miracle, and make it a foundation for any such system of religion' . . . , his argument is a question-begging failure" ("Hume's Concern with Religion," in Kenneth R. Merrill and Robert W. Shahan, eds., *David Hume: Many-Sided Genius* [Norman: University of Oklahoma Press, 1976], p. 77).

20. Lewis, *Miracles*, p. 106.

21. See Robert J. Roth, S.J., "Did Peirce Answer Hume on Necessary Connection?" *Review of Metaphysics* 38 (June 1985): 867–80.

22. David Fate Norton, *David Hume: Common-Sense Moralist, Sceptical Metaphysician* (Princeton, N.J.: Princeton University Press, 1982), p. 298.

23. Ibid., p. 299.

24. Hume, *Enquiry*, p. 114.

25. Swinburne, *Concept*, p. 28.

26. George Mavrodes, "Miracles and the Laws of Nature," *Faith and Philosophy* 2 (October 1985): 337.

27. Ibid.

28. R. S. Walters, "Laws of Science and Lawlike Statements," in Paul Edwards, ed., *Encyclopedia of Philosophy*, Vol. 4 (New York: Macmillan & The Free Press, 1967), pp. 410–11. See John Hospers, "Law," in E. D. Klemke, Robert Hollinger, and A. David Kline, eds., *Introductory Readings in the Philosophy of Science* (Buffalo, N.Y.: Prometheus Books, 1980), pp. 104–11; Charles E. Hummell, *The Galileo Connection* (Downers Grove, Ill.: Inter-Varsity Press, 1986), pp. 180–88; and Ernest Nagel, *The Structure of Science* (New York: Harcourt Brace, 1961), pp. 75–78.

29. Swinburne, *Concept*, p. 26. This view of scientific law as regular and predictable is echoed by Hummell, Walters, and Patrick Nowell-Smith. Hummell writes: "Since laws are based directly on experimental data, they can be tested at any time. They not only describe present natural phenomena but also precisely predict future results for a given set of conditions. Thus they also provide the basis for technology, the use of science for practical purposes" (*Galileo*, p. 184). Walters asserts: "Suppose it is a law, *s*, that sodium burns when exposed to air. This law . . . can explain why a given piece of sodium burns when exposed to air and can be used to predict that a given piece of sodium will burn when exposed to air" ("Laws," p. 412). Nowell-Smith, whose article is written in opposition to belief in miracles, writes that "a scientific explanation is an hypothesis from which predictions can be made, which can afterwards be verified. It is the essence of such an hypothesis—a 'law' is but a well-confirmed hypothesis—that it should be capable of such predictive expansion" (Patrick Nowell-Smith, "Miracles," in Antony Flew and Alasdair MacIntyre, eds., *New Essays in Philosophical Theology* [New York: Macmillan, 1955], pp. 249–50).

30. Swinburne, *Concept*, pp. 26, 27–28.

31. Ibid., p. 27.

32. Alastair McKinnon, "'Miracle' and 'Paradox,'" *American Philosophical Quarterly* 4 (October 1967): 308–14.

33. For example, see William Lane Craig, *Apologetics: An Introduction* (Chicago: Moody Press, 1984), pp. 121–22; Antony Flew, *David Hume: Philosopher of Moral Science* (New York: Basil Blackwell, 1986), pp. 81ff.; R. F. Holland, "The Miraculous," in John Donnelly, ed., *Logical Analysis and Contemporary Theism* (New York: Fordham University Press, 1972), pp. 226–35; and Noxon, "Hume's Concern," pp. 73–82.

34. Flew, *Hume: Philosopher of Moral Science*, p. 81.

35. Ibid., p. 80.

36. Referring to how Hume's argument affects the defender of miracles, Norton writes: "His conceptions are, to say the least, incompatible, and thus to argue that there are both uniformities and miracles is inconsistent" (*David Hume*, p. 299). Flew writes that Hume's work on miracles shows "what Hume never manages outright to say, that the critical historian, in

approaching the detritus of the past, has to assume whatever he knows, or thinks he knows, about what is probable or improbable, possible or impossible. For it is only upon these always fallible and corrigible assumptions that he becomes able to interpret any of that detritus as historical evidence at all; much less to erect upon it his account of what did and did not actually happen" (*David Hume: Philosopher of Moral Science*, p. 84).

This is not to say that Flew does not see the epistemological problem inherent in the concept of miracle as it relates to natural law, for he in fact has written on this problem elsewhere. However, in contrast to Norton, Flew denies that Hume himself specifically argues in this way: "All this argumentation, although (in spirit at least) thoroughly Humean, has little to do with the line of argumentation which Hume chose to develop in the section 'Of Miracles'" ("Miracles," *Encyclopedia of Philosophy*, Vol. 5, p. 349).

37. Hume, *Enquiry*, p. 110.

38. Hume writes of two types of probability, probability of chances and probability of causes. The former is similar to what probability theorists call the a priori theory of probability, and the latter is similar to what they call the relative-frequency theory of probability. An example of how both theories work can be seen in the odds of a flipped coin landing on heads. According to the a priori theory, prior to any flip, the odds are 1:2 that the coin will land on heads. In contrast, the relative-frequency theory measures the frequency of an event having occurred, and then a probability is calculated in light of this frequency. According to this theory, a coin that has landed on heads six times out of ten flips has a probability of 3:5, or .600. Irving Copi uses the following example to explain the relative-frequency view: ". . . the probability of a twenty-five-year-old woman surviving her twenty-sixth birthday is .971. . . . Of 1,000 twenty-five-year-old women, if 971 exhibit the attribute of surviving at least one additional year, the number .971 is assigned as the probability coefficient for the occurrence of this attribute in any such class" (*Introduction to Logic*, 5th ed. [New York: Macmillan, 1978], pp. 510, 513).

The probability of causes, which roughly corresponds to the relative-frequency theory of probability, is the view I believe Hume speaks of in his miracles argument. For the sake of covering all bases, however, in the text I will use examples of both improbable events (a priori and relative-frequency), which reasonable people should believe on the basis of sufficient evidence.

39. Richard Blodgett, "Our Wild, Weird World of Coincidence," *Reader's Digest* 131 (September 1987): 127.

40. Richard A. Epstein, *The Theory of Gambling and Statistical Logic* (New York: Academic Press, 1967), p. 222.

41. Hume, *Enquiry*, pp. 127–28.

42. Ibid., p. 128.

43. Ibid., p. 129.

44. See Beckwith, *David Hume*, pp. 12–13, 51–52, 54–63.

45. Alvin Plantinga, "Is Theism Really a Miracle?" *Faith and Philosophy* 3 (April 1986): 113. Another similar response to Hume's argument from probability along the same lines is Roy A. Sorenson's observation that "one cannot establish this kind of scepticism merely by showing that the low probabilities of the individual testimonies do not add up in such a way as to make probable 'There is at least one miracle.'" He concludes, "Hume's argument does not rule out the possibility that one accepts case by case scepticism and yet one knows through testimony that at least one miracle took place" ("Hume's Scepticism Concerning Reports of Miracles," *Analysis* 43 [January 1983]: 60).

My argument for the possibility of miracles that follows, based on the convergence of independent probabilities, could be viewed as an extrapolation of Sorenson's observation.

46. Gaskin, *Hume's Philosophy of Religion*, p. 115.

47. Ibid.

48. Hume, *Enquiry*, p. 116.

49. As cited in John Warwick Montgomery, "Science, Theology, and the Miraculous," in *Faith Founded on Fact* (New York: Thomas Nelson, 1978), p. 55.

50. See Swinburne, *Concept*, pp. 41–48. Montgomery explains that legal reasoning is an example of evidential criteria based on certain regularities: "The lawyer endeavors to reduce societal conflicts by arbitrating conflicting truth-claims. Inherent to the practice of the law is an effort to resolve conflicts over legal responsibilities, and such conflicts invariably turn on questions of fact. To establish a 'cause of action' the plaintiff's complaint must allege a legal right, which the defendant was duty-bound to recognize and which he violated; at the trial evidentiary facts must be marshaled in support of the plaintiff's allegations, and the defendant will need to provide factual evidence in his behalf to counter the plaintiff's prima facie case against him. To this end, legal science, as an outgrowth of millennia of court decisions, developed meticulous criteria for distinguishing factual truth from error" (Montgomery, *The Law Above the Law* [Minneapolis: Dimension Books, 1975], p. 86).

51. Swinburne writes: "So then a claim that a formula L is a law of nature and claims that testimony or trace of a certain type is reliable are established basically the same way—by showing that certain formulae connect observed data in a simple coherent way" (*Concept*, p. 43).

That simplicity and coherence are values, which the scientist seeks in formulating any law or theory, is defended by not a few philosophers of science. For example, see W. H. Newton-Smith, *The Rationality of Science* (London: Routledge & Kegan Paul, 1981), pp. 226–32; Karl R. Popper,

"Truth, Rationality, and the Growth of Knowledge," in his *Conjectures and Refutations* (New York: Harper & Row, 1963), pp. 240–41; Hilary Putnam, *Reason, Truth, and History* (New York: Cambridge University Press, 1981), p. 35; and J. P. Moreland, *Christianity and the Nature of Science: A Philosophical Investigation* (Grand Rapids: Baker Book House, 1989), Chs. 1–3.

52. A fine example of naturalism-of-the-gaps is Hume's defense of maintaining naturalism in his fictional account of Queen Elizabeth's resurrection (*Enquiry*, p. 128).

53. I am not the first to employ Hume's own view of probability against him. John King-Farlow cites a work of the little-known philosopher and scientist Charles Babbage, *Ninth Bridgewater Treatise* (1837), in which Babbage employs numerical probability to quantify the probability of a miraculous resurrection and the probability of witnesses to give accurate testimony of such an occurrence. He concludes that it is sometimes reasonable to believe that a miracle has occurred. Although I do not agree entirely with his approach, I believe Babbage was on the right track. See King-Farlow, "Historical Insights on Miracles: Babbage, Hume, Aquinas," *International Journal for Philosophy of Religion* 13 (1982): 209–18.

54. Beckwith, *David Hume*, pp. 121–38.

Religious and Scientific Uses of Anecdotal Evidence

8

Jesse Hobbs

ABSTRACT

Although frequently maligned, anecdotal evidence is commonly employed in revealed theology. I defend its epistemic value with four claims: (1) certain beliefs are justifiable anecdotally, and only anecdotally, and some beliefs about God are of this kind; (2) even in an epistemically paradigmatic science, beliefs are sometimes based on anecdotal evidence alone; (3) using anecdotal evidence is essential to human development and social functioning; and (4) occasionally it is superior to other forms of evidence. I answer objections that "you can prove anything with anecdotal evidence," and that its uniqueness makes it worthless because replicability is merely the societal equivalent of stability of perception.

One cannot carry on an extended epistemological discussion of revealed theology without encountering difficulties associated with anecdotal evidence, whether in scripture or in contemporary religious experience. The claim that Jesus rose from the dead, for example, is supported primarily by anecdotes taken from the four gospels. A question one hopes to avoid is whether beliefs can ever be justified on the basis of anecdotal evidence alone. A religion based on nothing but anecdotal evidence would be helplessly mired in contingency and the sands of shifting interpretation; a purely anecdotal science is impossible. So one hopes to find more reliable evidence relevant to any given question. Alternative forms of empirical evidence include (1) statistical or inductive evidence produced by sustained, systematic observation; (2) theoretical evidence produced by rational argumentation from theoretical premises enjoying independent support; (3) experimental evidence derived from instrumentation or controlled manipulation. Non-empirical evidence is also important, including (4) conceptual analysis, which functions more or less like a priori theoretical evidence.

None of these categories is sharply defined, and evidence will often fit more than one. For example, evidence produced by textual analysis is typically a combination of theoretical evidence and conceptual analysis. The purpose of typing evidence in this way is to alert us to customary strengths and weaknesses of the various groups. For example, theoretical evidence usually employs logically rigorous reasoning and a broadened base of empirical support, but is risky because of the epistemic gap between theory and supporting observations. Various of these tools have been embraced widely among theologians and sociologists of religion, but had at best a rudimentary existence in the early church.

Armed with this rough classification, we prefer to ask the question whether anecdotal evidence can contribute significantly to the justification of belief, as one among many forms of evidence. This still cannot be answered without knowing how much is being demanded from our epistemology. In particular, there are two demands traditionally placed on epistemology by religious people that anecdotal evidence is ill-suited to satisfy: (1) answering the skeptic, or establishing the truth of religious beliefs with certainty, and (2) providing a basis for rational consensus on religious questions. Many problems confronting religious epistemology are generic to epistemology and not peculiar to religion, including (1). The current wave of philosophical interest in naturalized epistemology signals the abandonment of the goal of answering the skeptic—a goal that has dominated epistemology since Descartes—as intractable. Sociologists of science openly question whether (2) can be accomplished even for scientific questions in the scientific community, although their doubts are not universally shared.[1] Hence, what religious people want from epistemology, although in line with what philosophers have traditionally sought, may not be forthcoming. On the brighter side, this raises the prospect that anecdotal evidence may not be in such bad company after all, if this is all that can be said against it.

Turning to the more modest epistemological aim of (3) providing adequate although corrigible legitimation for personal religious beliefs, several arguments indicate that anecdotal evidence can contribute significantly toward this end. Unfortunately, the issue is clouded by the fact that when anecdotal evidence works alongside other evidential forms, it is hard to tell how much of the load is being carried by each, or whether the evidential structure would be jeopardized if its anecdotal support were removed. Hence, for the sake of clarity, we must revert to the unrealistic question we were hoping to avoid. That is, to establish the usefulness of anecdotal evidence, we must look at cases in which it alone is bearing the epistemic burden, although our intention is not to make a practice of using anecdotal evidence this way.

Anecdotal evidence may be defended along the following lines: (1) apparently some kinds of belief can be justified anecdotally and only anecdotally, and beliefs about God are of this kind; (2) even in the supposedly paradigmatic science of physics, some beliefs formed solely on the basis of anecdotal evidence appear justified; (3) using anecdotal evidence is necessary for human development and functioning in society; and (4) under certain circumstances, anecdotal evidence may be superior to other forms of evidence. I defend these four claims in what follows, clarifying along the way the concept of anecdotal evidence and what counts as "adequate legitimation for belief." Nevertheless, I believe that using anecdotal material inevitably leads to idiosyncratic conclusions, and in concluding, I argue against two policies for handling anecdotal evidence purporting to have general applicability. Throughout the paper I apply 'evidence' and 'justifies' univocally, mindful of the enormous differences separating scientific and religious communities in their epistemic practices. In terms of Ian Barbour's fourfold classification of ways of relating theology to science, this puts me on the far end of considering them potentially integrable into a coherent structure yielding knowledge about the world.[2]

What Counts as Anecdotal Evidence?

For anything to count as evidence, it must be seen as supporting some belief or hypothesis—otherwise, an anecdote is just an amusing story. Current scientific parlance departs from ordinary usage, however, in that 'anecdotal evidence' has come to refer to a wider variety of supportive testimony than merely narrative accounts. The motive for thus broadening the concept is epistemic—the additional evidence to be included under the 'anecdotal' rubric is in the same epistemic 'bag' or natural kind as narrative testimony. Since the orientation of this paper is epistemic, I follow this broader sense rather than adhering to ordinary usage. Anecdotal evidence can then be explicated in terms of three characteristics: it is to an important extent (1) unique (not replicated), (2) uncontrolled (lacking a scientifically normative degree of control or rigor), and (3) taken to be an observed instance or consequence of the hypothesis in question (as opposed to an argument, explanation, or conceptual analysis of it). Thus, anecdotal evidence is always empirical. This conception is broader in that it includes firsthand nonverbal experiences, which often occur under unique and uncontrolled circumstances. Also, there is no prohibition against the evidence being experimentally derived. A novel experiment, such as the alleged creation of cold fusion in a test tube, counts as anecdotal evidence until it has been replicated enough times to say that it is not an isolated or unique occurrence. The anecdotal rubric also covers unique and uncontrolled occurrences that are witnessed by many people, although additional witnesses mean better corroboration. Case studies may be considered anecdotal because of their uniqueness, although they become less so the better they are controlled.

Whether evidence is unique or uncontrolled is a matter not only of degree but also of viewpoint. For control, the argument runs roughly as follows (more on uniqueness later). Before the placebo effect was widely recognized, many medical experiments failed to control for the effect of patient beliefs regarding the therapy being administered. The resulting evidence came to be treated as anecdotal once the need for blind trials was recognized. When these were also shown not to control adequately—this time for the effect of the physician's belief regarding the therapy—such single-blind trials were also relegated to the status of anecdotal evidence. Claims based on such evidence were seen as interesting stories that need better corroboration before a lot of confidence is put in them.

But not all scientific claims can be established on the basis of double-blind trials—the efficacy of coronary bypass surgery appears to be a case in point.[3] Although this expensive therapy undoubtedly produces positive results, the placebo effect also produces positive results, and it is difficult to determine how much of the efficacy of coronary bypass surgery is a consequence of the placebo effect. That is, because of the amount of faith our culture has in coronary bypass surgery, we cannot ethically set up a situation in which some patients are given it while others are given a treatment known to have no therapeutic value, with neither the patient nor the physician knowing who is receiving which. Other kinds of pragmatic limitations, such as the large number of subjects required for randomized double-blind trials to work, often mandate reliance on evidence that is not so well controlled.[4] Although it is impossible to say how weak the controls must be for evidence to qualify as anecdotal, these kinds of exigencies surely contribute to justifying the use of anecdotal evidence. Note that these non-blind and single-blind trials were replicated often, yet their status still came to be regarded as anecdotal once better-controlled procedures were available.

Some may reserve the term 'anecdotal' for pejorative use, but making it a term of abuse conflates judgments of fact and value. For the present purposes, every Bible story and every episodic religious experience could be classified as anecdotal, and hence as anecdotal evidence insofar as they are thought to teach us anything about the nature or existence of God—a fact that can be agreed upon independently of any assessment of their evidential value.

Anecdotal Evidence of Intelligence

My first argument for anecdotal evidence is that certain manifestations of intelligence can be attributed to an entity on the basis of anecdotal evidence, and cannot be attributed by any other means. This kind of intelligence is something we normally ascribe to God. Hence, we must rely on anecdotal evidence for this information.

Intelligence can be ascribed to God on a variety of grounds. One traditional argument is that God is perfect and intelligence is a perfection, but this does not tell us what intelligence is, and there are many theories to choose from. Plato says that intelligence is indicated by perfect regularity or orderliness of being. Given that rationality is unchanging, a perfectly rational being would never change according to this argument, and its works would exhibit similar regularity and order. Indeed, we find some regularity and order in creation, and an argument can be made on this basis to the intelligence of its creator.

We could go on in this fashion, but such conceptions of intelligence and rationality are far removed from what we would expect of a Being who made man, a "rational animal," in his own image. Even in humans 'intelligence' refers to many different properties, and people who excel by one measure may not by another. The kind of intelligence of interest here is exemplified by Solomon in the dispute of two women over a baby. In this case we have a flash of brilliance that solves a puzzle that otherwise appeared insoluble. To say that the puzzle was solved is to say that it was apparent, once the answer was given, that it met the constraints on an adequate solution. But if people could have predicted or anticipated this answer in advance, there would never have been a puzzle in the first place. Thus, there is a sense in which exhibitions of this kind of intelligence always come as a surprise, yet it need not be a complete surprise or we would not recognize Solomon as someone who can do this more often than most.

This kind of intelligence presents an epistemological problem noted by Daniel Dennett:

> a good scientist . . . knows how misleading and, officially, unusable anecdotes are, and yet on the other hand they are often so telling! The trouble with the canons of scientific evidence here is that they virtually rule out the description of anything but the oft-repeated, oft-observed, stereotypic behavior of species, and this is just the sort of behavior that reveals no particular intelligence at all—all this behavior can be more or less plausibly explained as the effects of some humdrum combination of "instinct" or tropism and conditioned response. It is the *novel* bits of behavior, the acts that couldn't plausibly be accounted for in terms of prior conditioning or training or habit, that speak eloquently of intelligence; but if their novelty and unrepeatability make them anecdotal and hence inadmissible evidence, how can one proceed to develop the cognitive case for the intelligence of one's target species?[5]

Undoubtedly, humans are capable of being conditioned in more complex ways than other animals—they can develop more complex stimulus-response patterns—and this is one way in which their superior intelligence manifests itself, but this is not what Dennett is talking about. Neither is it the intelligence measured by anything so replicable as standardized intelligence tests. Because such tests exhibit cultural biases, they must be revealing culturally conditioned responses, rather than unconditioned ability. The notion of intelligence that is relevant here is not a disposition that can be elicited on command, because we ascribe it to those who display flashes of brilliance on occasion, even though they cannot solve every problem set before them. And once it is established that someone such as Solomon outstrips us in this kind of intelligence, it seems uncharitable to judge the rest of his behavior unfavorably by means of standards devised by our admittedly inferior intelligence. Presumably, we must also be cautious in judging God in this way.

Evidence of God's intelligence is often found in events that are so serendipitous as to cry out for explanation. A nonreligious explanation may be available that accounts for why the event happened, but usually not for its teleological or serendipitous character—although sometimes it does this too. What a scientific explanation cannot offer that a religious explanation can is the ability to attribute unusual intelligence in the above sense to that part of the natural world outside human (animal) control, or to its Creator, as an explanation for such serendipity, because inanimate matter is conceived as passive and so unintelligent; and as Dennett says, this kind of intelligence may not be demonstrable without anecdotal evidence.[6]

Of course, we would like explanations for those times when the natural world exhibits unusual idiocy or senselessness as well, lest the appearance of serendipity turn out to be purely accidental. Skeptics often bring up this kind of point, emphasizing correctly that any adequate theory must be consistent with all available evidence. But by itself consistency leaves open many possible interpretations that can claim the anecdotal evidence in their favor. Since the anecdotal evidence will not be able to rule among these alternatives, it will not answer the skeptic. If the Dennett-inspired suggestion is correct that no other kind of evidence can better support the ascription of intelligence, then this kind of question will rarely have a definitive answer. Establishing by other means that instances of serendipity happen no more frequently than by chance would be question-begging. By its very nature, we are unable to anticipate where such intelligence is likely to manifest itself next, or how frequently these manifestations ought to occur, so we would probably reach a null statistical result because of our inability to choose appropriate reference classes. The most we can say is that if the world is intelligent in this way, or has an intelligent creator, this will manifest itself from time to time.

The Usefulness of Anecdotal Evidence

How, then, does anecdotal evidence provide adequate legitimation for belief, if such questions have no definitive answers? We must distinguish here between adequacy in the sense of rationally legitimating (permitting) belief and rationally compelling (obligating) belief. Historically, epistemologists and scientists have been more concerned with the latter sense, which allows one to eliminate opposing viewpoints as irrational. Thus, Thomas Hobbes says of dreams and religious experiences that none can *compel* him to believe, since the person relating them may be in error or lying.[7] This does not settle whether he would be *entitled* to believe on such evidence, or compelled *not* to believe. Religious people also have argued that religious belief is rationally compelled in order to explain why condemning the unbeliever is just. Classical foundationalism contributes to this program because what it permits and what it requires regarding beliefs are one and the same, making it unnecessary to give the "permitted" category separate treatment.

But classical foundationalism has been discredited as too austere to reconstruct most of what we count as knowledge; a more reasonable view is that evidence does not compel belief in much other than itself, because it is inevitably consistent with many conflicting theories or interpretations.[8] Thus, even the best evidence often does nothing more than legitimate belief in a theory or viewpoint—it makes such belief rationally permissible—in which case nothing more can be expected of anecdotal evidence. When I say that anecdotal evidence can provide adequate legitimation for belief, I mean that given such evidence, one is no longer rationally compelled to believe otherwise or suspend judgment. Without such evidence, principles of rationality such as Occam's razor, or that belief be proportioned to evidence, could mandate disbelief or suspension of judgment.

At this point one might object that, if this is all that anecdotal evidence does, how could any kind of evidence fail to accomplish at least this much? I don't say that it could; I am primarily opposing the view that anecdotal evidence is not really evidence at all—a view often defended by pointing out how frequently it is abused. Without denying that such abuses occur, my aim is to establish that anecdotal evidence has legitimate evidential value.

As an example will help to make clear, the central epistemological problem concerning anecdotal evidence is its uniqueness. Richard Nisbett and Lee Ross report the following incident:

> One of the authors recently was told by a respected colleague that an anthropologist friend of his, whom the colleague greatly respected, recently had been on a field trip to a remote African village. While sitting in the village one day, the anthropologist saw a man with a compound fracture of the shin being helped by two other men into the hut of the village shaman and healer. The seriousness of the injury was obvious. Both ends of the shin bone could be seen protruding from the torn tissue of the leg. Nevertheless, two hours after entering the hut, the man with the fracture emerged with a bandaged leg, walking under his own power.
>
> In a sense, all three parties—the author, the colleague, and the colleague's anthropologist friend—believe this story. The author trusts his colleague's veracity and judgment completely, and the colleague similarly trusts his anthropologist friend. Furthermore, the story, while surprising in some respects, is probably no more or less implausible to any one of the three parties than to the others. Yet we suspect that by placing each of them in a relevant test situation it could be shown that the three parties have not made the same inferences from the information. Imagine each of them finding themselves in a remote African village with a compound fracture of the shin! The author is confident that he would sooner ask for a revolver to put himself out of his misery than place himself in the hands of a shaman; his colleague no doubt would be terribly frightened but might take faint hope from the story he had heard from his anthropolo-

gist friend; and the anthropologist probably would quickly and calmly request that someone fetch the local practitioner of shamanistic medicine.[9]

In stating that this is probably what would happen, Nisbett and Ross are not necessarily endorsing these three responses, yet it is not hard to see how they could be justified. The anthropologist in question undoubtedly had to make a number of inferences to the best explanation to give the account that he did. He inferred that he did not mistake the nature or severity of the person's injury, that his eyes were functioning properly, that he is remembering the incident accurately, that the event was not being staged by the natives in order to deceive him, and so forth. His colleague must make *all of these same inferences, plus more.* Even if he knows the anthropologist well and is sure that the story wasn't fabricated deliberately, he still must infer that his friend is not unintentionally or even unconsciously misleading him, that he remembers and understands his friend's story correctly—not to mention his friend's interpretation—that his friend does not have greater credulity than himself, and so forth. The author, in turn, must not only make all *these* inferences, but also corresponding inferences about his colleague. Inferences to the best explanation, although in a sense inevitable and perhaps foundational to perception itself, are inferences that are prone to go awry. Thus, the more inferences involved in drawing a given conclusion, the more opportunity for error to creep in, and the more hesitant a person will be to trust such information, and rightly so.

An early formulation of this commonsensical principle was given by John Locke:

> . . . *any testimony, the further off it is from the original truth, the less force and proof it has.* The being and existence of the thing itself, is what I call the original truth. A credible man vouching his knowledge of it is a good proof; but if another equally credible do witness it from his report, the testimony is weaker: and a third that attests the hearsay of an hearsay is yet less considerable. So that in traditional truths, each remove weakens the force of the proof: and the more hands the tradition has successively passed through, the less strength and evidence does it receive from them.[10]

C. A. J. Coady rejects this claim, however, on the grounds that it implies the disappearance-of-history thesis, that "the evidential credentials of well-established facts will become negligible as they recede into the distant future."[11] I think the disappearance-of-history thesis is probably true, if only the time for evidence to degrade be made long enough, but Coady is wrong to say that Locke's view implies it. Locke did not say how much each change of hands weakens the evidence—this undoubtedly varies depending on *how* it changes hands. How *often* it changes hands also affects how rapidly it degrades. For example, orally transmitted histories disappear fairly quickly, whereas written histories disappear slowly. If the way it changes hands could be made progressively more secure, or the frequency of changes progressively reduced, the overall evidence for a well-established fact could decrease asymptotically toward a non-negligible positive value rather than to zero, in which case the history of that fact would never disappear entirely.

Locke's claim does require qualification to answer one of Coady's arguments, however.[12] A person who is more distant in time from the original truth may have better evidence for it if she has additional corroborating evidence not available to a more proximal person. Locke's claim implies monotonic degradation along lines of transmission taken singly, but not necessarily for the combined effect of all lines of transmission. If, as seems likely, our efforts to dig up new lines of evidence for the same event peter out over the long haul, then Locke's claim could eventually be reinstated for the totality of evidence. As for documentary evidence, no original document lasts forever, copies fail to duplicate the original precisely, and originals are sometimes altered by the hands they pass through. Bear in mind also that memory and rehearsal of firsthand experiences constitute intermediate hands through which they are transmitted. Ultimately, the disappearance-of-history thesis follows simply from the second law of thermodynamics.

If evidence weakens the more hands it passes through, then the only way all members of a community or institution can attain the same degree of warranted belief regarding an event would be to repeat the event for each one—thus the rationale behind replication. But the uniqueness of anecdotal evidence normally precludes this; we inevitably find ourselves at different epistemic distances from it. Hence, we cannot cope with anecdotal evidence "objectively," or independently of our peculiar vantage point. Two conclusions follow: (1) we cannot expect everyone to draw the same conclusion on the basis of anecdotal evidence, so it cannot be used to marshall a consensus; (2) if our ability to determine the epistemic position of others is impaired, we cannot as a rule determine whether their conclusions are legitimate either. That is, even if we can judge the veracity of their informant, we may not be able to judge "what they should have known" about the veracity of their informant.

This is not to say that anything goes. Keeping epistemological and metaphysical issues distinct, to say that the vantage point of others is difficult to judge is not to say that there is no fact of the matter what it is, or whether their conclusions are appropriate relative to it. Neither does it imply that we cannot evaluate our own vantage point and draw conclusions accordingly. But it does make room for pluralism in practice, or tolerance for the interpretation of others. This situation is not ideal; wariness of anecdotal evidence is proper when superior evidence is available. But religious people rarely possess an embarrassment of epistemic riches, in which case they ought to use whatever evidence is available.

If it is not the case that anything goes, then mightn't our vantage point be so ideal that belief on the basis of anecdotal evidence is rationally mandated, not just permitted? Yes. Fred Dretske asks the following rhetorical question: "We [all] know that we sometimes make mistakes about the whereabouts of our children, [but] is this relevant to whether I, while arm wrestling with my son, could be mistaken about *his* whereabouts?"[13] Only a Pyrrhonean skeptic could remain in doubt here, yet by varying the circumstances we could make the incident unique and the resulting evidence anecdotal. That is, we could replace Dretske with Jairus and his son with Jairus's daughter and conclude that Jairus ought to know his daughter's whereabouts when with her. What does this prove? After her death, recorded in Mark 5, most likely that something has happened which Jairus thought impossible on the basis of everything he had been taught; and being obligated to believe this, he would naturally be obligated to ask where he or his teachers had gone wrong, etc.[14] How far the obligation extends is not clear; I do not claim that it extends far.

Suppose the anecdotal evidence were verbal—could it still compel belief? Most of us would think a person quite irrational who, having been warned that the police strictly enforce a 25-mph speed limit on a certain street, and having been ticketed for speeding on it once already, continued to drive on it at 35 mph—and we would think this even if we ourselves drive 10 mph over the limit at times.

Further Arguments in Support of Anecdotal Evidence

My second argument takes its lead from what many regard as the epistemically paradigmatic science—physics—in how it deals with a phenomenon for which there is nothing but anecdotal evidence. Ball lightning has never been observed systematically, measured with scientific instruments, reproduced in the laboratory, or explained theoretically, yet most physicists believe it is a genuine phenomenon. S. Singer characterizes the current situation as follows:[15]

> Despite the extremely limited information available on ball lightning from measurements made during its appearance in nature, its general characteristics are well known. These have been obtained by study of approximately one thousand random observations by chance observers recorded over the past century and a half in the general scientific and meteorological literature.
>
> The glowing spheres are usually associated with ordinary lightning in severe thunderstorms. In contrast to the common flashes of lightning, however, these globes remain visible for an appreciable time while floating freely through the air in extended paths which may take them into houses. Their velocity is relatively moderate, as indicated by witnesses who have escaped being struck by the flying balls by leaping aside.[16]

Typically the globes are spherical, about 25 cm in diameter, and last from 1 to 10 seconds, although there is a great variation in size and some have been reported to last well over a minute.

Most often they move horizontally at 1 to 2 meters per second—not necessarily in a straight line—but a large number have been observed to fall directly down only to change suddenly to a horizontal path near the ground. They often appear to be spinning or making a hissing or crackling sound, and may disappear either silently or with an ear-shattering explosion. They have been known to enter buildings through doors and windows, and entrance through chimneys is surprisingly common. Incidents of burns, destruction, and death have been attributed to ball lightning, but more commonly it disappears without a trace.

Ball lightning has been subjected to considerable theoretical scrutiny by physicists, and many explanations have been proposed, but all are far enough from being adequate that even bizarre theories postulating antimatter or nuclear reactions cannot be ruled out as too unlikely. About the only matter of widespread consensus is that it is probably a globe of positive charge, yet a significant minority of physicists question its reality altogether. K. Berger is one such skeptic:

> The [a]uthor's 30 years of research in lightning phenomena on Mount San Salvatore near Lugano, Switzerland, including [scrutiny] of thousands of photographs and more than 1000 oscillograms, failed to confirm the existence of "ball lightning." On the basis of the extensive literature and his own experience, the author stresses the need to distinguish between subjective and objective observations. All published photographs of "ball lightning" have proved to have a physical explanation. To explain the numerous reported visual observations, the author recommends physiological research on "after-images" produced by lightning flashes on the human retina. New reports of ball lightning should be examined on the spot by high-voltage engineers and physicists.[17]

Why don't all physicists concur in this assessment? Perhaps because the following characterization of the scientific community by P. C. W. Davies is overly pessimistic:

> The appeal to physiology, then psychology, to explain embarrassing puzzles in physics epitomizes a quite general and interesting tendency in the scientific community. We are presented with two varieties of phenomena in science, which we may loosely call "laboratory" and "natural." The first variety is reproducible and can be subjected to

experimental manipulation, or is at least predictable in advance. The second variety is unreproducible and unpredictable (consisting of, for example, meteorites, ball lightning, novae) and if also transient the experimenter is fortunate indeed to have his apparatus at the right place at the right time. Consequently science must rely for its information on that much mistrusted individual, the layman, to whom is attributed the property of being able to observe objectively anything that can be explained, but imagining everything that can't. History is replete with examples, not least that of the meteorite. . . . The philosophy of this approach seems to be that if a naturally occurring phenomenon is hard to account for conventionally (i) decide that it has no physical reality; (ii) construct a physiological or psychological explanation; (iii) ignore the physical evidence that contradicts this explanation.[18]

It should not be hard for religious people to identify with Davies's position, since religion has often been the butt of such scientistic attacks. But granting that the believing majority is rational, apparently such belief is made rational solely by anecdotal evidence. I do not claim that those who suspend judgment are acting irrationally; perhaps people can reasonably differ over this issue.

A transcendental argument can also be given for the legitimacy of anecdotal evidence based on considerations advanced in recent years by philosophers such as Donald Davidson. The argument is that it is impossible to learn a language or function in society if one does not from infancy believe most of what one is told. That does not make everything we are told true, of course, but if too much appears to be false, this is not an argument for general skepticism regarding verbal reports, but that one has misinterpreted or misunderstood what one was hearing. Yet most of what one hears, insofar as it is evidential at all about the world, is not systematic, controlled, or replicable; and a person will never have an opportunity to verify more than a tiny fraction of it through more reliable means. Hence, reliance on anecdotal evidence is pragmatically unavoidable and hence justified, lest we violate the Kantian principle that 'ought' implies 'can.'

This argument does not preclude taking anecdotes with a grain of salt—the degree of belief proportionate to such evidence may not be high—but asserts only that we would be in a state of epistemic paralysis if we suspended judgment on everything that lacks non-anecdotal corroboration. When it comes to commitments of existential proportions, no one wants to rely on information that has to be salted. Scientists have good reasons for being loathe to rely on anecdotal evidence—many lives and reputations and much well-being are staked on the integrity of their theoretical structures. The same applies to religious institutions—the wariness of theologians regarding anecdotal evidence is understandable. But should individuals be less careful in the commitments they make? Two points are critical here. First, an individual may be privileged over the average third-person perspective by virtue of his proximity to the source of evidence, which permits placing greater confidence in it than would otherwise be warranted. Second, many scientists believe that *qua* scientists they *can* reconstruct reality adequately without the aid of anecdotal evidence, or they can confine their interests to those aspects of reality that can be so reconstructed. Thus, ball lightning's present status is as a curiosity; its epistemic infirmity prevents it from playing a structural role in the scientific edifice. The existential predicament of individuals often does not allow them to confine their interests so narrowly, however. Questions of what makes for ultimately meaningful existence can be tabled by scientists, but inevitably find a way of imposing themselves upon each of us as individuals.

If anecdotal evidence is generally inferior to other forms of evidence, does this mean that the systematically gathered statistical evidence of sociologists of religion should always be preferred to anecdotal evidence from religious sources with which it conflicts? Here it should be noted that using statistical evidence involves nontrivial assumptions about the objectivity of the investigator, both in how the statistics are collected and in the choice of statistics to be reported. Applying statistical evidence in practice also forces one to make judgments of whether the population studied and its circumstances are relevantly similar to one's own. What the statistician provides may not help us here except through the law of large numbers, which is of no avail against systematic bias.

With anecdotal evidence, although the sample is far smaller and therefore less likely to represent the population as a whole, one may be in a better position to estimate whether the circumstances of the informant are similar to one's own, what her biases are, and so forth. Anecdotal evidence often comes replete with a number of implicit cues to its use—intonations, gestures, or other information that can be processed even though never reaching our focus of attention. Such information is typically unavailable with statistical evidence. Of course, these cues can be used skillfully by hucksters to mislead us—but there is also the proverb, "You can prove anything with statistics." Defeasibility applies to any form of empirical evidence. Once again, I do not claim that anecdotal evidence is generally superior to statistical evidence, but beyond such broad generalities there may be any number of situations in which a person would justifiably trust anecdotal evidence more than the statistical evidence available, although hopefully with caution. Nisbett and Ross argue for the clear superiority of statistical evidence. I believe they exaggerate their case and their own abundant use of anecdotal evidence reveals much more than their argument.[19]

Objections to the Use of Anecdotal Evidence

A general observation of anecdotal evidence is that it is open to endless interpretation, and so is worthless in terms of evidential value. As Kant observed, if one needs to have a prior theory (or religious doctrine) in order to know which anecdotes to take seriously, then the anecdotes are ceasing to function as evidence and are only functioning as illustrations.[20] However, this foundationalist objection has been raised against all standard forms of evidence. In particular, Quine has argued that experimental "failures" are not localized: one can place blame on any of a number of statements when one's expectations are disappointed, and may reasonably call upon previously established theory for assistance in doing so.[21] Thus, there is a hermeneutic relation between theory and evidence—we use theories to interpret our evidence and evidence to choose, modify, and/or interpret theory. Nothing more than this hermeneutic relationship is being claimed here.

More serious is the Elvis Presley objection. I argued that some kinds of intelligence can only be revealed through anecdotal evidence because of their inherent unpredictability—one could only say that this kind of thing "will manifest itself from time to time." But the same could be said of posthumous Elvis Presley sightings—they are another phenomenon that "happens from time to time." Can such sightings legitimate any belief in the continuing existence of Elvis Presley? In a similar vein, at one time Sir Arthur Conan Doyle amassed anecdotal evidence in favor of the existence of fairies.[22] Does that legitimate belief in them?

It should be noted here that no general claim was made that anecdotal evidence legitimates belief; what it legitimates depends on one's distance from the evidence and one's assessment of the veracity of the storyteller, among other things. Not knowing personally any of the people who claimed to have sighted Elvis, and having no theoretical or other basis to ascribe to such claims non-zero probability, there is no reason why I should give them any credence. But how are sightings of ball lightning any different, given that physicists do not know the observers personally? Here are a few points to bear in mind. Some ball lightning sightings were made by scientists and engineers—skilled observers who are more likely to be aware of similar electrical or physiological phenomena, and so better able to rule them out. Were Elvis Presley sightings reported in publications of the same reputation for veracity as the sightings of ball lightning? Were they equally detailed? The overall number of sightings and the time frame over which they were made is also significant—with 1000 ball lightning sightings over 150 years, one can begin to make an inductive case for its existence that posthumous sightings of Elvis do not approach. If Elvis sightings are still prevalent as the *22nd* century dawns, then it might be time to reconsider. In one case, ball lightning was seen simultaneously by many people in an aircraft, but nothing similar has been reported for Elvis Presley.

Note also that some ball lightning sightings were reported by people with impeccable reputations—people who had more to lose than gain from making such a report. Although formally ad hominem, the appearance of a motive to fabricate is not irrelevant when it is a matter of taking the person's word essentially on faith. Motivational estimations are also notoriously fallible and may manifest only the estimator's prejudices, but what is the alternative? With excessive credulity, we would believe any number of contradictory claims, whereas excessive incredulity smacks of the misanthropic scientism criticized by Davies.

These and similar considerations may not settle the Elvis Presley question, but they bar easy legitimation for implausible beliefs. More importantly, they ultimately provide a more reliable basis for deciding the question than whatever uncritically held intuitions or prejudices we already have about Elvis Presley or his followers. When applied to religious contexts, such considerations exemplify a far more rational approach than that of Richard Swinburne's incredible Principle of Credulity.[23]

A different objection arises from the uniqueness of anecdotal evidence: failure of replicability impugns the reality of whatever the anecdote is being adduced as evidence for, because replicability is just the societal equivalent of stability of perception, and we do not normally ascribe reality to those contents of perception that are not stable. What makes dreams and hallucinations unreal is that they quickly vanish and do not reappear, as well as the fact that they are not intersubjective. All of this is quite unlike the observer- and time-independent objects we call real.

While serious, this objection trades on the vagueness of the concept of identity in terms of which uniqueness and replicability are defined. I am tempted to say that there is no notion of identity that is independent of the interests of the person making assertions about it. It seems obvious to me that I am not the same person I was four years ago, but it does no good to tell this to a police officer. In the case of ball lightning, each report is undoubtedly different in a number of ways, but there is a level of abstraction at which they are all instances of the "same" phenomenon. We can expect the same to hold with instances of intelligence or of religious experience as well. If one wants to deny the significance of the evidence, one can always point to the many differences in each manifestation of intelligence and cite failure of replicability; but if one has a different antecedent agenda, one can find something common to abstract from them after all. If they are all "the same" in that respect, then perhaps our perception is relatively stable after all. Pursuing this line of argument, is Frege correct that the morning star is identical to the evening star? Only on the basis of a theory that rejects the observed position relative to the sun as a criterion by which objects are individuated. In John's Gospel we have an account of a blind man who is healed and insists that he is the one who was born blind, while others are saying, "No, but he is like him." If receiving the gift of God makes one a new person, couldn't we say that both are correct?

Another aspect of replicability is the ability to reproduce the observation at will. It most surely is a sign that one is dreaming if one looks away from an object and, upon returning one's gaze to it again, finds that it has changed. Objects in the real world don't do that—indeed, we classify them as objects precisely because they are constant in perception over reasonably short periods of time. Thus, the objection that the results of parapsychology are not replicable is not that similar anomalous results never reappear, but that we can never count on them appearing. This is true of ball lightning, too, yet many people believe that the phenomenon is real and apparently are justified in so doing. Some phenomena are just like that. Nevertheless, it makes it effectively impossible to *do* anything with ball lightning. If intelligence in Dennett's sense were like this, then some might wonder, "What good is it?" But even if human intelligence is not something that can be exhibited on command—if it only manifests itself from time to time, and the rest of the time we are no better or worse off with it than without it—wouldn't those few times when it does appear make it worth having? In a similar vein, although we undoubtedly cannot make use of God or "do anything" with Him because of unreliability of His manifestations in our lives, don't the times that His presence manifests itself still make it worth having? We may just have to accept that it is characteristic of this kind of intelligence not to be present at all times or to be predictable in its appearance.

General Approaches to Verbal Testimony

Philosophers have occasionally proposed principles purporting to be generally valid rules for handling anecdotal evidence. Limiting discussion to the important subcategory of verbal testimony, I briefly examine in this section the views of Coady, representing the "believers," and Daniel Dennett, representing the "skeptics." Although their views are complex and hard to categorize, examining them briefly will prove instructive and provide an opportunity to articulate further why I favor neither a policy of generalized credulity nor generalized incredulity.

Coady believes that Davidson takes charity to excess in interpreting the testimony of others, but agrees with Davidson for the most part, saying, ". . . extensive commitment to trusting the reports of others [is] a precondition of understanding their speech at all."[24] He follows Swinburne's Principle of Testimony in excepting "special considerations to the contrary," but appears not to allow such considerations to invalidate a great deal of the testimony we receive.[25] We already saw one effect of this strong view in Coady's renunciation of the commonsensical principle that transmission diminishes the evidential force of testimony. It also leads to an attack on modern psychology, placing Coady further out on a limb.

His lead example of wrongheadedness is the psychologist Robert Buckhout who, from surveying a half century of psychological evidence on the reliability of human testimony, concludes that by and large it is not very reliable. Coady calls this "absurd to the point of idiocy," since Buckhout is relying on the testimony of other human beings as evidence that human testimony is unreliable, and has the gall to expect us to believe his testimony![26] Coady's criticism may be biographically accurate, but logical considerations favor Buckhout's conclusion rather than Coady's. First a terminological point: calling testimony reliable is calling it substantially correct, whereas calling it unreliable denies this—it is *not* the same as calling it substantially incorrect. I assume that 'substantially' means 'far more than 50 percent of the time.' Hence the testimony of psychologists and the population at large may both be unreliable if, say, both were correct 50 percent of the time and incorrect the other 50 percent, but they cannot both be reliable. Now for the argument: either the testimony of these psychologists can be relied upon or it cannot be. If their testimony is reliable, then human testimony in general is not; but if not, this is only so much more evidence for the unreliability of human testimony—you can't even trust the psychologists!—not evidence that human testimony is reliable by and large. We do not have a zero-sum game in which the only way for the psychologists to be wrong would be for the general population to be right.

Lest this strike the reader as logical hocus-pocus, let me reiterate that Coady's mistake is a common one, but the logic of the argument is a straightforward *reductio ad absurdum* of the reliability of human testimony. In a *reductio*, if one intends to prove some claim, say, *A*, then one assumes the denial of it, ¬*A*, and shows with the aid of uncontroversial assumptions that this leads to a contradiction. It leads to a contradiction if it implies anything that contradicts one of the original assumptions, including ¬*A* itself. Any collection of premises that implies a contradiction is inconsistent—they cannot all be true. If the other premises are uncontroversial, however, then the originally assumed denial *(¬A)* is most likely at fault, in which case what one intended to prove *(A)* is vindicated. What Buckhout intends to prove is that human testimony is by and large unreliable, so start by assuming the denial—that is, that human testimony *is* reliable—and see what this implies. Examining the available testimony, Buckhout finds a large body implying that human testimony is unreliable, in which case he arrives at the desired contradiction that human testimony is by and large both reliable and unreliable. The same would happen if he found collections of testimony that regularly contradict one another, as is often alleged of eyewitness testimony and of reports of religious experiences. One of our premises must be wrong, and the most obvious candidate is the premise that human testimony is reliable.

If the logic of Buckhout's argument is impeccable, he may still be wrong in point of fact. That is, perhaps most human testimony *is* reliable while only the testimony of certain groups, say, psychologists, is not. Or perhaps psychologists demand an unreasonably high standard of reliability. Nothing about this is so gallingly obvious that it would be "absurd to the point of idiocy" to suppose otherwise, however. It would be highly ironic for the only people to have undertaken systematic empirical study of the accuracy of human testimony to end up more mistaken or misled about it than the rest of us—but it could happen. It would not be surprising if Daniel Kahneman and Amos Tversky and Nisbett and Ross have exaggerated and sensationalized their negative findings somewhat to capitalize on their shock value, so why shouldn't other psychologists have done to human testimony what they have done to human inference? But in so doing they would be following a typical pattern of human motivation—people frequently exaggerate and sensationalize for the sake of personal gain. Hence this need not impugn their testimony as less reliable than the run of human testimony.

If these psychologists are at all correct, however, it dooms any sort of principle of testimony such as Coady, Swinburne, and Caroline Franks Davis advocate.[27] We may be entitled to accept the testimony of others to the extent that pragmatic considerations force our hand, but this does not license any blanket generalization regarding the reliability of human testimony, the burden of proof, or the need for special considerations before suspending judgment. One cannot both apportion credulity to the strength of the evidence and extend it to all anecdotal evidence willy-nilly. Perhaps the weasel phrase 'absent special considerations to the contrary' could be construed broadly enough to make the principle true, but I doubt that it would then be useful or have the advertised implications for religious experience.

By contrast, Dennett argues with respect to introspection that

> we are fooling ourselves . . . when we claim to be just using our powers of inner observation. [I suspect] we are always actually engaging in a sort of impromptu theorizing—and we are remarkably gullible theorizers, precisely because there is so little to "observe," and so much to pontificate about without fear of contradiction.[28]

I presume that his view generalizes to any kind of testimony regarding non-public experiences; reports of religious experiences are also controversial regarding the amount of theorizing that goes into them. His method for handling such testimony is to let the collection of reports constitute a "heterophenomenological" world much the way that a work of fiction constitutes the world that its characters live and act in. The text of these reports determines the world by fiat; whatever the text does not determine remains indeterminate. Dennett suspends judgment on whether any of the events reported are real unless they can be verified independently by physical evidence, on the grounds that people tend to confabulate, or make up theories and causal stories without realizing it. Since no alternative, physical evidential pathway exists for most religious experiences, Dennett would presumably adopt blanket incredulity for such reports. In answer to the charge that this approach gives only patronizing, "mock respect" to the testifier, who wants to be believed rather than bracketed, Dennett shrugs, ". . . deviation from normal interpersonal relations is the price that must be paid for the neutrality a science . . . demands."[29]

Why does Dennett's stance here differ from his statement regarding anecdotal evidence of intelligence? Presumably he is articulating here an "officially acceptable" scientific methodology, whereas before he was chafing under its restrictions. More importantly, his previous comments were about experiences of intelligence which are "public" in the sense that the intelligent entity is available for others to observe and either corroborate or dispute one's findings. Finally, not all "seemings" are born equal, since in some cases we receive ample feedback from the environment to educate our sense of how things seem to be, whereas in other cases our sense of how things seem operates in blissful ignorance. However, both of these factors vary by degrees, both for anecdotal evidence generally and religious experience in particular. Even paradigmatically private experiences such as of pain are subject to a measure of external corroborating and countervailing evidence. And whenever a person bases decisions on how things seem—as frequently happens in religious contexts—she creates the possibility of disappointed expectations that will educate her sense of seeming as surely as any behaviorist's schedule of reinforcement.

Dennett's explanatory principle amounts roughly to a principle of *incredulity*, absent special considerations to the contrary, and has already had a fairly extensive career in the sociology of scientific knowledge (SSK), where it is not religious believers but the claims of other scientists that are bracketed in the name of being "scientific." The fundamental problem underlying SSK is its lack of reflexivity or self-referential absurdity.[30] As typically practiced, the sociologist studies and believes to be real the sociological factors which theory indicates are causally and explanatorily active. Otherwise, he could not purport to explain the actions of other scientists in terms of interests, alliances, opportunism, and so forth. Meanwhile the scientists whom the sociologist studies, study and believe to be real the factors (physical, geological, astronomical, chemical, and so forth) that their theory indicates are causally and explanatorily active—factors in which the sociologist suspends judgment as the "price" to be "paid" for the neutrality that science demands. But if the sociologist wanted to be "scientific" about his own theorizing and his own peer group, he would have to suspend judgment in the existence of the sociological entities he postulates, in which case he would be unable to explain anything. What is unique about sociology that makes it a better basis for metaphysics than other sciences? If it is the sociologist's expertise, why should his expertise be more trustworthy with respect to social causes than the expertise of other scientists regarding the causes they study? If scientists by and large are scientific, why do they generally treat one another's findings as authoritative outside their own area of expertise, rather than suspending judgment on them? A consistent, reflexive, non-chauvinistic concept of 'being scientific' that sanctions a generalized principle of incredulity for testimony is lacking.

What we find here is typical of what is to be had in the literature at large. One readily recognizes in Dennett's hard-headed position the misanthropic scientism previously attacked by Davies, while philosophers of religion often seem prejudiced in favor of belief. Part of the problem stems from the desire to have a simple solution to a complex problem—something that can be formulated as a general principle. Assuming that God either exists or doesn't exist in a way that lends itself to being experienced, it is natural to reason either that most of these experiences are veridical or none of them are. But given the amount of disagreement among religious people, and the amount of impromptu theorizing that probably informs reports of religious experiences, I think the hypothesis should be entertained that God exists and yet most of the experience reports regarding him are false or significantly misleading. To borrow a Cartesian metaphor, God may exist while an "Evil Demon" exists also, bent on deceiving us. Such a scenario would defeat both policies of generalized credulity and generalized incredulity. If I am on the right track, the ultimately correct posture to take toward anecdotal evidence resists straightforward formulation; its epistemology is more complex than we want it to be.

Conclusion

Rationality does not require banning the use of unreplicated evidence arising in uncontrolled environments, yet such evidence naturally leads to idiosyncratic conclusions. Its evidential value will vary with our proximity to the original source, our knowledge regarding the source and its reliability, our experience with other anecdotal evidence, and whether we have had experiences similar to the ones being reported. Given that virtually all the revealed theological evidence for the nature and existence of God is anecdotal, the problem of finding a uniquely rational approach to religious questions becomes essentially irremediable at the institutional level, although not necessarily at the individual level. That is, there will be no canonical institutional "distance" from the evidence that is normative for all participants, but there is a fact of the matter regarding how distant each participant is from the evidence, from which normative conclusions follow.

In the foregoing, I examined anecdotal evidence in ways that most clearly elicit its strengths and weaknesses. The work that an adequate analysis of anecdotal evidence can do will be found in more controversial areas, however—areas in which much of the current discussion relies on uncritically held intuitions and prejudice. If what I have said is correct, it seems unlikely that a broadly based consensus can be reached on questions such as the reality of near-death experiences or multiple-personality disorder, except to the extent that these questions are amenable to other forms of evidence. Lack of a consensus need not be bad—not all knowledge need be scientific—but it poses problems in legal and political domains, since these implicate a societal scale at which uniformity is a prerequisite for adequate policy. Fashioning a uniform approach to religious uses of anecdotal evidence is similarly problematic: how can one steer between the Scylla of dogmatic overcommitment and the Charybdis of spineless undercommitment, admitting a measure of pluralism without going to the opposite extreme of "anything goes"? Any religion that relies on anecdotal evidence to a significant extent must find a way to do so, both in practice and in theology.

University of Mississippi

Notes

1. See, e.g., Steve Woolgar, *Science: The Very Idea* (Chichester: Ellis Horwood, 1988).

2. Ian Barbour, "Ways of Relating Science and Theology" in *Physics, Philosophy and Theology*, edited by Robert Russell, William Stoeger, and George Coyne (Notre Dame, Ind.: University of Notre Dame Press, 1988), pp. 21–48. Reprinted in Barbour's *Religion in an Age of Science* (New York: Harper & Row, 1990), pp. 3–30.

3. Herbert Benson and David McCallie, "Angina Pectoris and the Placebo Effect," *New England Journal of Medicine* 300, 25 (1979): 1424–29.

4. See Thomas Cook and Donald Campbell, "The Causal Assumptions of Quasi-Experimental Practice," *Synthese* 68 (1986): 141–80.

5. Daniel Dennett, *The Intentional Stance* (Cambridge, Mass.: MIT Press, 1987), p. 250 (emphasis his).

6. Dennett is not giving up on the scientific method just yet. He believes the process can be kept scientific if one devises better controls on the situations in which the anecdotes are generated (ibid., pp. 252, 271). This requires conducting what amounts to a case study, and the resulting evidence would be like what one commonly finds in anthropology or sociology—rarely enough to quell a controversy. Dennett himself is pessimistic that such studies will reveal anything more than a spotty and inconsistent pattern, because this is the most that human (or animal) imperfection will allow (p. 255). Thus, my pluralistic conclusion seems vindicated, although Dennett would undoubtedly take exception to religious applications of the intentional stance.

7. Thomas Hobbes, *Leviathan*, Ch. 32.

8. This, at any rate, appears at the heart of Quine's three indeterminacies—indeterminacy of translation, reference, and the underdetermination of theory by evidence. It also flows from Saul Kripke's analysis of rule-following in *Wittgenstein on Rules and Private Language* (Cambridge, Mass.: Harvard University Press, 1982). Neither philosopher turns this into an issue of

rationality, however. For that, see Bas van Fraassen, "Glymour on Evidence and Explanation," in *Testing Scientific Theories*, edited by John Earman, pp. 165–76 (Minneapolis: University of Minnesota Press, 1983); and "Empiricism in the Philosophy of Science," in *Images of Science*, edited by Paul Churchland and Clifford Hooker, pp. 245–308 (Chicago: University of Chicago Press, 1985).

9. Richard Nisbett and Lee Ross, *Human Inference: Strategies and Shortcomings of Social Judgment* (Englewood Cliffs, N.J.: Prentice-Hall, 1980), p. 50.

10. John Locke, *Essay Concerning Human Understanding*, Book 4, Ch. 16, Sec. 10 (emphasis his).

11. C. A. J. Coady, *Testimony* (Oxford: Clarendon Press, 1992), p. 199.

12. Ibid., pp. 212–13.

13. Fred Dretske, "Why Information?" *Behavioral and Brain Sciences* 6 (1983): 85 (emphasis his).

14. Some would argue that this incident does not function as evidence at all, because the text (Mark 5:36) indicates that Jairus had to believe already for Jesus to raise his daughter from the dead. I do not deny that Jairus had to believe *something* appropriate for letting the work of God manifest itself, but neither here nor elsewhere does the text say precisely what. Even an experimenter must entertain appropriate beliefs to set up her experiment and give it a chance to work, but she need not believe that the outcome will be precisely what happens. Surely the beliefs of Jairus and his household were changed by what happened, and textual evidence that this was considered proper appears in many places, including Jesus' admonition that if you don't believe Him, believe the works. So the raising of Jairus's daughter from the dead appears intended to have evidential value.

15. Most of the information on ball lightning in this section comes from S. Singer, "Ball Lightning," in *Lightning*, Vol. 1, edited by R. H. Golde (London: Academic Press, 1977), pp. 409–36.

16. Ibid., p. 409.

17. K. Berger, "Ball Lightning and Lightning Research," *Naturwissenschaften* 60 (1973): 485–92.

18. P. C. W. Davies, "Ball Lightning or Spots Before the Eyes?" *Nature* 230 (1971): 576–77.

19. Nisbett and Ross defend their use of anecdotal evidence by claiming that it contributes to comprehension, or has illustrative value, but lacks inferential value (op. cit., p. 282)—a distinction I deny. Illustrations assist us in constructing psychological schemas for the thing being illustrated, and there is no doubt that psychological schemas function inferentially, as they themselves point out (ibid., pp. 32ff.).

20. Immanuel Kant, *Grundlegung zur Metaphysik der Sitten*, pp. 408–9.

21. W. V. Quine, "Two Dogmas of Empiricism," *Philosophical Review* 60 (1951): 20–43.

22. Sir Arthur Conan Doyle, *The Coming of the Fairies* (London: Hodder & Stoughton, 1922). See also Edward Gardner, *Real Fairies: The Cottingley Photographs and Their Sequel* (London: Theosophical Society, 1945). Both have been reprinted.

23. Richard Swinburne, *The Existence of God* (Oxford: Clarendon Press, 1979), p. 254.

24. Coady, *Testimony*, p. 176.

25. Ibid., pp. 145–51; Swinburne, *The Existence of God*, p. 272.

26. Coady, *Testimony*, p. 265; Robert Buckhout, "Eyewitness Testimony," *Scientific American* 231, 6 (1974): 23–31.

27. Caroline Franks Davis, *The Evidential Force of Religious Experience* (Oxford: Clarendon Press, 1989), pp. 99–102.

28. Daniel Dennett, *Consciousness Explained* (New York: Little Brown, 1991), pp. 67–68.

29. Ibid., p. 83.

30. See the essays in *Knowledge and Reflexivity*, edited by Steve Woolgar (London: Sage, 1988).

Intellectual Virtue in Religious Epistemology

Linda Zagzebski

ABSTRACT

It is common for contemporary epistemologists to borrow concepts from moral theory in their analyses of the normative aspects of epistemic states, but virtually all epistemologists take an act-based theory as their normative model, even those that use the concept of intellectual virtue. The most common normative concepts in epistemology are justification and warrant, both of which are properties of beliefs, and both of which are typically analyzed in ways which parallel either deontological or conse-quentialist ethics. In this paper I argue for the benefits of using a true virtue ethics as the normative model in epistemology. I show how some of the most important advantages of a virtue ethics over an act-based ethics would also make a virtue-based epistemology preferable to a belief-based epistemology. I then show how the advantages of this approach should be particularly appealing to the religious epistemologist.

1. Introduction

Some thirty-five years ago Roderick Chisholm observed that "many of the characteristics which philosophers and others have thought peculiar to ethical statements also hold of epistemic statements."[1] Since then we have seen epistemologists routinely referring to epistemic *duty*, to epistemic *responsibility*, to the fact that we *ought* to form beliefs in one way rather than another, to epistemic *norms* and *values*, and more recently to intellectual *virtue*. The use of these moral concepts in epistemic discourse is not superfluous, but is central to the attempt to explicate the normative aspects of epistemic states, a goal that has justifiably become one of the central concerns of contemporary epistemology. It is generally acknowledged, then, that moral concepts are important to epistemological inquiry. What is not often acknowledged, however, is that when epistemologists borrow moral concepts, they implicitly borrow the theoretical background of those concepts. An awareness of the differences in function of concepts in different types of moral theory can illuminate their use in epistemology. If there are problems with the moral theory epistemologists use as their normative model, these problems may adversely affect the epistemological project. On the other hand, any advantages of a particular approach to moral evaluation may also prove advantageous to epistemic evaluation.

In this paper I call attention to the fact that virtually all contemporary theories in epistemology take an act-based moral theory as their normative model, even those that promote the concept of intellectual virtue. Contemporary epistemological theories are belief-based, just as most contemporary ethical theories are act-based. Next I argue that a virtue-based epistemological theory has certain advantages over a belief-based theory which parallel some of the advantages of a virtue-based ethical theory over an act-based ethical theory. I then consider the principal recent objections to virtue ethics and argue that these objections either do not apply or do not jeopardize the virtue approach to epistemology. I conclude with reasons why this approach should be of particular interest to religious epistemology.

2. Contemporary Epistemological Theories and Their Normative Models

Contemporary discussions of justification and knowledge almost always focus on particular instances of beliefs, just as most modern ethical theory until recently has focused on the morality of particular acts. The epistemologist assumes that the normative concepts of interest to their inquiry are properties of beliefs in one of two senses of 'belief': either they are properties of the psychological states of believing, or they are properties of the propositional objects of such states. The dispute between foundationalists and coherentists and between externalists and internalists are disputes about the nature of such properties.

The epistemic analogue of the concept of a right act is that of a justified belief. To be justified is a way of being right. Alternatively, epistemologists may speak of a warranted or well-founded belief. In these cases also it is the epistemic analogue of a right act. Just as the right act is usually the primary concept for moral philosophers, the justified (warranted, well-founded) belief is the primary concept for epistemologists. Roderick Firth expresses the position which is almost universal among contemporary epistemologists: "The ultimate task of a theory of knowledge is to answer the question, 'What is knowledge?' But to do this it is first necessary to answer the question, 'Under what conditions is a belief warranted?'"[2] What Firth calls "the unavoidable first step" is generally the major part of the theory. It is not surprising that the answer to this question often involves the concept of epistemic duty and the application of epistemic rules, both of which are closely associated with the deontological concept of right. Alternatively, the answer may involve the idea of a reliable process for the obtaining of the good of truth, the epistemic analogue of the consequentialist concept of right.

Contemporary epistemology, then, is belief-based and it is no surprise that the type of moral theory from which moral concepts are borrowed is almost always an act-based theory. In those cases in which the theory identifies justification or the normative element in knowledge with epistemic duty, the theory is clearly and usually consciously deontological. In those cases in which justification or the normative element in knowledge is identified with reliability in the obtaining of truth, the theory is consequentialist, though generally only implicitly so. An interesting variant is the theory of Ernest Sosa, who identifies justification with intellectual virtue. Sosa argues that the concept of intellectual virtue can be used to bypass the dispute between foundationalists and coherentists on proper cognitive structure.[3] But Sosa does not adapt his concept of virtue from a virtue theory of morality; rather, his model of a moral theory is act-based, and his definition of virtue consequentialist: "An intellectual virtue is a quality bound to help maximize one's surplus of truth over error."[4] Sosa does not distinguish between intellectual virtues and faculties, and his examples of intellectual virtues are nothing like virtues in the Aristotelian sense. While Sosa is welcomely sensitive to the importance of the social conditions for believing in his understanding of intellectual virtue, he does not attempt to benefit from the history of the concept of virtue. In any case, he makes no attempt to integrate intellectual virtue into the broader context of a subject's psychic structure, as that has been done by many philosophers for the moral virtues.

John Greco and Jonathan Kvanvig also define an intellectual virtue in such a way that reliabilism is a form of virtue epistemology, and Greco gives as examples of intellectual virtues such faculties as sight, hearing, introspection, and memory.[5] Kvanvig's primary examples of virtue epistemology are the theories of Armstrong, Goldman, and Nozick, all of which are forms of reliabilism.[6] None of these theories attempts to analyze intellectual virtue as a *virtue*, nor do they look to moral philosophers for help in understanding the nature of virtue. Even when Kvanvig traces the roots of virtue epistemology to Aristotle, it is to Aristotle's epistemology that he briefly turns, not Aristotle's theory of virtue. Kvanvig's subsequent rejection of what *he* calls the virtue approach, then, has no bearing on the project I am proposing here, nor do the objections offered by Greco.

Two theories which come closer to the one I wish to promote are those of Lorraine Code and James Montmarquet. In *Epistemic Responsibility* Code gives a provocative account of intellectual virtue, stressing a "socialized" approach to epistemology, pointing out the connections between epistemology and moral theory, and exhibiting a sensitivity to the epistemological importance of other aspects of human nature than the purely cognitive.[7] Code justly credits Sosa with the insight that epistemology ought to give more weight to the knowing subject, her environment, and epistemic community, but argues that Sosa's reliabilism does not go far enough in that direction. Code urges a move to what she calls a "responsibilist epistemology":

> I call my position "responsibilism" in contradistinction to Sosa's proposed "reliabilism," at least when *human* knowledge is under discussion. I do so because the concept "responsibility" can allow emphasis upon the active nature of knowers/believers, whereas the concept "reliability" cannot. In my view, a knower/believer has an important degree of choice with regard to modes of cognitive structuring, and is accountable for these choices; whereas a "reliable" knower could simply be an accurate, and relatively passive, recorder of experience. One speaks of a "reliable" computer, not a "responsible" one.[8]

Although this suggestion is promising, Code looks only at consequentialist and deontological ethics for analogies with epistemology rather than at a virtue theory.[9] And even that much she does not pursue very far, saying, "Despite the analogy I argue for . . . between epistemological and ethical reasoning, they are not amenable to adequate discussion under the rubric of any of the traditional approaches to ethics, nor under any reasonable amalgam thereof."[10] Code's account supports the rejection of the atomistic approach to epistemology, also argued in the later book by Kvanvig, but she neither makes such a rejection explicitly, nor does she see the problem in using act-based moral theory as the analogue for epistemic theory when such a rejection is made. She seems, then, to identify with Sosa's theory more than she should, given the insights she develops in her book.

Montmarquet gives a very interesting defense of the claim that epistemology ought to focus on the epistemic virtues in a sense of virtue that is at least similar to the moral virtues.[11] He says:

> I characterize the epistemic virtues as traits of epistemic character which, if they are not epistemic conscientiousness itself, are desired by the epistemically conscientious person in virtue of their apparent truth-conduciveness under a very wide variety of ordinary, uncontrived circumstances. Partly for this reason, they possess the kind of entrenchment Aristotle describes the moral virtues as having.[12]

The most important classes of such virtues, as described by Montmarquet, are the virtues of impartiality and the virtues of intellectual courage. The former include such qualities as openness to the ideas of others, the willingness to exchange ideas with and learn from them, the lack of jealousy and personal bias towards other people's ideas, and the lively sense of one's own fallibility. The latter include the willingness to conceive and to examine alternatives to popularly held beliefs, perseverance in the face of opposition from others, and the Popperian willingness to examine, and even actively seek out, evidence that would refute one's own hypotheses. Montmarquet considers these virtues to be complementary because they concern opposite sides of the balanced intellectual personality:

the inner-directed virtues of a person of intellectual integrity and the other-directed virtues necessary to sustain an intellectual community.

Montmarquet's approach is roughly, though somewhat vaguely, Aristotelian, but like the others, his epistemology is belief-based. Montmarquet links the concept of epistemic virtue to justification; he claims that the idea of virtuously formed belief forms an important partial account of the concept of epistemic justification. He does not link epistemic virtue with reliability, explaining virtue in terms of a certain motive, namely, the desire for truth. Montmarquet's account is insightful, but it seems to me that once we give up the atomistic approach in favor of a virtue approach, there is no reason to link intellectual virtue and justification. The latter is a property of a belief, while the former is a property of a person.

3. Some Advantages of Virtue-Based Theories

Until recently contemporary moral theories were almost exclusively act-based, with more and more subtle forms of consequentialism vying with more and more subtle deontological theories for the allegiance of philosophers. Lately there has been a resurgence of interest in virtue theories, as well as some strong and well-known attacks on contemporary act-based theories, although curiously, the latter is not always associated with the former.[13] The mark of a virtue theory of morality is that the primary object of evaluation is persons rather than acts. To describe a good person is to describe that person's virtues, and these theories maintain that a virtue is not reducible to the performance of acts independently identified as right nor to a disposition to perform such acts. Furthermore, a virtue is not reducible to a disposition to perform acts which can be independently identified descriptively. There is both more and less to a moral virtue than a disposition to act in a specified way. There is more because a virtue also includes being disposed to have characteristic feelings, desires, motives, and attitudes. There is less because a virtuous person does not invariably act in a way that can be fully captured by any set of independent criteria; morally right action is not strictly rule-governed.[14]

This means that virtues and vices are conceptually prior to right and wrong acts and cannot be adequately defined in the manner favored by act-based theories. The approach to ethics I have just described would not be agreeable to all adherents of virtue theories. Nonetheless, it is clearly conceptually opposed to both consequentialist and deontological styles of ethics. As far as I know, no one has proposed an epistemological theory which is closely modeled on such a theory. Considering the fact that contemporary epistemology has reached an impasse on the important question of the nature of the normative aspect of knowing and other epistemic states, it is worth investigating such an approach.

Let us now consider some of the principal advantages of a virtue-based ethics.

One of the first major attempts in recent philosophy to call attention to the advantages of focusing ethics on virtues rather than acts was Elizabeth Anscombe's important paper "Modern Moral Philosophy," which appeared in 1958.[15] In this paper Anscombe argues that the principal notions of modern moral discourse, namely, *right, wrong,* and moral *duty,* lack content. On the other hand, concepts such as *just, chaste, courageous,* and *truthful* are substantively rich. Furthermore, she argues, *right, wrong,* and *duty* are legal concepts which make no sense without a lawgiver and judge. Traditionally, such a legal authority was God. In the absence of an ethic grounded in theism, however, legalistic ethics makes no sense. It would be far better to return to an Aristotelian virtue ethics which contains neither a blanket concept of wrong, nor a concept of duty.

In the same year that Anscombe made her appeal for a return to the virtues, Bernard Mayo wrote that the virtues are more natural categories for making moral judgments than are principles.[16] Virtue categories allow for nuances of judgment that principles can handle only with grave difficulty. Consider, for example, the virtue of truth-telling. Mayo says:

> Telling the truth, for Aristotle, is not, as it was for Kant, fulfilling an obligation; again it is quality of character, or, rather, a whole range of qualities of character, some of which may actually be defects, such as tactlessness, boastfulness, and so on—a point which can be brought out, in terms of principles, only with the greatest complexity and artificiality, but quite simply and naturally in terms of character.[17]

While moral philosophers have not widely accepted Anscombe's position that the concepts favored by legalistic, act-based ethics are incoherent or unnatural in the absence of a divine lawgiver, it is hard to find fault with the claim that virtue concepts have the advantage of greater richness. In fact, the distinction between "thin" and "thick" moral concepts is now well known.[18]

A second set of considerations favoring a virtue approach to ethics is that now fewer philosophers are convinced that morality is strictly rule-governed. With the exception of act-utilitarianism, act-based theorists have been faced with the problem that more and more complex sets of rules are necessary to capture the particularity of moral decision-making. Philosophers such as Martha Nussbaum have argued for a more particularist approach, using literature as the basis for proposing a model that does not begin with the rule or principle, but with the insight into the particular case.[19] While particularists are not necessarily virtue theorists,[20] dissatisfaction with attempts to force the making of a moral judgment into a strictly rule-governed model is one of the motivations for contemporary virtue ethics.

A third reason favoring the focus of morality on virtues rather than acts and principles is that some virtues do not seem to be reducible to specifiable acts or act-dispositions. Gregory Trianosky, for example, has argued that higher-order moral virtues cannot be analyzed in terms of relations to acts. He points out that it is a virtue to have well-ordered feelings. A person with such a virtue has positive higher-order feelings towards her own emotions. Similarly, it is a virtue to be morally integrated, to have a positive higher-order evaluation of one's own moral commitments. These are virtues that cannot be analyzed in terms of some relation to right action.[21] Furthermore, while Trianosky does not say so explicitly, such higher-order virtues are connected to the virtue of integrity since integrity in one of its senses is the virtue of having a morally unified self, and it is difficult to see how such a virtue can be explicated in terms of dispositions to perform acts of a specified kind.

The resurgence of interest in virtue ethics in recent philosophy is obviously not due solely to the three sets of considerations to which I have just alluded. Nonetheless, these reasons are important and are generating serious discussion in the literature. I call attention to these three sets of reasons in particular because all of them have analogues in the evaluation of cognitive activity. In fact, some of them are even stronger in the epistemic case than in the moral case.

I have said that contemporary epistemology is belief-based, just as modern ethics is act-based. Epistemic states are evaluated in terms of properties of beliefs or belief-dispositions, just as moral evaluations are given in terms of properties of acts or act-dispositions. Epistemic states which are evaluated positively are called 'justified,' just as acts evaluated positively are called 'right.' Some epistemologists go farther with the act-based moral analogy and speak of epistemic duty.

Now if Anscombe is right that legalistic moral language makes no sense without a divine lawgiver, such language in epistemology is even more peculiar. We can at least find practical reasons for continuing to judge acts and render verdicts in the moral case, but it is hard to see the point of such a conceptual system in the evaluation of beliefs and cognitive activities. What purpose is served by declaring that Jones has violated her epistemic duty in believing in UFOs? Is she to be declared epistemically guilty? What follows from *that?*

As was said above, however, the stronger point is not Anscombe's claim about the need for a divine lawgiver, but the claim that the concepts of right, wrong, and duty lack content. This is clearly applicable to the case of epistemic evaluation. The concept of justified is even more artificial and lacking in content than the concept of right. Ordinary people will speak of what is right and wrong, but never of what is justified or unjustified. This is not to say that ordinary people lack the idea of evaluation in the cognitive area. It is simply that they direct their evaluations to persons themselves and call them narrow-minded, careless, intellectually cowardly or rash, prejudiced, rigid, obtuse. People are accused of jumping to conclusions, ignoring relevant facts, relying on untrustworthy authority, lacking insight, being unable to "see the forest for the trees," and so on. Of course, the beliefs formed as the result of such defects are evaluated negatively, but the lack of a blanket term for this negative evaluation in ordinary discourse suggests that the content is given by the concepts just named. All of these terms are names for either intellectual vices or for categories of acts exhibiting intellectual vice. It is possible, of course, that all of these defects involve using improper procedures; the point is that there does not seem to be any single property of epistemic impropriety or wrongness which can be explicated in a way that is not excessively complex and unnatural. A virtue approach to epistemic evaluation, then, has the same advantage of naturalness and richness of content possessed by a virtue approach to moral evaluation.

The second set of reasons for preferring a virtue approach in ethics also applies to epistemology. There is no reason to think that being in an epistemically positive state is any more rule-governed than being in a morally positive state. Insight, for example, is an intellectual virtue that is not rule-governed, but differs significantly in the form it takes from one person to another and from one area of knowledge to another. Insight is necessary for another virtue, trust, which has an intellectual as well as a moral form. One cannot know who or what is trustworthy by following a specified procedure, even in principle. Not only does one need insight into the character of others to have trust in its virtuous form, but trust also involves certain affective qualities that are not describable in procedural terms. In addition, such intellectual virtues as adaptability of intellect, the ability to recognize the salient facts, sensitivity to detail, the ability to think up explanations of complex sets of data, as well as such virtues as intellectual care, perseverance, and discretion are not strictly rule-governed. In each case, the virtue involves an aspect of knowing-how that is learned by imitation and practice. If those philosophers who advise a more particularist approach to moral evaluation are right, it is reasonable to think the same point applies to epistemic evaluation. An interesting consequence is that the recent turn to literature for help in understanding the right way to act might also help us in understanding the right way to think and to form beliefs.

Consider next the epistemic analogue of the third objection to act-based theories. The type of higher-order moral virtue identified by Trianosky has a cognitive parallel. It is an intellectual virtue to be cognitively integrated, just as it is a moral virtue to be morally integrated. A person who is cognitively integrated has positive higher-order attitudes towards her own intellectual character and the quality of the beliefs and level of understanding that such a character produces. When belief-based theorists, such as William Alston, attempt to identify this desirable quality, they say that it is not only epistemically valuable to *be* justified in one's beliefs, it is epistemically valuable to be justified in believing one's beliefs are justified. But this way of approaching this virtue is inadequate because the quality in question is not a property of a single belief, not even a belief about all of one's beliefs. To have a good intellectual character, it is not sufficient to simply pile up justified beliefs and judge that they are justified. A person who is cognitively integrated has epistemic values that determine such things as the proportion of one's time spent gathering evidence or the epistemic worth of one belief over another. Cognitive integration is partially constitutive of intellectual integrity, the virtue of having an intellect with an identity. Therefore, at least some intellectual virtues cannot be analyzed in terms of a relation to good (justified, warranted) beliefs. The virtue of intellectual integrity requires a virtue approach to epistemic evaluation.

Besides the three advantages I have mentioned, several epistemologists have recently criticized contemporary epistemic theories on grounds that would make a virtue approach more promising. A common objection is that contemporary epistemology is too atomistic and insufficiently social. We already noted this objection in the work of Sosa and Kvanvig. The complaint here is that it is a mistake to attempt to evaluate beliefs singly since a belief cannot be separated from other beliefs of the same person or from beliefs of other persons. Furthermore, evidence suggests that beliefs cannot be separated from non-cognitive psychic states such as feelings, desires, and motivations. Elsewhere I have argued that there are intimate connections between cognitive and feelings states and, concomitantly, between intellectual and moral virtues.[22] Such connections make a belief-based approach to evaluating epistemic states awkward at best. Virtues, however, are naturally understood as connected with desires and motivations, even in the case of intellectual virtues.

4. Objections to Virtue Theory

Along with the new interest in virtue theory in recent philosophy, there have been objections to the aretaic approach by
those who favor an act-based theory. It is illuminating to see
how little these objections threaten a virtue approach in epistemology. Perhaps the most serious objection to virtue ethics is
that it is imperative to have concepts of rights and duties in
order to single out a certain class of acts which are intolerable.[23]
Aristotelian virtue ethics may seem soft precisely because it
lacks such a category. Regardless of the strength of this objection to virtue ethics, however, it is irrelevant to the virtue
approach to epistemology since no one speaks of violating
other people's epistemic rights, and those who find the idea of
epistemic duties illuminating do not imply anything close to
the severe kind of moral judgment which accompanies such talk
in ethics. While it may sometimes be helpful to speak of a duty
to weigh evidence or to proportion one's belief to the evidence,
no one claims that such a way of speaking is the only one
capable of expressing the idea that one should conduct oneself
cognitively in certain ways.

A second common objection to virtue ethics is that it is too
vague to be of much use in making moral decisions in difficult
cases, say, a decision concerning abortion or euthanasia. This
also does not have an analogue in an objection to the virtue
approach to evaluating epistemic states and cognitive activities.
Rarely, if ever, do we think of a single cognitive act as having
the level of significance often given to moral decisions. The fact
that an account of intellectual virtue will leave unspecified the
precise manner in which a particular cognizer should proceed
is something we can live with. Vagueness is never welcome, of
course, but its presence is not as threatening in the epistemic
case as in the moral case.

A third objection to virtue ethics is that our society is so
pluralistic that we cannot hope for agreement on the virtues
which a moral person aims to acquire. This objection also does
not seriously jeopardize the virtue approach in epistemology
since there is little disagreement that the qualities I have called
intellectual virtues are in fact virtues. Almost everyone admires
intellectual care, perseverance, discretion, open-mindedness,

fair-mindedness, insight, sensitivity to detail, thoroughness, the ability to understand the whole picture, and so on. Of course, there are disagreements about how these virtues operate in the particular case, but that is to be expected. The objection as it applies to the moral virtues goes far beyond the application to particulars. The problem there is said to reside in the identity of the virtues themselves. Again, I cannot say how great this problem is for virtue ethics, but it is unlikely to pose a serious problem for virtue epistemology.

5. Virtue Theory in Religious Epistemology

The approach to epistemology I advocate ought to be particularly pleasing to the epistemologist of religion. Religious practice unifies the self in a way that mere beliefs do not, and so religious people have an appreciation for the importance of integrity. Religions are forms of life, not just coherent (or not so coherent) systems of beliefs, and it is important that this not be ignored when religious beliefs are evaluated. It does violence to the reality of religion to evaluate religious beliefs individually, in isolation from the character of the believer and the community with which the believer identifies. This is not to say that religious belief can get by with lower standards of rationality or justification than other sorts of belief. It simply means that religious belief calls attention to features that most of our beliefs have anyway but which are sometimes overlooked. One such feature is their connection with non-cognitive states of the person. This not only means that sets of beliefs must be evaluated as a whole, but that there is no autonomous whole to evaluate independently of non-belief states. Virtue theory has gone the farthest in explaining both this connection between beliefs and other states of a person's psyche, and the connection between the cognitive processes of an individual and that of a community. Virtue theory is therefore a promising alternative to a belief-based theory for an understanding of the normative aspect of religious belief.

How would we proceed with such an approach? In the first place, the emphasis would not be on isolating individual beliefs, such as "There is a God" or "Jesus rose from the dead," in an attempt to identify features of the belief that can then be tested against some criterion for justification or warrant. Instead, it would be appropriate to consider the kind of intellectual character to which we all should aspire, and then we would ask whether people with such a character in the requisite circumstances have such beliefs. The Christian emphasis on living a life in imitation of saintly persons would extend to imitating the cognitive activities of persons of intellectual virtue. Some qualities of intellectual character may turn out to be causally connected with qualities of moral character, in which case, moral properties would be relevant to *epistemic* evaluation, and conversely.

The virtue approach promises a richer analysis of the normative element in epistemic states than that given by the well-known approach of Alvin Plantinga.[24] Plantinga defines the normative element of knowledge—what he calls "warrant"—as that quality which a belief has when it is formed by faculties functioning properly in the appropriate environment, according to a design plan aimed at truth. It is interesting that in ancient Greek philosophy a virtue is a quality that permits a creature to perform properly those functions specific to its nature. Those qualities of a person which permit the proper functioning of faculties designed for the obtaining of truth would therefore be what I call virtues. If so, my virtue approach and Plantinga's proper-functioning approach should yield the same results. The difference is that Plantinga does not link his account of warrant with a tradition that guides us in explicating the content of the character of persons with properly functioning faculties. The virtue tradition does provide such guidance with a long history of investigation on the nature of virtue and the connection between a virtue and human ends. The study of this tradition, I believe, yields an understanding of intellectual virtue that is more internalist and voluntarist than Plantinga's, as well as more social.[25] In any case, since Plantinga says very little about what proper functioning actually amounts to, this approach provides a much richer and more detailed content.

I suggested above that perhaps the particularist interest in investigating literature for its moral insight should be extended to investigating literature for insight into good cognitive behavior as well. Religious epistemologists might find helpful models of the nature of rational religiosity in the study of narratives with religious themes. Theologians are more familiar with this method than are philosophers, but philosophers are well suited to investigate the connections among virtues, feelings, beliefs, and cognitive activity in a well-ordered psyche. As far as I know, the use of literature by philosophers has been limited to the area of moral philosophy. I suggest that epistemologists, including religious epistemologists ought to turn to it as well.

The implication of adopting a virtue-centered approach to analyzing the normative aspects of belief-forming and other cognitive behavior is that one should give up the current focus on justification as the key normative concept in epistemology. The primary focus of inquiry simply should not be a belief, and that means that no property of a belief can be the primary normative property in epistemology. Replacing justification by the concept of warrant will not solve the underlying deficiencies of the belief-based approach either, since warrant also is a property of a belief.

Recently there has been a lot of interest in philosophy in finding new models of rationality. Considering how poorly religious belief fared under the restricted model of rationality favored since Descartes, religious epistemologists have a special interest in finding such models. I hope that an approach centered on the virtues will prove a rich source for such investigations.

Loyola Marymount University

NOTES

1. Roderick Chisholm, *Perceiving: A Philosophical Study* (Ithaca, N.Y.: Cornell University Press, 1969), p. 4.

2. Roderick Firth, "Are Epistemic Concepts Reducible to Ethical Concepts?" in Alvin I. Goldman and Jaegwon Kim, eds., *Values and Morals: Essays in Honor of William K. Frankena, Charles Stevenson, and Richard Brandt* (Boston: D. Reidel, 1978), p. 216.

3. Ernest Sosa, "The Raft and the Pyramid," *Journal of Philosophy* 75 (October 1978): 509–23.

4. Ernest Sosa, "Knowledge and Intellectual Virtue," *The Monist* 68 (April 1985): 226–45.

5. John Greco, "Virtue Epistemology," in Jonathan Dancy and Ernest Sosa, eds., *A Companion to Epistemology* (Cambridge, Mass.: Basil Blackwell, 1992).

6. Jonathan Kvanvig, *The Intellectual Virtues and the Life of the Mind: On the Place of the Virtues in Epistemology* (Lanham, Md.: Rowman & Littlefield, 1992).

7. Lorraine Code, *Epistemic Responsibility* (Hanover, N.H.: University Press of New England, 1987).

8. Ibid., pp. 50–51.

9. Ibid., pp. 40–42.

10. Ibid., p. 68.

11. James A. Montmarquet, "Epistemic Virtue," *Mind* 95 (1986): 482–97.

12. Ibid., p. 484.

13. A good example of this is Susan Wolf's paper, "Moral Saints," *Journal of Philosophy* 79 (1982): 419–39. Wolf's provocative and convincing attack on both utilitarian and Kantian theories is not accompanied by a call to bring back classical Aristotelianism. In fact, she explicitly denies that our conception of the moral will permit this move.

14. Several philosophers have argued recently that virtues cannot be tied to act-descriptions, e.g., James Wallace, *Virtues and Vices* (Ithaca, N.Y.: Cornell University Press, 1978). Gregory Trianosky says that primary and secondary actional virtues are conceptually or causally tied to right action respectively, but what he calls spiritual virtues are not so tied in "Virtue, Action, and the Good Life: Towards a Theory of the Virtues," *Pacific Philosophical Quarterly* 68 (June 1987): 124–47.

15. Elizabeth Anscombe, "Modern Moral Philosophy," *Philosophy* 33 (January 1958): 1–19.

16. Bernard Mayo, *Ethics and the Moral Life* (London: Macmillan, 1958); excerpt reprinted in Louis Pojman, *Ethical Theory* (Belmont, Calif.: Wadsworth, 1989), pp. 302–4.

17. Ibid., p. 302.

18. Bernard Williams makes this distinction throughout *Ethics and the Limits of Philosophy* (Cambridge, Mass.: Harvard University Press, 1985). Williams's examples of thick ethical concepts include *courage, treachery, brutality,* and *gratitude.* Clearly not only virtues are "thick," but virtues are among the paradigm examples. Allan Gibbard also uses this distinction in *Wise Choices, Apt Feelings* (Cambridge, Mass.: Harvard University Press, 1990).

19. Martha Nussbaum takes this position in numerous places. See especially *Love's Knowledge* (New York: Oxford University Press, 1990).

20. W. D. Ross is an example of a particularist, act-based theorist.

21. Trianosky, "Virtue, Action, and the Good Life."

22. "Theology and Epistemic Virtue," in Stephen T. Davis, ed., *Philosophy and the Future of Christian Theology* (New York: Macmillan, 1993). I am presently working on a theory of the intellectual virtues as forms of moral virtue in a book to be called *Virtues of the Mind*.

23. Robert Louden, "Some Vices of Virtue Ethics," *American Philosophical Quarterly* 21 (1984): 227–36.

24. Plantinga's fullest and most recent presentation of his theory appears in *Warrant and Proper Function* (New York: Oxford University Press, 1992).

25. My criticisms of Plantinga's approach for its externalism, non-voluntarism, and individualism appear in "Religious Knowledge and the Virtues of the Mind," in my edited collection, *Rational Faith: Catholic Responses to Reformed Epistemology* (Notre Dame, Ind.: University of Notre Dame Press, 1993).

Reformed Epistemology and Epistemic Duty

James F. Sennett

ABSTRACT

One of the most common reasons for thinking that Alvin Plantinga's notorious "Reformed epistemology" claim is false is that religious belief without evidence must violate some epistemic duty. In this paper I identify a plausible epistemic duty and defend the claim that most, if not all, basic theistic belief violates it. I then entertain a substantive objection to the duty and revise the duty in response to the objection. I conclude that it is possible that basic theistic belief does not violate the revised duty, but only if Reformed epistemology is conceived of in a way foreign to the spirit of Plantinga's original intentions.

Introduction

Alvin Plantinga has "gained notoriety and caused much anxiety"[1] during the past decade with his outspoken support of a doctrine he calls "Reformed epistemology," which I will formulate:

> RE: Theistic belief need not be based on propositional evidence in order to be justified.[2]

That is, theistic belief can be *properly basic*—justified though not grounded in any propositional evidence.[3] A theistic belief is a belief that obviously entails the existence of God. A belief B obviously entails a belief B* just in case it is impossible for a cognizer to justifiably believe B without previously or simultaneously being justified in believing B* (where *S is justified in believing B* does not entail *S believes B*).[4] Examples Plantinga uses are *God made this flower* or *God disapproves of what I have done*. It is propositions such as these, rather than *God exists*, that Plantinga thinks are believed in a properly basic way by some theists. Belief of the proposition *God exists* is properly basic only indirectly, in that it is obviously entailed by a directly properly basic belief.[5]

Needless to say, there are many in the philosophy of religion community who are not convinced that RE has the ring of truth about it. One of the most common reasons for rejecting RE is the view that theistic belief without evidence violates some epistemic duty.[6] However, Plantinga asks, if S holds basic theistic belief, then what duty does she violate by virtue of which such belief is not justified?

In part one of "Reason and Belief in God," Plantinga entertains several possible answers to this question, and finds all of them wanting. For example, he claims that arguments for the improbability of *God exists* will not do, since epistemic improbability is a function of given noetic structures; and it is possible that some cognizer S has a rational noetic structure, yet there be no arguments against the existence of God that are supported by S's noetic structure. Plantinga similarly dismisses suggestions by Flew and Scriven that there is an epistemic "presumption of atheism" or obligation to accept atheism unless one is supplied with good evidence to reject it.[7] In short, Plantinga does not see how a case can be made for epistemic duties that categorically rule out properly basic theistic belief, even for contemporary Western cognizers.

In this paper I will examine one plausible epistemic duty and argue that basic theistic belief fails to meet it, despite Plantinga's contentions to the contrary. I will then introduce a plausible modification of that duty and argue that basic theistic belief may meet the modified duty, but only in a way foreign to Plantinga's intentions for RE.

Quinn on Defeaters of Justification

Plantinga's claim that there is no epistemic duty that is both plausible and rules out RE has been challenged by Philip Quinn.

[A] proposition is not *prima facie* justified if one negligently ignores good reasons for thinking one of its potential defeaters is true which would be sufficiently substantial to undermine the proposition's *prima facie* justification to such an extent that it would not be *prima facie* justified. Such epistemic negligence would constitute an epistemic deficiency.

[I]t also seems initially plausible to say that conditions are right for . . . propositions . . . to be properly basic for me only if I have no sufficiently substantial reasons to think that any of their potential defeaters is true and this is not due to epistemic negligence on my part.[8]

Quinn's comments offer the foundation for the following epistemic principle:

EP: For any cognizer S and belief B, S is justified in holding B in a basic way only if
  (i) Either
    (a) S has no good reason to think that any potential defeater D of B is true; or
    (b) if S has some such reason, then either she has an even better reason for thinking D false or she does not have reason to believe D to be a defeater of B;[9] and
  (ii) Condition (i) was not brought about by S's epistemic negligence.[10]

Quinn argues that most contemporary Western theists[11] do have sufficient reason to accept a defeater of theistic belief, such that they have reason to believe it a defeater of theistic belief and they do not have better reason to believe it false. That is, most contemporary Western theists are such that their theistic beliefs fail to meet condition (i) of EP.
Consider

(1) God does not exist.

There are many prima facie good reasons for any contemporary Western theist to believe (1). The problems of evil—both philosophical and existential[12]—are as good starting places as any. It is safe to say that many theists today have reasons grounded in observed or experienced evil that are sufficient to support (1) for them, and many of these theists have very little in the way of reasoned response to this evidence. Perhaps the fact that there are many normally functioning non-theists is also adequate reason to believe (1). Why, after all, should God make his presence so obscure that many intelligent people concerned with truth fail to see justification for accepting his existence?[13]

Or consider the fact that a great number of brilliant and informed people of the twentieth century have eschewed theistic belief. Suffice it to say that a culture as replete with atheistic testimony as ours is one in which reasons for (1) abound, and it is purely ad hoc to conjecture that most theists in this culture have good reasons to reject every plausible reason for (1) they have encountered. If they do not, then the theistic belief of most theists fails the constraints of EP and does not qualify as justified if basic.[14] (Of the preceding reasons for (1), only the problem of evil—specifically the inductive argument from evil—is mentioned and developed by Quinn. But the others could just as easily be proffered and undoubtedly function in the noetic structures of many to justify belief of (1).)

Finally, consider the following epistemic duty:

ED:	Cognizers should not hold any beliefs in a basic way that fail to satisfy the consequent of EP.

Quinn's point can be stated: any contemporary Western cognizer holding basic theistic belief is unjustified by virtue of her violating ED.

Plantinga on Intrinsic Defeater-Defeaters

Plantinga has responded to Quinn, charging first that there are good reasons to reject (1) and second that a phenomenon he calls the intrinsic defeater-defeater shows EP to be either false or no objection to properly basic theistic belief.[15]

Concerning the first claim, Plantinga charges, "So far as I can see, no atheologian has given a successful or cogent way of working out or developing a probabilistic argument from evil; and I believe there are good reasons for thinking it can't be done."[16] But Plantinga's objection seems irrelevant to Quinn's point. Quinn does not claim that the problem of evil actually *does* confirm (1) or make it highly probable. Rather, he claims first that the presence of evil in the world "confirms highly *for me* the propositions expressed by [(1)]," and second that "most intellectually sophisticated adults in our culture are in an epistemic predicament similar to mine."[17] Quinn's point is one about what one *would take to be* good evidence for (1), not what *actually is* good evidence for (1).[18] In other words, Quinn asserts that it is very common among contemporary Western theists that their noetic structures support (1) to the extent that it defeats *for them* any basic belief entailing its denial. This is perfectly consistent with what Plantinga has claimed above.

Plantinga himself has done extensive work designed to reject both the logical and probabilistic arguments from evil.[19] These rejections are highly complex and sophisticated, relying on technical features of modal logic, possible-worlds semantics, and probability theory. If such a path is required to rebut these atheological claims, it is certainly plausible to assume that most Western contemporaries confronted with evidence for (1) from the presence of evil will not succeed in carving such an intellectual path out of their "epistemic dilemma."[20] In short, the fact that *Plantinga* understands the arguments from evil to fail to confirm (1) entails nothing about how most people in our culture will understand the evidential relationship between the presence of evil and (1).

In addition, there are other reasons for (1) in the noetic structures of many (if not all) contemporary Western theists. I previously alluded to some, and there are undoubtedly others. Although Quinn has chosen only one reason, it is easy to expand to the others, and it becomes increasingly difficult to claim that every reason is defeated by the noetic structures in question.

Plantinga's second objection to Quinn is more formidable, though (I believe) no more successful. Plantinga charges that EP fails to consider what he calls "intrinsic defeater-defeaters." A proposition P is an intrinsic defeater-defeater of some potential defeater Q for S just in case P defeats Q's potential defeat of P itself for S. That is, Q is a potential defeater of P for S, but S's belief of P is itself adequate to defeat Q for her. To illustrate this phenomenon, Plantinga offers what I will call "the purloined letter case."[21]

Smith is accused of stealing a letter from his dean's office containing evidence of his professionally unethical behavior. He has a good motive and is known to have done such things before. Furthermore, several reliable witnesses testify that they saw Smith enter the dean's office at the time in question. Smith has nothing to say to rebut this evidence. But, as a matter of fact, Smith did not take the letter, but was alone all day walking in the woods. Furthermore, he distinctly remembers that he was in the woods all day and nowhere near the dean's office. Under such circumstances, Smith's belief of

> (2) I was alone in the woods all day and did not steal the letter

is potentially defeated by the above-cited body of evidence— evidence against which Smith has no defeating evidence. Yet his belief of (2) remains properly basic.

Plantinga asserts that (2) *itself* can serve to defeat its own potential defeaters. Although (2) has no *extrinsic* defeater-defeaters, it can serve as its own *intrinsic* defeater-defeater and therefore preserve its own proper basicality. This is so because *it is more rational for Smith to believe (2), given his memorial experience, than it is for him to believe that (2) is false given the collected evidence against it.* Thus, Plantinga's argument against EP can be stated: Either condition (i)(b) of EP includes intrinsic defeater-defeaters among the reasons for thinking defeaters false or it does not. If it does not, then the purloined letter case seems to be an obvious counterexample—S need not have *extrinsic* defeater-defeaters to preserve the proper basical-ity of a belief. If it does, then the purloined letter case suggests a scenario under which basic theistic belief can meet the conditions of EP and thus be a candidate for proper basicality. If theistic belief, like (2), could function as its own defeater-defeater, then it could be properly basic.

Basic Theistic Belief and Intrinsic Defeater-Defeaters

I believe that the first horn of Plantinga's dilemma for EP cannot be escaped. If Quinn intends his principle to allow only extrinsic defeater-defeaters to rescue potentially defeated basic belief, then the purloined letter case indeed proves it false.

However, it seems to me that the second horn can be avoided. I can think of at least three good reasons why we can allow (2) to be its own defeater-defeater, yet preclude such right from basic theistic belief, at least for our now-familiar contemporary Westerner.

First, the purloined letter case has intuitive force precisely because memory belief is generally accepted as properly basic. All of us understand the phenomenon of vivid memory belief with substantial external evidence against it. We understand what it is to reject such evidence in favor of the memorial force and to feel justified in doing so. But the claim that basic theistic belief might be so vindicated loses such phenomenological force for many. The purloined letter case relies only on intuitive force to make its point—not on argument at all. Such force is legitimate regarding an example concerning memory precisely because the intuitive appeal is so widespread. Once the example is applied to theistic belief, however, this widespread appeal is lost. Hence, the intuitive force is lost, and there is need for argument—yet no argument is given. Such is the danger inherent in points resting solely on the intuitive force of an example without analysis of why the example has such force.[22]

Second, Plantinga has argued in response to the famed Great Pumpkin objection to RE that there is nothing in committing to properly basic theistic belief per se that commits one to the proper basicality of any other kinds of beliefs.[23] One way to explicate Plantinga's reasoning is to note that proper basicality involves an appropriate relation between certain experiences and the beliefs to which they give rise.[24] The experience, the belief, and the relation between the two are all relevant when considering the proper basicality of a belief. Therefore, one cannot simply infer from the fact that a certain belief kind can be properly basic on a certain kind of experience that any other belief kind could rate that privilege, or that any other kind of experience could confer it.

I will put this point more precisely. Experience kinds are not sanctioned as properly basic belief grounders per se, nor are belief kinds sanctioned as properly basic per se. Some belief kinds can be properly basic *under certain circumstances*, and some experience kinds can basically ground *certain kinds of beliefs*. To oversimplify, a foundationalist epistemology will specify belief/experience pairs (B/E pairs) such that only the proper match-ups can produce properly basic beliefs. So the foundationalist who pairs beliefs of kind BK with experiences of kind EK need not worry, without good reason, that a belief of kind BK might be properly basically grounded in an experience of kind EK*, or a belief of kind BK* properly based on an experience of kind EK. The integrity of the B/E pairs must be maintained. To say that beliefs of kind BK can be properly basic when produced by experiences of kind EK is to say nothing about whether or not beliefs of kind BK* can be properly basic at all, or of whether or not experiences of kind EK* can properly ground any beliefs at all.

This reasoning can be used against the supposition that the purloined letter case has application in the defense of RE. The purloined letter case notes circumstances under which memory belief is properly basic—namely, in the face of unanswered defeaters of a certain order. But, by the preceding point, this gives no reason to suppose that theistic belief would be properly basic under similar circumstances. Without argument that shows why (2) is properly basic for Smith and that such reasoning is applicable to basic theistic belief in similar circumstances, it is best to conclude that the purloined letter case is inconclusive regarding intrinsic defeater-defeat of (1), despite first appearances.

These first two reasons for rejecting the purloined letter case allege that the case fails to establish that the circumstances under which (2) is properly basic for Smith are also circumstances under which some theistic beliefs might be properly basic. But suppose I am wrong, and theistic belief under such circumstances could be properly basic. The third reason to reject intrinsic defeater-defeater status to theistic belief addresses this possibility. I maintain that the purloined letter case still fails to defeat Quinn's charges, because it does not represent the defeating circumstances Quinn describes for basic theistic belief.

Consider

(3) God made this flower.

My basic belief of (3), under Quinn's analysis, is not defeated by direct evidence against (3), as in the purloined letter case. My evidence is not, for example, that God did not make *this* flower (but perhaps he made others), or that making flowers is not the kind of thing God does. Rather, the evidence is against the general proposition *God exists*, the falsity of which entails that (3) *and all theistic propositions* are false. The evidence is not against a given theistic belief, but against the belief *kind* itself.

In the purloined letter case, however, the evidence Smith has is against a given memory belief and not against memory beliefs per se, or even against *his* memory beliefs per se. Suppose that we revise the purloined letter case thus. Smith is told by his dean that he has had alleged memories many times that had similar evidence against them. He goes home and relates the whole story to his wife, who tells him, "Your dean is right, dear. There have been many times when you 'remembered' something that the children and I swear never happened. In fact, you seem especially likely to have such memory beliefs when they will help get or keep you out of trouble." Under such circumstances, (2) ceases to be an intrinsic defeater-defeater. The evidence is not just against (2) itself, but against a whole category of beliefs to which (2) belongs. In the purloined letter case, (2) counts as an intrinsic defeater-defeater only if Smith is justified in trusting his memory beliefs in general, or at least in the circumstances at hand. When the evidence is expanded to count against such beliefs in relevant circumstances, Smith is no longer justified in so trusting, and is therefore no longer justified in basically believing (2) in the face of the defeating evidence against it.[25]

The revised purloined letter case gives impetus for an additional epistemic principle, specifying certain necessary conditions for intrinsic defeater defeat.

AEP: For any cognizer S, belief B, and belief kind BK such that B is of kind BK, B can serve as an intrinsic defeater-defeater for S only if

(i) Either

(a) S has no good reason to think that any potential defeater of all beliefs of kind BK is true; or

(b) if S has some such reason, then either she has an even better reason for thinking that the

defeater is false or she does not have reason to
think that it is a defeater of all BK beliefs; and
(ii) Condition (i) was not brought about by S's epistemic negligence.

A belief B satisfies EP by virtue of its being an intrinsic
defeater-defeater only if it satisfies AEP. In the revised purloined letter case, (2) fails to be properly basic for Smith
because it fails to satisfy AEP and hence fails to satisfy EP.

Now (3), if basic, is defeated for contemporary Western
theists because *God exists* is defeated by (1), and (3) obviously
entails *God exists*. In fact, for any theistic belief B, B is defeated
if *God exists* is. That is, (1) serves to defeat not just (3), but an
entire kind of beliefs—namely, theistic beliefs. But here is an
exact parallel to the revised purloined letter case: (3), too, fails
to satisfy AEP. So, if (2) fails as an intrinsic defeater-defeater in
the revised purloined letter case, then (3) fails as an intrinsic
defeater-defeater under Quinn's analysis of its defeat. Hence,
(3) as a basic belief does not satisfy EP.

So Plantinga's purloined letter case faces a dilemma of its
own. Either the circumstances it invokes are transferable to
consideration of basic theistic belief or they are not. If they are
not, then of course he has no case against Quinn. If they are,
then the case fails as a counterexample because the circumstances explicated in the purloined letter case do not accurately
represent the circumstances Quinn understands the contemporary Western theist to be in. And, when the example is revised
to represent those circumstances more accurately, the justification of the basic belief is lost. In either case, Quinn's case
against Plantinga remains firm so far—EP seems to be a
plausible epistemic principle under which basic theistic belief
fails to be proper for most members of contemporary Western
culture; and ED, a plausible epistemic duty that such basic
theistic belief violates.

Epistemic Duty and Evidence Essentiality

In the remainder of this paper, I will offer reasons to reject EP
as formulated. I will then revise EP in response and argue that

theistic belief may, in one sense at least, be properly basic according to the emendation.

Stephen Wykstra has observed a parallel between the way many theistic beliefs are in fact formed basically—in a context of unquestioned theistic assumptions and testimony from elders and authority figures—and the way many other beliefs are formed.

> [W]e might recall that most of us acquired most of our beliefs about scientific matters—that the sun is larger than the moon, say, or that electrons exist—in [this] way, when our grade school teachers taught us these things, and we trustingly believed them. Were we irrational in so doing? Surely not. But if we allow that it can (under certain conditions) be rational to believe in a basic way in electrons, must we not also allow that it can be rational to believe in a basic way in God? To claim the contrary . . . seems utterly extravagant.[26]

However, Wykstra notes, distinction should be made between *individual* and *communitarian* evidence. Though I personally may be unaware of good propositional evidence for the existence of electrons, the justification of my belief in them is contingent on there being such evidence somewhere in my epistemic community. The ground of my belief is testimonial, but that ground is not sufficient alone to justify the belief. It must be accompanied by the assumption that someone has grounding for it that is not merely testimonial but propositional.

Wykstra asks us to imagine discovering that there really is no propositional evidence for the existence of electrons— "say, that the entire presumed case for electrons was a fraud propagated by clever con-men in Copenhagen in the 1920's."[27] If such a discovery were made, we would not consider ourselves epistemically entitled to hold on to our electron beliefs just the same. Knowledge that communitarian evidence is lacking is sufficient to defeat the justification of electron beliefs. Wykstra labels beliefs dependent on communitarian evidence as "evidence essential." I need not have propositional evidence for them myself to justifiably believe them, but I must be justified in presuming that there is such evidence within the community.

The concept of evidence essentially offers the Reformed epistemologist a response to ED. Perhaps all that is required for a cognizer holding a belief B basically to be justified in doing so is that she be justified in believing

(4) There is communitarian evidence sufficient to justify belief that any potential defeater D of B is false or that D is not an actual defeater of B.

It seems that many theists have reason to accept (4) as applied to their theistic beliefs. After all, there are any number of philosophers, theologians, and scientists who are well acquainted with the evidence against the existence of God, yet remain firmly planted in the faith. A very reasonable explanation of this phenomenon is that these professionals have evidence that the potential defeaters in question either are false or are not actual defeaters.

(It is important to note here that I am applying the notion of evidence essentiality differently from the way Wykstra applies it. Wykstra suggests that acceptance of

(3) God made this flower

and other theistic beliefs is evidence essential—that is, S can properly basically believe (3) only if S is justified in believing that there is communitarian evidence for *God exists*.[28] I, on the other hand, am suggesting that belief of (3) can be properly basic for S only if S is justified in believing that there is communitarian evidence *against the evidence S has for (1)*. This is consistent with, though it neither entails nor is entailed by, Wykstra's suggestion.)

Recall a point made above. Plantinga has devoted much of his philosophical career to arguing against the arguments from evil. I mentioned that his arguments are highly complex and technical and quite out of the grasp of understanding of most contemporary Western theists—very much like evidence for the existence of electrons. As it stands, EP does not allow the fact that Plantinga has arguments against the evidence for

(1) God does not exist

to count toward the rationality of rejecting the evidence for (1) for anyone unacquainted with and unappreciative of the defeating evidence. But perhaps many contemporary Western theists may rest comfortably in their rejection of (1), despite the evidence they have for it. Perhaps such rejection need not be based on any defeating evidence they personally have, but on the knowledge that such evidence is to be had in the community—say, by Plantinga.

So I suggest the following revision of EP:

EP*: For any cognizer S and belief B, S is justified in holding B in a basic way only if
(i) Either
(a) S has no good reason to think that any potential defeater D of B is true; or
(b) if S has some such reason, then either she has an even better reason for thinking D false or she does not have reason to believe D to be a defeater of B; or
(c) S has reason to believe that there is communitarian evidence to justify belief that D is false or that D is not a defeater of B; and
(ii) Condition (i) was not brought about by S's epistemic negligence.

The addition here is condition (i) (c). I suggest that EP* is more plausible than EP, since the former does and the latter does not allow for the plausible notion of epistemic justification grounded in communitarian evidence against defeaters of the belief. I also suggest that our contemporary Western theist may very well have basic theistic belief that meets the criterion of EP* and is thus a candidate for proper basicality.

Here it is important to note that EP* suggests only a *necessary* condition on proper basicality. I am not arguing that basic beliefs that satisfy EP* are thereby properly basic. It may well be (and most likely is) the case that there are further constraints on proper basicality, and it may also be that no basic theistic belief can meet all of these.[29] My argument is not one for the proper basicality of some theistic belief. Rather, my argument is that it is possible, and perhaps quite common, that basic theistic belief

satisfy EP*, and therefore it is not this condition that disquali-
fies such belief from proper basicality.

One objection that could be raised against EP* vis-à-vis
basic theistic belief is that, even for the professionals in the
community who possess the evidence against potential defeaters of theistic belief, theistic belief is generally not grounded in
the evidence they possess. That is, such theists would be theists
even if they did not have evidence against the case for (1). There
seems to be something inappropriate about grounding a community's justification for accepting theistic belief in evidence
that does not serve to ground the belief of the one possessing
the evidence.

Two words can be said in response. First, it is not obvious
that the charge is true. It is at least more likely that a professional to whom evidence for a defeater of theistic belief is not
adequately defeated will be dissuaded from such a belief than
will one who has not been so diligent in seeking such defeater
defeat.[30] Second, even if it were true that such professionals
would, by and large, still hold theistic beliefs in such circumstances, this point seems irrelevant to the question at hand. If
the evidence they have against the potential defeaters can be
rationally taken as good evidence, this should be all that is
required. Facts about how they would respond in counterfactual situations does not affect the actual justificatory circumstances.

Another possible objection to the claim that basic theistic
belief might satisfy (i)(c) of EP* is that there is widespread disagreement in the professional communities over the strength
of evidence against (1) as a defeater of theistic belief. Although
there are many professionals who believe there is such evidence, there are also many who reject the strength of any of it
and who see (1) as well established. But this situation is not
unique to the theism debate. The communitarian evidence
supporting electron belief is not universally accepted in the
professional world. Instrumentalist theories and other explanatory scenarios abound. Yet the controversy over realism with
respect to theoretical entities does not count against the
properly basic acceptance of electron belief grounded in the
communitarian evidence for the existence of electrons. Hence,
it is not clear why such controversy should negate the properly

basic acceptance of theistic belief grounded in the communitarian evidence against (1) as a defeater of theistic belief.[31]

Now, what does the suggestion that basic theistic belief must satisfy EP* to be properly basic entail about the status of such theistic belief? EP* entails that justification in believing

(5) Evidence for (1) need not concern the theist

is evidence essential. Being justified in believing (5) is essential for basic theistic belief to satisfy EP*. Hence, there is some evidence-essential justification that is a necessary condition for holding properly basic theistic belief. Hence, EP* entails that evidence essentiality is a necessary condition for theistic belief, though it is evidence essentiality regarding *defeaters* of the theistic belief and not the theistic belief itself.

It seems that basic theistic belief may indeed satisfy EP*. But it must be noted that any account of properly basic theistic belief that admits EP* as a condition on proper basicality departs from the intentions of Plantinga and other Reformed epistemologists. Such philosophers wish to draw parallels between theistic belief and beliefs that are clearly non-evidential, even in the communitarian sense—e.g., perceptual and memory beliefs and beliefs about the psychological states of others.

For example, Wykstra contrasts electron beliefs with beliefs about physical objects. Someone might think, for example, that Descartes's argument for the existence of physical objects is a good argument. Nevertheless, if he were to be convinced that this argument is deeply flawed—or even that there can be no good argument for the existence of physical objects—his physical object beliefs would still be justified. Furthermore, if he were confronted with evidence against his physical object beliefs—the argument of Bishop Berkeley, for example—against which he had nothing to offer, it still seems right to say that he may properly basically retain his physical object beliefs.[32] Both electron and physical object beliefs can be (and often are) properly basic. We may accept the former sheerly on testimony and the latter sheerly on perceptual experience. Nonetheless, electron beliefs are evidence essential, while physical object beliefs are evidence non-essential. (Note that evidence non-essentiality is a function of a belief's being qualified to serve as its own defeater-defeater. That is, a basic belief is evidence non-essential only if it satisfies AEP.)

If theistic beliefs can be properly basic, their proper basicality is more similar to that of electron beliefs than physical objects beliefs, contrary to Plantinga's intentions. Furthermore, I have argued elsewhere that belief of *God exists* itself is evidence essential, and that all theistic beliefs, therefore, are evidence essential because they obviously entail a belief that is evidence essential.[33] Thus, in an even stronger sense, theistic belief can be properly basic only if it is evidence essential. Therefore, if the RE thesis can be saved by appeal to EP*, it can be so saved only by revising the thesis away from its original force.[34]

Palm Beach Atlantic College

NOTES

1. With apologies to Tom Lehrer ("Poisoning Pigeons in the Park" on *An Evening Wasted with Tom Lehrer*, Reprise Records, 1959).

2. Plantinga develops this doctrine in a number of papers produced throughout the early 1980s. The magnum opus of this corpus is "Reason and Belief in God," in Alvin Plantinga and Nicholas Wolterstorff, eds., *Faith and Rationality: Reason and Belief in God* (Notre Dame, Ind.: University of Notre Dame Press, 1983), pp. 16–93.

3. Throughout this paper, I will use the absolute term 'evidence' to signify *propositional* evidence.

4. See James Sennett, *Modality, Probability, and Rationality: A Critical Examination of Alvin Plantinga's Philosophy* (New York: Peter Lang, 1992), Ch. 1. Note that this is an epistemic, rather than a semantic notion. One important consequence of this fact (though it is, I think, irrelevant to the present paper) is that it is possible that B obviously entail B* *for S*, but not *for S**.

5. Plantinga, "Reason and Belief in God," p. 81.

6. This internalist approach is most often stated in deontological terms, though it might also be expressed in aretaic or axiological terms. For sake of simplicity, I will use only deontological vocabulary—though translation into either of the other two modes is, I believe, a simple task. Hence, it is not to be understood as committed to an ontology of epistemic duties or obligations. Throughout "Reason and Belief in God," Plantinga seems to demonstrate a latent frustration with the whole concept of epistemic duties. This frustration continues throughout the RE corpus and culminates in

"Justification in the 20th Century," *Philosophy and Phenomenological Research* 50 supplement (1990): 45–71, where he argues against the internalist approach to epistemology in general.

7. Plantinga, "Reason and Belief in God," pp. 21ff., 25ff.

8. P. Quinn, "In Search of the Foundations of Theism," *Faith and Philosophy* 2 (1985): 480.

9. I am grateful to Albert Casullo for pointing out to me that this second disjunct is needed, though it is not explicitly stated in Quinn's paper. Clearly it is possible that (i) S has good reason to believe that D; (ii) D is a potential defeater of B for S; (iii) S does not have reason to believe that D is a potential defeater of B for her; and (iv) S is justified in holding B in a basic way. For sake of simplicity I will refer only to S's reason to believe a potential defeater true or false, though the additional reason to believe it a defeater must always be understood as a necessary condition. In working with (1) below, for example, it is utterly obvious that most contemporary theists will have good reason to think it a potential defeater of *God made this flower* and any theistic belief.

10. Conditions (i) and (ii) (absent the second disjunction of (i)(b)—see note 9) are paraphrased from Quinn's conditions numbered identically on p. 483.

11. Quinn actually speaks of "most intellectually sophisticated adults." However, as will be seen, I believe that there is justification for expanding this claim to the wider domain, which makes it more useful for discussion and more in line with Plantinga's purposes.

12. See Sennett, *Modality, Probability, and Rationality*, Ch. 4, on this distinction.

13. Recall Bertrand Russell's legendary reply when asked what he would say to a God who asked why he did not believe—"Evidence, God. Not enough evidence!"

14. One might ask why EP is restricted to properly basic beliefs. Why not make it a principle concerning all belief? It seems that a non-basic belief P may be grounded in a set of reasons R for S, yet potentially defeated by Q for S, such that S has better reason for Q than she has for ¬Q. This is so because S has reasons for P (R), and R may be more compelling for S than is Q or her reasons for Q. Hence S might believe that P, have substantial reason for Q, have no defeater for her evidence that Q, yet be rational in believing that P on the strength of R. It seems that this available out is missing from the basic beliefs precisely because there is no R. However, see Plantinga's purloined letter case in the following section.

15. Plantinga, "The Foundations of Theism: A Reply," *Faith and Philosophy* 3 (1986): 309ff.

16. Ibid., p. 309.

17. Quinn, "In Search of the Foundations of Theism," p. 481 (emphasis mine).

18. It need not be the case that the cognizer in question actually does take the evidence in question as evidence against (1). What I have (and, I believe, Quinn has) in mind here is that the person's noetic structure is such that the evidence *should* count against (1) for her—perhaps *would* so count upon proper reflection. That is, the only explanations for her not taking it to be good evidence against (1) would involve some sort of epistemic negligence.

19. See *God and Other Minds* (Ithaca, N.Y.: Cornell University Press, 1967), Chs. 5 and 6; *The Nature of Necessity* (Oxford: Clarendon Press, 1974), Ch. 9; "The Probabilistic Argument from Evil," *Philosophical Studies* 35 (1983): 1–53; and "Epistemic Probability and Evil," *Archivio di Filosofia* 56 (1988): 557–84.

20. At a public presentation at the University of Nebraska in February 1989, Plantinga stated that he would need to explain many issues in modal logic and go into quite complex detail to show the logical argument from evil to be unsound—it would be no simple task. So even Plantinga recognizes what a difficult task providing defeaters of (1) is.

21. Plantinga, "The Foundations of Theism," p. 310.

22. In *Modality, Probability, and Rationality*, Ch. 5, I introduce the notion of *universal sanction*—a property borne by belief types whose rationality is affirmed by virtually everyone under normal circumstances. They are all such that everyone holds many beliefs of the type routinely and as a matter of normal living. They are all such that general denial of the rationality of beliefs of the type would be unthinkable for virtually all cognizers. They help structure, and seem indispensable to, the normal functions of human beings. Examples include perceptual beliefs, rational intuition beliefs, memory beliefs, beliefs about the psychological states of others, personal identity beliefs, testimonial beliefs, and certain beliefs about the past and future. I then argue that theistic belief lacks universal sanction. My point in the present paper can be stated thus: the purloined letter case is forceful because memory belief bears universal sanction. Its application to theistic belief loses such force because theistic belief lacks universal sanction.

23. Plantinga, "Reason and Belief in God," pp. 74ff.

24. By "experiences," I mean any non-doxastic belief-producing phenomena.

25. I am not claiming that one could never justifiably hold a belief B belonging to a defeated belief kind BK. My claim, rather, is that, given the defeat of BK, one cannot justifiably hold B merely on those grounds that normally justify BK beliefs. This is precisely because she has sufficient reason to suspect any BK belief without further corroboration. One may be able to hold B justifiably, but only if she has more reason than normal grounding circumstances would supply.

26. "Toward a Sensible Evidentialism: On the Notion of 'Needing Evidence'," in William Rowe and William Wainwright, eds., *Philosophy of*

Religion: Selected Readings, 2nd ed. (San Diego, Calif.: Harcourt Brace Jovanovich, 1988), pp. 429ff.

27. Ibid., p. 430.

28. Recall that *S is justified in believing P* does not entail *S believes P.*

29. In "Universal Sanction and Proper Basicality" (in progress), I develop an account of proper basicality that is both plausible and unsatisfiable by any theistic belief (see also note 22).

30. This is not to suggest, however, that theistic belief for such a professional is evidential. Evidence that a potential defeater D for a belief B is false or not an actual defeater of B is not evidence *for* B.

31. Certainly there are disagreements in professional communities in which there is consensus of the mainstream against a radical or extremist fringe, and the position of the fringe may not be adequate to provide communitarian evidence for the position. The creationist/evolutionist debate in theoretical biology and geology might be a good example. But certainly the realism/instrumentalism debate in the philosophy of science is not a matter of the mainstream against the fringe. There are any number of obviously mainstream, acceptable scholars on both sides of the issue (though realism clearly holds the majority). Theism is represented in philosophy, theology, and science by many in the mainstream of those disciplines and is thus more like the realism/instrumentalism controversy than it is like the creationist/evolutionist controversy. Hence, although the "radical fringe" testimony on the professional level may not supply adequate communitarian evidence for a position, this is not a problem that plagues the suggestion that scholarly testimony to theism might provide such evidence.

32. This point is mine, not Wykstra's.

33. Sennett, *Modality, Probability, and Rationality,* Ch. 6. Wykstra likewise argues that belief that God exists is evidence essential.

34. Thanks to Robert Audi, Albert Casullo, Phil Hugly, and Alvin Plantinga for conversations and comments on previous work that contributed significantly to the formation of this paper and to Keith Cooper, Philip Quinn, and Thomas Senor for helpful comments on earlier drafts. I also thank my colleagues at Pacific Lutheran University, who read and discussed a previous version in colloquy, and the participants of the 1991 Pacific Northwest meetings of the American Academy of Religion, before whom a draft was read.

Skepticism, Religious Belief, and the Extent of Doxastic Reliability

Michael A. Brown

ABSTRACT

Two forms of doxastic reliabilism are distinguished, practical and theoretical, both of which are responses to skepticism. William Alston's version of theoretical reliabilism is considered in terms of the ideals of internal coherence, dialectical adequacy, and usefulness for determining how far reliability extends among religious practices. The conclusion is that Alston's theory cannot be used to make that determination and at the same time satisfy the other two ideals. Accordingly, there is no reason to prefer Alston's reliabilism over its practical counterparts.

It goes almost without saying that epistemology is often done in the shadow of skepticism. The shadow is not so ominous or well defined as it once was when the dissolution of Romanized Christianity, the birth of experimental science, and the newly available writings of Sextus Empiricus were culturally dominant. However, there is no denying that skepticism still provides a helpful backdrop for developing, understanding, and assessing theories of knowledge, justification, and belief formation.

Often epistemic theories are compromised into apparent circularity by what may appear to be conflicting goals. Since explanation requires a coherent *explanans*, these theories are designed to be internally consistent. But since they are also used to cull from the theoretical field at least some competitors, they must be dialectically adequate. For modern epistemologists, being "dialectically adequate" seems to mean that an epistemic theory must include or at least imply a refutation of both local skeptics, who deny the first principles upon which the theory is based, and more global skeptics, who challenge and eventually deny all first principles, epistemic and otherwise.

A common intuition is that the elimination of theoretical competitors should proceed according to the best available standards of fairness. In a distinctly modern combination of fair play and the commitment to show skeptics precisely how they refute themselves, this means theoreticians are supposed to assume for the sake of argument that their first principles are false and only then proceed to show that, nonetheless, these principles can be demonstrated to be true.

Two questions highlight the apparent circularity of epistemic theories developed in this modernist context. How can we say that the assumptions that fuel the *reductio* are based on the best available standard of fairness rather than on an unjustified and perhaps unselfconscious refusal to accept any belief that does not seem consistent with beliefs already held? Is the distinctly modern approach to skepticism responsible and heuristically efficacious, or is it a disguised form of what Wittgenstein called "contempt for the particular case," a contempt without which it may be impossible to create self-sealing theories? Of course, Descartes thought he could answer these dialectically charged questions without giving up on internal consistency, and anyone who adopts his modernist orientation runs the risk of building yet another version of the Cartesian circle.

Doxastic reliabilism is conspicuous among recent attempts to answer those dialectically charged questions without surrendering the goal of internal consistency and without supposing that dialectical adequacy must be construed in terms of refutation. By "doxastic reliabilism" I mean any theory that maintains that the reliability of certain belief-forming practices is sufficient to ensure dialectical adequacy, and that such reliability is a necessary condition for explaining justification and knowledge. In other words, doxastic reliabilists reject the Cartesian circularity implicit in the project of both refuting skepticism and purging the rational life of non-rational accretions through arguments normally found in the skeptic's repertoire. Doxastic reliabilists insist that the dialectical ideal has been set too high. Instead of initially conceding too much to skepticism by supposing that it needs to be refuted, which would require showing in a specific case that we do possess knowledge or justified belief, we should at most rebut skepticism by showing that its "arguments" or tropes do not establish the general impossibility of achieving traditional epistemic desiderata.

So far, I have described doxastic reliabilism in terms of the relation between skepticism and a distinctly modern approach to epistemology. In what follows, I consider what I take to be a paradigm case of doxastic reliabilism, the one William Alston has started to articulate in recent years, especially in "A 'Doxastic Practice' Approach to Epistemology"; and I argue that when considered in terms of the epistemology of religious belief, his theory is not both internally consistent and dialectically adequate.[1] At least when considered in those terms, Alston's epistemology is compromised by circularity that looks suspiciously like its Cartesian predecessor.

I

At first glance it seems that doxastic reliabilism could be developed in one of two ways, depending on where we attach reliability to the rational life. Does it attach to belief-forming practices exclusive of any ensuing commitment to the likely truth or rationality of statements generated from them, or does it attach to those practices precisely because they lead to such commitments? If doxastic reliabilism is developed in the first direction, we get roughly the view of thinkers like Heidegger and Wittgenstein, for whom epistemic evaluation stops naturally since it occurs against the background of shared practices that are not objects of analysis. As analysis approaches asymptotically that truly "first" or fundamental level, it presumably stops in a manner impervious to the skeptic's charge that all justification ends in a trilemma of circularity, infinite regress, or arbitrary suspension of the principle of sufficient reason.

If doxastic reliabilism is developed in the second direction, reliability is primarily a function of commitment to the truth or rationality of explicit statements rather than a result of shared patterns of behavior. This is roughly the view of many contemporary analytic epistemologists. Although there is disagreement about the exact terms in which this type of reliability should be understood, it is commonly believed that the desired understanding should be rigorously theoretical, a retrieval and reworking of classical metaphysical and epistemic concepts. Ideally, once the reworking of a given concept is finished, we will have a localized explanation of why it is rational, though not obligatory, not to accept skepticism.

Each of these versions of doxastic reliabilism has been construed by proponents of the other to be an inducement to skepticism, rather than a rebuttal of it. Proponents of the second version think proponents of the first play into the hands of the skeptic. When the skeptical tropes have done their work and the ladder of justification has been pulled up and discarded, the skeptic unthinkingly acquiesces in whatever patterns of behavior define the given social context. The similarity to the acquiescent tendency in Heidegger and Wittgenstein is only too obvious. But from the opposing perspective, the second version seems similarly misguided. It continues to concede too much to skepticism by failing to recognize that by so acquiescing skepticism dismantles itself, and that any commitment to the primacy of theory over practice obscures this fact and thus gives skepticism a foothold from which it cannot be dislodged theoretically.

These parties disagree, in other words, on just which aspects of the rational life are non-rational accretions and which actually define that life. Is brute-behavior the culprit or is it theorizing that can in principle be detached from any specific pattern of behavior? The question can be rephrased rhetorically. Does the reliability we naturally associate with the rational life, and which is sufficient to dialectically defeat skepticism, attach to belief-forming practices exclusive of any commitment to the likely truth or rationality of statements generated from them, or does it attach to those practices precisely because they lead inexorably to such commitments? This question has an unnerving bite, especially in a religious context, in which the question of truth is decisively linked to the meaning of life.

Alston wants to have it both ways, or so it seems. He is indebted to practical reliabilists like Wittgenstein and Thomas Reid, but at the heart of his approach lies the idea that our chief cognitive goal is to believe what is true and not believe what is false. This seems to mean that Alston's cognitive doxastic reliabilism (hereafter, CDR) refuses to concede that the final meta-epistemological work is a clash of incommensurable theories that are embedded in practices that are believed to be reliable, but that cannot be shown to be reliable in any theoretically meaningful way. In order to see if Alston can have it both ways, I want now to explore the relation between the CDR mechanism for initially disqualifying a doxastic practice and one principle of the mechanism for making such disqualifications at the next highest epistemic level.

II

Any appeal to standards of reliability will elicit from the skeptic a familiar reaction. If there is anything less than complete parity of reliability for all doxastic practices, then making the relevant discrimination requires a standard, and that standard requires a meta-standard, and so on, until we note the trilemma staring us in the face. After detailing the Reidian, roughly Wittgenstein-ian, principles of his doxastic practice approach to epistemology, Alston says that he will not directly address the skeptic's meta-epistemological challenge. Instead, he considers the resources available for determining whether a given practice is rationally acceptable.

Alston admits if we eschew epistemically circular support for principles of reliability, we will not be able to establish the reliability of any doxastic practice; and if we do allow such support, an airtight case can be made for any such practice. He believes, nonetheless, that there is a way to responsibly disqualify doxastic practices. As I would put it, he grants the "circular" horn of the skeptic's trilemma, assumes that the justificational regress cannot be infinite, and argues that it stops non-arbitrarily when the appropriate criteria of rationality are used.

Alston is well aware that CDR will be criticized both for conceding too much and conceding too little. It might seem insufficiently restrictive since it grants prima facie reliability to practices that are not followed universally. Universality is an unreasonably high standard, Alston says, since it would exclude socially established religions like Christianity and Hinduism.

However, CDR might also seem to be inadequately permissive since not being socially established is sufficient to show that a practice is not prima facie reliable.

> It is a reasonable supposition that a practice would not have persisted over large segments of the population unless it was putting people into effective touch with some aspect(s) of reality and proving itself by its fruits. But there are no such grounds for presumption in the case of idiosyncratic practices. Hence we will proceed more reasonably, as well as more efficiently, by giving initial, ungrounded credence only to the socially established practices.[2]

Alston knows that this "social establishment principle" (hereafter, SE) is potentially chauvinistic. In fact, CDR is animated by recognition that non-doxastic approaches to epistemology seem to encourage that error. And so he suggests a mechanism for checking at a higher level the practices that make the first cut.

According to Alston, "massive and persistent inconsistency between the outputs of two different practices is a good reason for disqualifying at least one of them." He goes on to say that the only principle for determining which contender to eliminate—the only principle he sees as both "unchauvinistic and eminently plausible"—is the conservative principle (hereafter, CP) that we should give preference to the more firmly established practice. Here I am not directly interested in how Alston would determine what is to count as "more firmly established," though he does mention subprinciples that might be used for making those judgments. Note, rather, how Alston nails down another meta-epistemic thread left dangling by the introduction of CP. He mentions what I think is the chief corollary of CP.

> But mightn't it be the case in a particular conflict that the less firmly established practice is the more reliable? Of course that is conceivable. Nevertheless, in the absence of anything else to go on, it seems the part of wisdom to go with the more firmly established. It would be absurd to make the opposite choice; that would saddle us with all sorts of bizarre beliefs.[3]

III

So far as I can tell, the oddity of a religious practice cannot do the theoretical work it must do if CP is to be both plausible *and* unchauvinistic. Let me try to make this point by working with CP and then linking the problems associated with that effort to similar problems associated with SE.

Try to imagine "massive and persistent" conflict between the belief outputs of what may be called roughly the "Christian doxastic practice" and some other socially established, non-Hebraic counterpart. So-called great world religions like Buddhism and Hinduism would not be good candidates since it is difficult if not impossible to imagine both massive and persistent conflict. For example, I take standard beliefs found in Judaism and its descendants to have been in persistent conflict with standard beliefs in Hinduism and its descendants. But I can't imagine that this conflict would ever be "massive," ranging over most of the areas in which we have come to expect that Christianity and, for example, Buddhism will have belief outputs that do not conflict significantly.

There are two relevant possibilities here. Either this failure of imagination results from what Alan Donagan has called "a muddle characteristic of our age"—namely, the supposed impossibility of both respecting these two great religious traditions and denying that more than one of them can be true—or it suggests how the Christian doxastic practice has changed since the Enlightenment, probably in response to material forces beyond the direct control of any specific human institution.[4] If my failure of imagination is in fact the result of a "muddle," then we should be able to reveal that fact by trying to use CP both efficiently and unchauvinistically.

Assume that Christianity and Hinduism are in persistent and massive conflict. CP indicates that one must be rejected as unreliable, but which one? Here we would appeal to Alston's subprinciples, principles such as being more widely accepted, having more of an innate basis, being more important in our lives, and so forth. As I understand them, these principles divide naturally into two groups: those that clearly could be used to fuel social scientific research and those that could not, at least at this stage in the development of the social sciences.

The crucial issue here is how these principles would be used. I don't know how things would turn out if we used them to fuel social scientific research, but I suspect we would be left with a mass of data and no answer to our question. On the other hand, we might try to overcome the supposed value-neutrality of social science and use the principles "philosophically," but without allowing distinctly Christian values to guide the process.

Here a great deal of caution would be required. No doubt pre-Enlightenment Christian philosophers are not to be blamed for granting more credibility to their own doxastic practices than to their non-Christian rivals. In William James's words, the rivalry was not between "live" options, and so their philosophy was essentially an outgrowth of prior religious commitment. It was a tool for articulation and defense of the faith, but it stopped short of calling into question key Christian beliefs. However, the options have become increasingly "live" since the Enlightenment, so that contemporary Christians *may* have an obligation unthinkable to their predecessors. They may be obliged to make philosophical judgments about competing religious practices by first abstracting from specifically Christian values and practices.

Add substance to this caution by considering an example. Say that you discover in your locale a small but flourishing group of religious Appollonians—followers of that Appollonius who lived in the early years of the first century, until about 96 or 98 A.D., and who is sometimes referred to as having been a serious rival of Christ. Say, moreover, that there is massive conflict between the outputs of Appollonian and Christian doxastic practices. The conflict has persisted over the centuries, even though you were unaware of this before your encounter with the Appollonians. Finally, say that as a doxastic reliabilist you want to adjudicate the conflict in terms of CP and its subprinciples. Which of the two practices is more "firmly established"?

You begin to address that question by taking those subprinciples amenable to social science and using them to do, for example, the appropriate historical research. You discover that the Gospels and, for example, Philostratus's account of Appollonius both contain well-established facts, as well as historical inaccuracies. So far it seems unreasonable to decide in favor of one practice over the other. Then you note that the texts contain features with which social-scientific history or any other social science is not equipped to deal. They describe "miracles," incidents in which Christ or Appollonius seem to contravene or suspend the laws of nature. Again, without going further, there seem to be no reasonable grounds for deciding one way or the other. In order to proceed you must find a "philosophic" strategy unencumbered by the supposed value-neutrality of science, a strategy that does not also beg the comparative question posed by CP.

Now consider an argument that I take to be a model for this type of strategy, one which illustrates how one of Alston's subprinciples *might* be used "philosophically"; although, so far as I know, he does not recommend that they be used in this way. It has been argued that the principles of the Christian doxastic practice are more "obviously true" than their Appollonian counterparts since in the second case miracle accounts are interspersed with fantasy; whereas in the Gospels there is no fantasy, only miracle accounts firmly embedded in historical claims. The point is that in Philostratus

[Y]ou get miracle stories a little like those in the Gospels, but also snakes big enough to eat elephants, kings and emperors as supporting cast, traveler's tales, ghosts and vampires. Once the boundaries of fact are crossed, we wander into fairyland. But the Gospels are firmly set in the real Palestine of the first century, and the little details are not picturesque inventions but the real details that only an eyewitness or skilled realistic novelist can give.[5]

This argument turns on the distinction between "fantasy" and "miracles." A combination of miracles and historical fact yields more "obvious truth" than miracles plus historical fact *and* fantasy. But doesn't this distinction collapse under its own weight, as I believe it does?

Assume plausibly that the known laws of nature at a given time indicate that the eating of elephants by snakes and the curing of certain diseases are scientifically inexplicable. If either of these events occurs, then from the perspective of the known laws of nature they are inexplicable. Both involve what seem to be the suspension or contravention of the laws of nature. For any god endowed with the requisite powers, it would be just as easy to make a snake big enough to eat elephants as it would be to cure presently incurable diseases. If a god could suspend or contravene the laws of nature, it could do so without being bound by the max-min principles that govern our efficiency calculations, especially those purporting to describe nature.

What may blind us to this fact is the presumption that there is a third option for understanding how the Christian God, and only the Christian God, performs miracles. These miracles are often believed to be consistent with the laws of nature, whereas their non-Christian counterparts do not have that apologetic advantage. When performing miracles, Christ *was* bound by the principles governing our max-min calculations; although given the present state of knowledge of these principles, especially as they are applied to nature, it is not evident how this is so. However, it is also supposedly evident that in Philostratus we get accounts of fantasy-miracles that are obviously inconsistent with *any* scientifically respectable view of nature.

My point is that the strategy in question seems to assume that Christianity is more closely aligned with science than, say, Appollonian religion, but that it can also be plausibly assumed that the two beliefs are both inconsistent with science. When held uncritically, the first assumption makes it difficult for Christian philosophers to use CP unchauvinistically. I will specify the relevant sense of "impossibility" in a moment. Here it suffices to say that in one way my point is not startling. There is a long tradition in Christianity that says belief in God is not compatible with a scientific outlook, in any of its forms; therefore, the grafting of Biblical religion onto Greek and early modern science was a mistake, tantamount to idolatry. I am aware of arguments designed to show that in a culture like ours, where commitment to science is firm, the only option for the Christian apologist is to insist that Christian belief and a scientific outlook are compatible. My point is that although this assumption may be necessary for apologetic purposes, it clouds the philosophical issue when confused with what is required of an adequate *dialectical* defense of typical Christian knowledge claims. An adequate dialectical "defense" would not simply assume that the key tenets of Christianity are true. If religious epistemology only clarifies and defends beliefs given uncritically, where "defense" does not include doubt that any given belief may be false, then I do not see how religious doxastic reliabilism can have any dialectical aspirations.

IV

It may seem that the Appollonian example was badly chosen. I should have been trying to show that my inability to imagine "massive and persistent conflict" between Hebraic and Hindu religions is not the result of confused ecumenical zeal, but the result of how the Christian doxastic practice has changed since the Enlightenment. Instead, I showed at most that this practice generates beliefs that are dialectically tendentious when used for adjudicating conflict with a religion as admittedly odd as the Appollonian.

I chose that example because it suggests why the usual taxonomy of religions is misleading when using CP to respond to the challenge of skepticism in a religious context. No doubt my hypothetical Appollonian religion would be odd, but so is Hinduism, Buddhism, and any other religion not descended from the Hebraic root, even if it is a so-called great world religion. These religions have characteristics that show that perhaps the crucial distinction when trying to use CP is not between well- and less well-established religions, but between those that square with our cultural commitment to science and those that do not.

Say that you discover in your locale small but flourishing groups devoted to Buddhism, Hinduism, or any other religion not descended from the Hebraic root. These groups will present live religious options only if, unlike the hypothetical Appollonians, their doxastic practices do not encourage belief in antiscientific fantasy. Since all such religions reserve some role for "fantasy," this means that they will be candidates for disqualification on Alston's second level of evaluation only if the fantasy element is retained. Only then will the relevant conflict be both "massive and persistent." But if it is retained, the religion will fail to make the cut. It will be judged to be odd, less "obviously true" than its Christian competitor.

What characteristics make these religions seem "odd"? Unless I'm mistaken, two characteristics are relevant here.

First, when compared to forms of Christianity that suppose that Christianity is consistent with science, they emphasize nature in an odd manner. Those committed to these religions either deny outright that certain deities transcend nature—to us they confuse religion and science—or if they admit some transcendence, they are nonetheless more inclined to identify the actions of certain deities with what we call natural processes than are Christians. If pressed, Christians will parade the oddity of their beliefs. They will admit that in some sense, however tenuous and poetic, the blowing of the wind is an act of God. These other religions make that type of identification more readily, without being pressed.

Second, the deities in question are often linked to specific natural features and geographic locales and fail to have significance without this linkage. Again, a comparison with religion in the Hebraic tradition is instructive. With the influence of Canaanite religion, there was a danger that Israel would come to believe that Yahweh was tied to the land. The prophets worked to obviate the danger, arguing that Yahweh is tied not to the land but to the nation, thus ensuring the possibility that Christianity could be for all people, regardless of locale. By contrast, what I will call natural religion forges stronger links between divinity and specific natural features and geographic locales. This may not be obvious to us in Buddhism and Hinduism—we tend to obscure this fact by our tendency to delete from them "bizarre" beliefs—but it is manifest in non-Christian Celtic religions, many Native American religions, the native aboriginal religions of Australia, and many others, all of which we typically dismiss as primitive when compared to religions that derive from the Hebraic root.

In the case of these primitive religions there *could* be "massive and persistent" conflict with the doxastic outputs of Christianity. So CP indicates that we go with the more firmly established practices. Doing otherwise would be absurd because it would saddle us with "bizarre" beliefs.

But why would it be absurd to adopt and cultivate a religious belief just because it is, in Alston's words, "bizarre"? We can now answer that question. Consider the beliefs that Jesus was Christ in the full-blown sense, the scientific belief that the sun is, roughly speaking, a fusion reactor, and the religious aboriginal belief that the sun is a white cockatoo. Taken in isolation from the relevant doxastic practices, none of these beliefs is more bizarre than any other. And unlike our pre-Enlightenment predecessors, we can take them, it seems, in that manner.

Still, the aboriginal belief *does* strike us as bizarre, but not simply in the sense that it is something that has no place in the doxastic practices that typically form our religious beliefs. No, the oddity runs deeper than that, or perhaps I should say that it is more shallow than that. It would be absurd for us to come to believe as the aborigines do, not because their belief happens to be one we do not accept—that would obviously beg the interesting question—but because it would be so practically difficult for us to engage in the doxastic practices that make that belief second nature and thus not at all "bizarre."

If we try to use CP dialectically, by appeal to its chief corollary, we can thus discover that a religion is "bizarre" if its beliefs are inconsistent with the belief outputs of experimental science. Belief in Jesus as Christ is presumably not bizarre in that sense. The credibility of that belief is typically guaranteed by appeal to a supernatural realm, and it is precisely with respect to that realm that the aboriginal belief lacks credibility. It competes with the account of nature given by experimental science; and since that science has no genuine competitors, the doxastic practices that generate it are not comparatively reliable.

Is it "impossible" for us to come to believe as the aborigine does? Surely that is not logically impossible. Any of us could conceivably give up the scientific outlook and, along with it, any religious beliefs believed to be compatible with it. We could acquire whatever knowledge there is of aboriginal practices, move to the appropriate locale, and begin to live as aborigines. We could even overcome our scientific or Christian tendency to remain detached from that locale, and the given practices, by chemically or surgically inducing the right amount of amnesia. Eventually, as every good evangelist and pastoral counselor will tell us, the uncomprehending repetition of behavior would lead to the right kind of belief. Perhaps we overlook this plain feature of belief-acquisition because, as Nietzsche pointed out, Christians have lost the sense of just how odd it is to say that God became man and died on the cross.

Radical conversion to aboriginal or other natural religions is unlikely because that would involve eliminating a doxastic practice that continues to inform both Christianity—even the severely attenuated forms that still dominate the West—and experimental science. This is the practice of acting as if the natural world is maximally free of anthropocentric conceptions, which tie both humans and gods to specific geographical features and locales and thus obviate the possibility of experimental science and supernatural religion. Thomas Nagel, Charles Taylor, and Bernard Williams offer noteworthy descriptions of this practice; but for purposes of understanding its relation to CDR, perhaps the best description is given by Paul J. Griffiths, in terms of what he calls "denaturalized discourse."

> In sum: formally, a denaturalized discourse is one that, in its ideal-typical form, shows no evidence of rooting in any sociocultural context; exhibits no essential connections with any natural language; and is completely unambiguous. Functionally, a denaturalized discourse is aimed primarily at making available to its users what really exists, a function that, from the viewpoint of a user of such discourse, cannot be performed by ordinary, nondenaturalized, discourse.[6]

As I understand it, denaturalized discourse is the linguistic version of the practice(s) of acting as if anthropocentric conceptions are not applicable to the natural world in any philosophically illuminating way. CP marks the boundary between the denaturalized discourse CDR assumes to be normative and the non-denaturalized discourse used in natural religion.

V

If this "absolute" doxastic practice does inform CP and if, as I have suggested, its presence is a necessary condition for becoming "socially established," then we would expect to find the same evidence of it on CDR's first level of reliability evaluation. We would expect that because there, too, the operative contrast is between being doxastically odd and being socially established.

Take Alston's example of an initially unreliable practice. Cedric consults sun-dried tomatoes to determine the future of the stock market. Change the example slightly so that the consultation presumably reveals the will of a certain god, and correct forecasts are expressions of that god's beneficence. Why shouldn't we immediately accord this practice reliability? No doubt the guiding intuition for not doing so is sound. We need to distinguish charlatans from reliable religious authorities. I am raising a question not about the intuition, but about the mechanism Alston proposes for justifying the reports of the intuition. Again, according to SE, being "socially established" means that we can assume that the practice puts people into effective touch with reality, an assumption that is proved reasonable by its fruits.

Say that Cedric consults his tomatoes and announces that his god wants me to do X, and that if I do X, I will be justly rewarded with correct predictions of market fluctuations. For whatever reason, I follow the recommendation; and when my investments are profitable, I return to Cedric for an explanation. I note that the principles to which he alludes resemble the principles found in the *I-Ching*. Does this mean that Cedric's practice is "socially established," despite what might be his claim to the contrary? If it does, then especially in view of my success, Cedric's practice seems to be reliable, at least to the degree appropriate to this level of evaluation. If the resemblance with the *I-Ching* is not sufficient to make it socially established, then we might ask why it isn't sufficient.

My point in raising these questions is twofold. Obviously, Alston's example is contrived, and so is my extension of it. Nonetheless, my example shows that the manner in which his example is contrived is illuminating. It disregards what I am tempted to call the "historical" or "phenomenological" fact that no matter how unprecedented it claims to be, for any new yet recognizable doxastic practice there will be a revealing analog somewhere, if only we look for it. In other words, there do not seem to be any "idiosyncratic" practices in the sense necessary for the case Alston is trying to build. This point is an extension of Wittgenstein's arguments against so-called private language. The activity of subsuming particulars under general terms cannot be adequately justified without an ungrounded evaluative element that is irreducibly public, behavioral, and non-theoretical.

Now we may object that once again the conclusion is under-determined by an ill-chosen example. Surely a truly idiosyncratic example could have been chosen, even by the standards I have suggested. I have my doubts. Like the Cedric example, any practice that suggests itself would not be "idiosyncratic" in the sense required for SE and CP to work unchauvinistically *and* efficiently, but would be socially unestablished, relative to some expression of the absolute doxastic practice, or at least that is my suspicion. It would be "bizarre," but not socially unprecedented, meaning that like natural religion, it would seem to compete directly with the scientific doxastic practice. Alston has argued persuasively elsewhere that such competition does not characterize Christianity's relation to that practice, but without an argument showing that natural religions do indeed compete with science, only half the needed story has been told.[7]

VI

What I have offered is clearly not a conventional criticism of CDR. It was an exercise in dialectic, the activity of arguing to establish first principles, especially those concerning the choice between denaturalized and non-denaturalized discourses, rather than an exercise in arguing from principles already established. I have tried to show that, at least to the degree it has been developed so far, CDR fails to do justice to what I described in Section I as the tension between practical and theoretical versions of doxastic reliabilism. When considered in terms of its dialectical aspirations and the epistemology of religious belief, CDR doesn't go significantly beyond the circularity so common when theoreticians assume that skepticism must be refuted.

In Section III, I tried to show that if one common taxonomy of religions is accepted, in which Christianity is a "great religion" and certain others are not just in case they are not socially established, then CP can't be used unchauvinistically because it uncritically assumes that Christianity is more closely aligned with science than the competing religion. On the other hand, if one changes the taxonomy to reflect the oddity Christian beliefs have against a scientific background, then I tried to show in Section IV that CP cannot be used efficiently since that would require our willingness to acquire beliefs that are practically impossible for us to acquire. Again, it is unlikely anyone will make a conversion journey to the outback, but not because it would be logically impossible to do so, and even though if Christianity is inconsistent with science, we would have an obligation to do so in order to tell whether it or the competition is more "bizarre."

Which taxonomy should we adopt when the reliabilist tries to use Alston's CP? In Section V, I suggested that at best Alston has answered half that question. He may have satisfactorily completed the apologetic task of showing that Christianity does not compete directly with science; but without a religiously neutral argument showing that socially unestablished, natural religions do compete with science, CDR remains impaled on the horns of the dilemma sketched in Sections III and IV. Without some way between the horns of that dilemma, we might just as well say with the skeptic that believing falsely can have prolonged, practical benefits and therefore the social success of religions derived from the Hebraic root is consistent with the most extreme skepticism. We might just as well embrace the deep-seated natural skepticism that Wittgenstein expressed by yearning to replace the "contempt for the particular case," fostered by the values of the absolute doxastic practice, with what he called the "elder days of Art, in which the gods are everywhere."[8,9]

Creighton University

NOTES

1. William Alston, "A 'Doxastic Practice' Approach to Epistemology," in Marjorie Clay and Keith Lehrer, eds., *Knowledge and Skepticism* (Boulder, Colo.: Westview Press, 1989), pp. 1–29.
2. Ibid., pp. 16–17.
3. Ibid., p. 18.
4. See Alan Donagan, "Can Anybody in a Post-Christian Culture Rationally Believe the Nicene Creed?" in Thomas Flint, ed., *Christian*

Philosophy (Notre Dame, Ind.: University of Notre Dame Press, 1990), pp. 92–117.

5. Richard Purtil, "Miracles: What If They Happen?" in Richard Swinburne, ed., *Miracles* (New York: Macmillan, 1989), pp. 201–2.

6. Paul J. Griffiths, "Denaturalizing Discourse: Abhidharmikas, Propositionalists, and the Comparative Philosophy of Religion," in Frank E. Reynolds and David Tracy, eds., *Myth and Philosophy* (Albany: State University of New York Press, 1990), p. 65.

7. See his "Religious Experience and Christian Belief," *Nous* 16 (1982), and "Christian Experience and Christian Belief," in Alvin Plantinga and Nicholas Wolterstorff, eds., *Faith and Rationality* (Notre Dame, Ind.: University of Notre Dame Press, 1983).

8. See G. P. Baker and P. M. S. Hacker, *An Analytical Commentary on Wittgenstein's Philosophical Investigations* (Chicago: University of Chicago Press, 1983), p. 5. For a discussion of Wittgenstein's "polytheism," see James Edwards, *The Authority of Language: Heidegger, Wittgenstein and the Threat of Philosophical Nihilism* (Gainesville: University Presses of Florida, 1990).

9. I would like to thank Stephen Maitzen, Russell Reno, and Richard White for helpful comments on earlier versions of this paper.

Index

In the following index, the modification *Cited* signifies a simple reference crediting a quotation or claim in the text to the subject indicated. The word *Mentioned* before a page number indicates a brief mention of the subject's views, frequently in the form of "See . . ." in an endnote or a passing reference in the text. Where appropriate, these modifications are grouped with sub-headings under a particular entry.

Russell, Robert. *Cited as editor:*
167n. 2

Santayana, George. *Mentioned:* 54
Schrodinger, Erwin. *Mentioned:*
63n. 24
Science: confirmation of hypotheses, compared with religious
hypotheses, 13–17; confirmation
of hypotheses, detecting variables
in, 14–15; confirmation of
hypotheses, use of control
groups, 16–18, 23–24; evidence
used in, types of, 141–42 (*see also*
Anecdotal evidence); physics as
paradigm of, 153; priority in
Western culture of, xviii–xix,
219–25; sociology of, 142,
154–55, 156, 164–65; sociology
of, contrasted with religion,
154–55, 156
Scriven, Michael. *Mentioned:* 190
Sennett, James F., ix, xvii. *Cited:*
204n. 4, 206n. 29. *Mentioned:* xix
Sessions, William Lad, ix, xii, xv
Sextus Empiricus. *Mentioned:* 209
Shahan, Robert. *Cited as editor:*
136n. 19
Singer, S., 153. *Cited:* 168n. 15
Skepticism, xiii–xiv, xv, 104, 113,
114n. 5, 142, 152, 155; circularity of, 58–59; doxastic practices
and, 209–13, 225; transcendental
arguments against, 155
Sociology of science and religion.
See Religion, Science
Solomon (king of Israel). *Men-
tioned:* xv, 146
Sorenson, Roy A., 139n. 45
Sosa, Ernest, 173–75. *Cited:* 185nn.
3, 4. *Mentioned:* 181
Spirituality: characteristics of, 5–6,
18–19; conditions for the devel-

opment of, 6–7, 19–20, 22–23;
detecting, 16–18, 23–24; evidence for God's existence based
on, 1–5, 7–13, 21–22, 24–30;
non-Christian forms of, 19–20,
29–30; social factors in, 26–29.
See also Christian, promised spiritual fulfillment
Stark, Rodney. *Mentioned:* 33n. 3
Statistical evidence, 156–57
Stich, Stephen, xi, 41–43, 45, 62nn.
11, 13. *Cited:* 62n. 9, 63n. 17
Stoeger, William. *Cited as editor:*
167n. 2
Swinburne, Richard, on: Hume,
124; natural law, 124, 136nn. 14,
25; Principle of Credulity, xiii,
103, 104, 105–7, 109, 110, 111,
112–113, 113n. 3, 114n. 7 (*cited:*
114n. 4; *mentioned:* 115n. 12,
159); Principle of Testimony,
114n. 6, 139n. 51, 169n. 23 (*cited:*
139n. 50; *mentioned:* 161, 163);
religious experience, 69, 113n. 2,
159 (*cited:* 169n. 23; *cited as editor:*
226n. 5)

Taylor, Charles. *Mentioned:* 222
Testimony: approaches to verbal,
149–53, 160–64; conflicting
claims in, 36, 103, 108–113,
114nn. 7, 8, 9, 10 (*mentioned:*
119); miracles or extraordinary
events supported by, xiv–xv,
119–21, 128–35, 139n. 45,
149–53; professional, 199–204,
207n. 31. *See also* Anecdotal evidence; Beliefs, social and communitarian influence on; Swinburne, Principle of Testimony
Theism, theistic beliefs: knowledge
and, xi, 51, 60–61, 64n. 27; miracles supporting, 132; religious